D0061312

Lower
East Side
Memories

Lower East Side Memories

A JEWISH PLACE IN AMERICA

Hasia R. Diner

PRINCETON UNIVERSITY PRESS

PRINCETON AND OXFORD

Copyright © 2000 by Princeton University Press
Published by Princeton University Press, 41 William Street,
Princeton, New Jersey 08540
In the United Kingdom: Princeton University Press,
3 Market Place, Woodstock,
Oxfordshire OX20 1SY

Second printing, and first paperback printing, 2002
Paperback ISBN 0-691-09545-0

The Library of Congress has cataloged the cloth edition of this
book as follows

Diner, Hasia R.
Lower East Side memories : a Jewish place in America /
Hasia R. Diner.
p. cm.
Includes bibliographical references and index.
ISBN 0-691-00747-0 (cloth : alk. paper)
1. Jews—New York (State)—New York—social life and customs—20th
century. 2. Jews—New York (State)—New York—Intellectual life—20th
century. 3. Immigrants—New York (State)—New York—Social life and
customs—20th century. 4. Lower East Side (New York, N.Y.)—Social life
and customs—20th century. 5. New York (State)—New York—Ethnic
relations. I. Title.

F128.9.J5 D56 2000
974.7'1004924—dc21   00-021148

British Library Cataloging-in-Publication Data is available

This book has been composed in Baskerville Typeface

Printed on acid-free paper. ∞

www.pup.princeton.edu

Printed in the United States of America

10 9 8 7 6 5 4 3 2

In memory of my mother,

ESTHER KITE SCHWARTZMAN,

whom I do not remember,

but wish that I did.

And, in honor of my sister,

VARDA, *who shares all the*

other memories.

CONTENTS

ACKNOWLEDGMENTS

THIS BOOK has one author, but multiple points of origin, and as such a number of people helped make it possible. The first starting place for this book is personal, and I briefly touch upon what the Lower East Side has meant to me, and how I have experienced it as a site of Jewish memory despite the absence of any personal or family linkages to the neighborhood. The second source is scholarly. I had long been struck by the number of books and articles in the scholarly literature that referenced the Lower East Side, although the specific setting had little, often nothing, to do with that particular place. I kept noticing how many historians invoked the name of the neighborhood without probing the meaning of the place. Eventually I decided that I wanted to understand the Lower East Side as this singular point of reference.

Other sources for this book were actually more concrete, and it is because of them, and the individuals involved, that the book actually took shape. In the summer of 1997 the District of Columbia Jewish Community Center (DCJCC) invited me to give the first Bernard Wexler Lecture on Jewish History. Honored to be asked to give a Wexler lecture, particularly the inaugural one, I cast about for a subject. I was deeply involved in another project and did not want to talk about it yet. I was too mired down in the minutiae of research and did not yet see the forest amid the many trees.

I knew that the audience would be composed of a large number of people who knew me well and who had heard me speak many times. As such I wanted to tackle something new and a topic that would be engaging to a broad public. In preparing for a community lecture, I needed to strike a balance between the concerns of scholarship and the presentation of a compelling story.

At that time I was working with two colleagues and fellow historians, Jeffrey Shandler and Beth Wenger, on planning a conference entitled "Remembering the Lower East Side," scheduled for the following summer at New York University. At that point we were collecting names of speakers and potential topics, but I had not yet formulated for myself a conceptual framework for the meaning of those memories of American Jewish geography. Given that I had the Lower East Side on my mind, I decided to think about it as the sacred space of the American Jewish past as the topic for my Wexler lecture. It seemed appropriate for this occasion: it was instantly recognizable to the listeners as important, yet its history and memory involved some of the key issues with which historians have been struggling.

Likewise, the very setting of the talk inspired me to think about histories, memories, and places. The District of Columbia Jewish Community Center, at Sixteenth Street, just north of the White House, had been a locus for organized Jewish life in the nation's capital from its founding in the 1920s until it followed the movement of the city's Jews out to the suburbs in the 1960s. In 1968 the Jewish community of Washington had sold the imposing building, exchanging the lofty structure, with its steep marble stairs, for a sprawling campus in Maryland beyond the Beltway. The old DCJCC stood as a kind of silent reminder of the past, a curious relic to be looked at from the windows of a passing car.

But by the 1980s the number of Jews in the city had grown, and so had their consciousness of themselves as urban dwellers. They organized themselves to reconstitute a Jewish community center and by the 1990s had bought back the old building. After they raised millions of dollars to renovate it, the "old/new" DCJCC's magnificent edifice declared, phoenix-like, the reemergence of the city's Jewish presence. One of the earliest exhibits in the art gallery focused on other American Jewish spaces that like this one, had once been lived in, had been abandoned, and at that moment were undergoing the process of resuscitation. Given all this, I was predisposed to talk about sacred spaces in American Jewish memory, and that is what I did on June 18, 1997.

I liked the talk but understood that the narrative was much more complicated than that which I had presented. It needed more details, more nuance, and more explanation. I received wonderful comments and suggestions from audience members, several of whom were historians. Others were the interested and engaged people from the community who generally come to lectures of this kind and who have made the DCJCC the remarkable institution that it is. I decided to expand the talk, flesh it out, and transform it into an article.

What emerged was too long for an article but not yet as complex and fully-developed as the topic required. I understood that the meaning of the Lower East Side to post–World War II American Jews needed more intensive nuancing to give its many facets the luster they deserved.

The article was stowed away in a drawer in my office in New York and sat there facing an uncertain future. In fact, when Brigitta van Rheinberg, the History and Classics Editor at Princeton University Press, came to speak with me about my research, I had another project in mind. In the midst of our conversation, however, the Lower East Side came up, and I mentioned my article, which I thought was worth a book-length treatment. She liked the idea, and read and critiqued the article. It is a result of her guidance that this book was born.

Let me now get on with the wonderful task of thanking people. To the DCJCC, to its Executive Director, Arna Mayer Mikelson, and to Natalie Wexler, who chose to honor the memory of her father, Bernard Wexler, with a lecture series focusing on the history of the Jewish people, I begin my pleasant chore of writing acknowledgments. It is indeed a tribute to the institution and to the Wexler family that of all the ways they could have enshrined Bernard Wexler's memory, they chose to focus on the past.

I thank Beth Wenger and Jeffrey Shandler for drawing me in to the planning of the conference. "Remembering the Lower East Side" was their baby first, and they allowed me to share it with them. I have learned much from working with them on this project.

Brigitta van Rheinberg has been exceedingly helpful and encouraging. A skillful editor, she has been a pleasure to work with. In her quiet and understated way, she gave me space at the same time she made sure that I paid attention to what others had advised.

I presented another version of this project as a lecture at Binghamton University. There I received very helpful comments from Lance Sussman, Kitty Sklar, and Thomas Dublin, and I offer my thanks to them. On another happy occasion I spoke at the University of Wisconsin–Madison, delivering a Lower East Side talk as the Kutler Lecturer in American Jewish history. Stanley Kutler, who made the lecture possible, was my teacher when I was an undergraduate student at the University of Wisconsin. I was honored to give the lecture bearing his name, and at that talk I was challenged by some provocative questions asked by him, David Sorkin, Anthony Michaels, Donald Downs, and a number of students at my alma mater.

Several colleagues read and commented on the manuscript, and it is a better book for their efforts. Stephen Whitfield and Martha Hodes, in particular, gave it a good deal of attention and asked stimulating questions. I particularly want to thank Lawrence Levine for his insights. I have admired his writing for a long time, have enjoyed his company as a friend, and have reveled in hearing his many stories, told with great aplomb. Now I understand why his students are so devoted to him. He is a superb reader and critic, and he forced me to write a better book than I would have without his valuable help. Moses Rischin was one of the readers to whom Princeton University Press sent the manuscript, for which I am grateful. I also appreciate that he let it be known that the comments were his. He started this field, carving out the Lower East Side as the locus for historical research, and his remarks greatly informed the final product.

Additionally, a cadre of students read this book in its manuscript form and offered me much help. Jane Rothstein, who also worked with me as a research assistant through the Skirball Department of Hebrew and Judaic Studies at New York University; Ari Kelman, also of NYU; and Shelby Shapiro, at the University of Maryland, all played a part in making this book possible. Shelby Shapiro, in particular, wields a wicked red pen. I am thrilled that he, and the other students, felt comfortable enough to point out my errors, inconsistencies, and clumsy formulations. I thank them and look forward to seeing their careers unfold.

Without the generosity of the Skirball Department of Hebrew and Judaic Studies, particularly its chair, Lawrence Schiffman, this book would not have been possible. He saw to it that I was able to get graduate student research assistance, as well as financial help to secure the rights for the images that appear on the pages that follow. He and the department have provided me with an intellectually stimulating and supportive environment that is truly sustaining. Alex Molot provided meticulous help and good cheer.

Other friends and colleagues have helped with advice, suggestions, references, and snippets of Lower East Side memory. I thank Max Ticktin, Jeffrey Rubenstein, Mario Maffi, R. Gordon Kelly, and Beryl Benderly. Likewise, whole sections of this book needed the words of the creators of texts. I have relied on interviews with Rabbi Kenneth Roseman, Amy Waterman, Rabbi Philip Warmflash, Joan Micklin Silver, Stephen Long, Ruth Abram, Seth Kamil, Wendy Rosenthal, Allison Gottesegen, Antonia Coffman, and Bobbie Malone. Omer Davidson took some of the photographs. The help of all these people brought to life the artifacts and texts that have demonstrated the power of the Lower East Side in shaping an American Jewish culture. Several of these individuals went out of their way to find photographs of the artifacts, without which this book could not have happened. Likewise, my daughter, Shira, not only encouraged me—as always—but also took pictures when she ran across Lower East Side icons far removed from the lower reaches of the island of Manhattan. I also relied on the photographic skills of my son Eli, who just moved into a student apartment on Avenue D, on the northern reaches of the Lower East Side, and thus is the first Lower East Side Jew in his family.

Steve Diner has always read my drafts, from my horribly written master's thesis, which I was working on when we first met, through this book. In the years that he was *just* a professor, he had somewhat more time to perform this invaluable service for me. Although he now is a dean and infinitely more busy, he still found the time to read, critique, and discuss this book. I owe him thanks for this and for everything else good that he has shared with me.

*Lower
East Side
Memories*

The Stirrings of Memory

W<small>E INSTANTLY</small> recognize the photographs. We have seen them many times before and know, without a moment's hesitation, that we are viewing the Lower East Side. In these black-and-white pictures, the streetscapes of the end of the nineteenth century and the early years of the twentieth, we observe people teeming out of doors, milling about, pressing into each other, with little regard for privacy or personal space. The women and men rush about, crowding and shoving. They shop from pushcarts, bending over these rickety outdoor emporiums and critically inspecting the merchandise—squeezing, touching, tugging, and probing.

They talk with their hands, and if pictures could talk, we would hear their shouts—in heavily accented English, but mostly in Yiddish—resonating through the clogged streets. Our ears would pick up bits and pieces of their arguments. They debate with peddlers about the prices of the goods for sale, relative to their quality. They clash among themselves, shouting out their differences about politics, religion, children, parents, America.

The buildings in these scenes, so firmly fixed in our collective minds, are tall and narrow. They have a name, "tenements," and it is as though the structures have a will of their own. They, like the immigrant Jews who live in them, aggressively push into each other, leaving no room for lawns and trees and open skies. Laundry flaps about on lines, waving in the air with an intensity matched only by the pace and passion of the people on the streets below.

If the photographs could engage our sense of smell, we would pick up an array of pungent odors. We would smell the garbage,

Figure 1. Photographers created a vast compendium of images of the Lower East Side in the years that it served as a neighborhood of eastern European Jewish immigrants. These "classic" shots have been reproduced widely in books and exhibits. (Library of Congress)

Figure 2. "Classic" Lower East Side photographs emphasized the narrow streets, the throngs of people, and the jumble of pushcarts. The overall impact of the photographs was to emphasize the absence of sharp distinctions between sidewalk and street. (Photofest)

wrinkle our noses, and feel sorry that these immigrants and their children had to live that way.

But we would also whiff the stuff of the carts: the roasting chestnuts, sour pickles, steaming sweet potatoes, and spicy chickpeas. If only our sense of taste could be activated, we would sample with pleasure from these foods. Though the food would be served on greasy paper, handed to us by the vendors' bare hands (no tongs or plastic gloves to protect us from germs), we would devour the briny herring, chewy bread, and smoked meats.

This is the Lower East Side of memory, a place of beginnings, of engaged senses, of passionate ideologies, and of life lived to its

Figure 3. Lower East Side imagery emphasized the public nature of private matters. The billowing laundry, common in visual and verbal descriptions of the neighborhood, made that point. (Photofest)

fullest. These images, captured in the photographs and reproduced far and wide, have made their way into film, television, historical scholarship, the graphic arts, public ritual, journalism, and
fiction—actually into most texts where Jews have explored their
past in America.

The Lower East Side has become fixed in American Jewish
memory as the site from which a singular story has been told. It
has all the markings of an apocryphal tale: a people persecuted in
the "Old World" picked up their featherbeds, Sabbath candlesticks, and samovars and fled to the Atlantic ports. They never
looked back as they traveled in steerage across the ocean to a land
of freedom, their landing welcomed by a massive statue grasping
the beacon of liberty.

What they found, however, was a warren of dark, crowded
streets, the Lower East Side of New York. Dirty and dank, this
neighborhood, with its jumble of buildings that made no room
for light or fresh air, became their new home.

It was as though the neighborhood tested their mettle as Jews
and as potential Americans. Here they endured a series of trials.
Here they often struggled with poverty, disease, and family discord. They clashed among themselves, but ultimately, on the
streets of the Lower East Side, they learned that compromise was
their passport to success. In the end, it was here where they tri-
umphed, becoming educated, middle-class Americans who re-
tained their Jewishness, albeit in new forms. And in their achievements, they left the neighborhood behind.

As the focal point of American Jewish remembrance, the neighborhood was canonized into its mythic status well after the Jewish
crowds dwindled, after less and less Yiddish could be heard on the
streets, after the accents of eastern Europe were replaced by those
of China and the Caribbean, as synagogues became churches, and
as the vendors started selling the foods of other cultures, redolent
with the smells and tastes of other peoples.

The Lower East Side story as the locus for the American Jewish
founding myth bears a striking resemblance to the Pilgrims' tale.
A band of women and men, united by their persecution, the Pilgrims left their homes to pursue religious freedom in the "New

World." They were not the first of their "group" to make the dangerous voyage across the Atlantic, but because of their idealism, their tribulations, and their ultimate achievements, the big story got told in their name and through their experiences.

The Lower East Side has become the American Jewish Plymouth Rock. It has come to stand for Jewish authenticity in America, for a moment in time when undiluted eastern European Jewish culture throbbed in America.

The mythic dimensions of the story of the Lower East Side of memory actually do not fit the history. Other Jews, not from eastern Europe, lived on these streets well before the 1880s, the date when the story takes off in memory. The immigrants from eastern Europe came with a mix of motives, and economic ones played as much a role in their decision to emigrate as did political-religious ones. Many non-Jews also lived on the Lower East Side, and there is little compelling evidence that the Jews who lived on what we now consider the Lower East Side ever thought of themselves as living in a single, bounded neighborhood.

American Jews, however, since the end of World War II and particularly after the 1960s, wanted the Lower East Side to be the place of their memories. They wanted to have that story be peopled by refugees from the pogroms, exploited workers who struggled for their daily bread, who scrimped and saved, but sent their children to American schools. They wanted to tell their story, to themselves and to their non-Jewish neighbors, from this singular place, closed off from the rest of New York, and indeed from the rest of America. They felt, because of the pressures and opportunities of their experiences of the last half of the twentieth century, the need to turn back to the immigrant era and project a particular past, told through the themes of a particular space.

This book explores the evolution of the Lower East Side as American Jewish sacred space. It probes the ways American Jews made the Lower East Side their common heritage, regardless of where they live at the end of the twentieth century. Nearly all of them claim a piece of the Lower East Side, and I want to understand why they do so.

How and why did this sacralization occur? Why did the Lower East Side emerge as American Jews' special place? What undergirds the Lower East Side walking tours, flavored as they are with the cadences of the return pilgrimage to sacred ground? Why do those photographs reappear, and what lessons do they teach? How did this neighborhood, almost a century removed in time, become familiar and sacred to late-twentieth-century American Jews?

I, too, have participated in the Lower East Side's veneration. As a place, it spoke to me despite my never having been there. I grew up in Milwaukee. None of my family members, as far as I know, had ever set foot on the Lower East Side. My father spoke of Phila-delphia and Los Angeles as the places where he had lived in America after immigrating from Russia in the 1920s. The latter city, in particular, emerged in the stories about his early life in America as a place pulsating with Jewish culture, where he learned about America as an immigrant Jew. My extended family on my mother's side made their home in our region's big city, Chicago, having landed in the lesser and less sacred port of Baltimore.

But even in faraway Wisconsin in the 1950s, without any family anchors to New York, I had two encounters with the Lower East Side that drew me emotionally eastward, pulling me into that neighborhood's culture. First, neighbors of ours, our landlords, were involved with a local Yiddish theatrical group. By necessity in Milwaukee, it had to be at the amateur level. But they talked about New York's Second Avenue in reverential terms, as the standard to which they aspired, as the wellspring of all that was authentically Jewish and worthy of drawing upon for Jewish artistic inspiration. Every few years the leaders of this troupe, the Perhift, went to New York to find out what was being staged there. They came back with wondrous tales of this intensely Jewish cultural milieu. Their visits took the form of pilgrimages, journeys to the source of "real" Jewish culture, where they could learn from the experts, the high priests of Yiddishkeit, about what we in the "provinces" should be seeing.

To make their pilgrimage complete, they always brought back rye bread from the Lower East Side. Although it must have been stale by the time they returned to Milwaukee, the loaves of bread served as physical, digestible reminders of having been in New York, the only place, they said, where you could get real Jewish rye bread, just as Second Avenue, a place I did not see until I was in my twenties, served as the source of Jewish culture.

I also came to my romantic engagement with the Lower East Side through the children's book *All-of-a-Kind Family*. A voracious reader, I always went to the library on Friday afternoons to load up with books for the weekend and beyond. Sometime in elementary school I stumbled upon Sidney Taylor's book set on the Lower East Side. Although I had already read most of the classic Jewish children's books then available, such as *The Adventures of K'tonton* and *Hillel's Happy Holidays*, these books had not found their way to the shelves of the Milwaukee Public Library, and the characters never seemed real (one, indeed, centered on the magical K'tonton, "the Jewish Tom Thumb"). They did not move me.

All-of-a-Kind Family was the first book I ever read with Jewish characters, Americans, with whom I could identify. The minute I pulled the book off the shelf and looked at the cover, I knew instinctively that the family in the book was Jewish and that its pages contained stories that would affect me deeply. I am not sure how I knew this, but I distinctly remember the pleasure of that moment of recognition and the hours of delight (since I read it over and over again) that it, and the other volumes in the series, brought. While it would be too much of a leap to say it changed my life, finding this book did give me a sense of validation and a rush of belonging that I never experienced again as a reader.

In the first chapter of the book, the girls in the family, Jewish children in immigrant New York, go to the library—on Friday afternoon—on their weekly foray for books. Here I was reading a book that I found in the public library on a Friday afternoon in which the main characters, a family of little girls, did exactly what I did: get their library books on Friday afternoon, light Sabbath candles, eat kugel, celebrate Passover, speak English to their Yiddish-speaking parents, argue with each other, get in trouble, get out of trouble, and so on. Despite the fact that the book was set in a city I had never seen and that the actions took place a half century earlier than the years of my growing up, I felt an instantaneous bond with these girls and their neighborhood. I could not think of anyplace I wanted to visit more than New York, and I expected that the Lower East Side would look and sound just like it did when Henny, Ella, Gertie, Sarah, and Charlotte ran down the steps of the library, rushing home before the Sabbath began.

Figure 4. Sydney Taylor's *All-of-a-Kind Family* was one of the first post–World War II texts, distributed to a broad juvenile market, that located the Lower East Side as the site of American Jewish memory. (Reprinted by permission of GRM Associates, Inc., Agents for the Estate of Ralph Taylor, from the book *All-of-a-Kind Family* by Sydney Taylor. Copyright © 1951 by Follett Publishing Company; copyright renewed 1979 by Ralph Taylor.)

I have subsequently learned that my engagement from afar with the neighborhood through *All-of-a-Kind Family* was not unique or idiosyncratic. A young Jewish girl growing up in San Antonio, Texas, in those same years, in the affluent but decidedly non-Jewish neighborhood of Alamo Heights, also stumbled upon Sydney Taylor's Lower East Side book. She, too, experienced a deep personal encounter with her Jewishness through the Lower East Side, with the book as a springboard to the past. Bobbie Sharlack, however, was much more creative than I was. I just read the book, repeatedly, once writing a book report on it. She was so "predisposed to find 'romance' in the tales of these urban pioneers of the Lower East Side," she remarked years later, that she wrote a play about it, and her little Lower East Side drama was staged at San Antonio's Reform congregation, Temple Beth El, as a Purim play one year in the mid-1950s.

So the Jewish children of the temple, deep in the heart of Texas—instead of dressing up as Queen Esther, who saved her people in ancient Persia, or King Ahashverush, who decided their fate, or the noble Mordecai, Esther's uncle who advised her, or the evil Haman, who sought to destroy them—put on the imagined immigrant garb of fifty years earlier. They reenacted the stories of the five girls of the Lower East Side and, without knowing it, launched the beginnings of American Jewish memory culture.[1]

That culture was in full swing when for the first time I, with my husband and children, took a walking tour of the Lower East Side sometime in the 1980s. I felt that I had "come home." It was an emotional, intense afternoon in which everything was new, but also absolutely familiar. I looked for my parents on Delancey Street, on Essex and Rivington, as they appeared in the black-and-white photographs of our family album. I knew that they had never lived here, but I kept trying to superimpose the pictures that had been taken of them in Venice, California, and Chicago in the 1930s and 1940s onto the streetscapes of the Lower East Side of the 1980s.

The historian in me wants to know why I felt that this constituted a homecoming. Why did I devour Sidney Taylor's books? Why did my Milwaukee neighbors think that day old-bread from the Lower East Side was somehow more Jewish, more tasty, and more authentic than the rye bread sold at the kosher bakeries two blocks from our house, which could be gotten hot and fresh?

All of this was made possible by a series of historic events unleashed by the closure of World War II and the realities of American Jewish life in the 1950s. A community made up primarily of the children of immigrants, Jews in America were now, for the first time, fully American and fully middle class. Having just witnessed, but from afar, a harrowing period in the history of their people, they embraced an expansive set of American opportunities fostered by postwar liberalism.

In this book I want to link that moment, and the details of the subsequent five decades, to the memorialization of the Lower East Side. I shall explore the texts, including Taylor's book, that connect America's Jews to these particular sidewalks of New York. The American Jewish consecration of a particular piece of land in Manhattan did not just happen.

Rather, it can be placed in the context of time. It developed as a result of a series of historical events, the devastation of World War II, the destruction of European Jewry and Jewish places where they had lived, and the opening up of America's bounty to its Jews, the descendants of the eastern European immigrants.

The memory culture developed because a broad range of writers, artists, scholars, and other producers of culture participated in constructing the Lower East Side. It developed because what those creators produced touched the broad masses of American Jews, stirred something in their identities, as they experienced the second half of the twentieth century.

The story of the Lower East Side has become almost universally understood to be synonymous with the story of Jewish life in America. The neighborhood is understood as different than any other place where Jews lived. It emerged, and still serves, as the point of reference for all other American Jewish stories in its singularity and its mythic status. Transformed from being just a swath of urban space where many Jews lived for some period of time and then moved on, leaving in their wake some buildings with Jewish markers on them, it became sacred.

In the process of making the profane holy, the history of the neighborhood in all its complexity has somehow gotten lost. Because the history of the neighborhood got written during the same time that the sacred memory became fixed in place, the nuances, ambiguities, and complications of Jewish immigrant life in New York took second place to a reified and singular Lower East Side.

We actually have no history of the designation "Lower East Side," its coinage, usage, and why this name, as opposed to others, stuck. It is not even clear if events took place "in" or "on" the Lower East Side, and where the boundaries of that neighborhood ought to be drawn, who lived there, how they defined themselves, and how they used space.

I want to examine the idea of the Lower East Side in American Jewish memory of the last half of the twentieth century not as a cynical debunker of conventional wisdom but rather as a historian interested in furthering our understanding of how American Jews made sense of their past as they contended with a particular kind of present.

At no point will I challenge the truth, proven in ample detail by many before me, that most eastern European Jewish immigrants after 1880 disembarked in New York, flocked to the more southerly and easterly area of the city, and, in that space now designated by the phrase "Lower East Side," created an institution-rich community unmatched by any other American Jewish area of first or second settlement. Not only did they build a vast network of institutions for their own use, but some of those institutions—the press, the publishing houses, the theaters—produced cultural texts that went forth from their neighborhood to the rest of American Jewry and to the larger world beyond. Those artifacts became the sources that historians in later generations, who rightly decided that this neighborhood, now called the Lower East Side, had a history that deserved to be written, turned to, in order to reconstruct that past.

By a twist of fate, that neighborhood happened to be in America's largest city and the place where the producers of American culture also found themselves. That same moment in time, by happenstance, perhaps, coincided with the explosion of investigative journalism, documentary photography, the birth of motion pictures, and the upsurge in Progressive reform touching Americans around the country, but with New York as the center of those activities. Because of that coincidence, New York's eastern European immigrant Jews in the era after the 1880s, the women and men of the Lower East Side, may be the most written about, observed, commented upon, described, and photographed Jews in the long history of the Jewish people, with the possible exceptions of the victims of the Holocaust and contemporary Israeli Jews. No wonder, then, that historians and the creators of mnemonic culture seized upon the Jews of the Lower East Side and their urban space as the means to understand and represent the American Jewish experience.

The power of the Lower East Side in American Jewish expressive culture cannot be explained solely as a result of the size of either the community or the body of sources available for contemplation. These factors certainly ought to be thought of as the necessary prerequisites for constructing the grand narrative. Rather, they came together with certain powerful realities in the years after World War II, as new generations of American Jews faced challenging issues particular to their time and place. It is within the context of that moment that I want to explore the sacralization of the Lower East Side, focusing much less on what we know about that history as produced by many fine historians and more on the question of why the neighborhood came to take on mythic proportions in the memories of American Jews.

It is risky business to look at individual texts as pivotal in shaping popular culture. Yet I recognize that no one did more for the memory of the Lower East Side and for the popularization of the history of the eastern European Jewish immigration to America than Irving Howe, author of the neighborhood's greatest tribute, *The World of Our Fathers*, timed to appear in the year of America's bicentennial. Jewish readers embraced the book with passion, whether or not they plowed through all of its 646 pages. In an era when Americans sought to explore their roots, here were theirs uncovered in bold relief.

In the chapters that follow, I place Howe's book into the context of other popular works that reflected, and contributed to, the culture of memory embodied in the Lower East Side. Indeed, I consider it here alongside romance novels, children's books, films, parodic songs, television shows, and other artifacts of popular culture that put the Lower East Side in the foreground of the American Jewish experience. These artifacts stengthened the bond between the idea of the American Jewish experience and the Lower East Side as the site of its origins.

I draw upon a wide array of sources, invoking texts in which American Jews have enshrined the Lower East Side as their special place, as the place by which they perform their conjoined Jewish and American identities. I ask why the sacralization of the Lower East Side happened when it did, and what that timing might tell us about historical memory and about American Jewry in the half century since the end of World War II.

This deconstruction may seem cynical, but it is not. After all the research, the months of writing, and the unraveling of the skeins of memory, I still feel an emotional tug when I cross into the "Lower East Side." I start searching for relics of the past, trying to find the markers of the Jewish culture of a bygone age. I savor the sights, look for the hints of what was once there. I imagine tastes and smells that somehow can connect me to this very sacred space.

CHAPTER ONE

The Lower East Side
and American
Jewish Memory

I'm Jewish because love my family matzoh ball soup.
I'm Jewish because my fathers mothers uncles grandmothers said
  "Jewish," all the way back to Vitebsk & Kaminetz-Podolska via Lvov.
Jewish because reading Dostoyevsky at 13 I write poems at restaurant
  tables Lower East Side, perfect delicatessen intellectual.

—ALLEN GINSBERG, *"Yiddishe Kopf"*

THE POET Allen Ginsberg, born and raised in Newark, New Jersey, returned in his later years to a narrative style of expression, shifting gears from the anger and fire of his early career. In this poem from 1991 he also touched down again, after a long hiatus spent exploring Buddhism and Eastern philosophy, upon some Jewish themes, as a way of remembering the world of his youth. He described that world in one poem, "Yiddishe Kopf," literally, a Jewish head, but more broadly, a highly distinctive Jewish way of thinking, based on insight, cleverness, and finesse.

That world for him stood upon two zones of remembrance. The world of eastern Europe, of Vitebsk, Lvov, and Kamenets-Podolski gave him one anchor for his Jewishness. That space of memory gave him a focus for continuity and inherited identity, tied down by the weight of the past, by family in particular. The other, the

Lower East Side, nurtured and fed him. It also offered him his passport out of and into the bigger world. Here he wrote his youthful poetry, he told his readers, at delicatessen tables, influenced by the great ideas of Western civilization—in this poem, through reading Dostoyevsky.

This formulation, while captivating in Ginsberg's distinctive rapid-fire, challenging style, was actually less original and much more formulaic than the poet might have thought. Since the late 1940s, American Jewish memory had been bounded by these two mythic places, eastern Europe and the Lower East Side. Each one stood, and still stands, as a point of memory, replete with an instantly recognizable set of images of people and places, described with a sensual trope built around sounds, smells, and tastes, stimulating a process of remembering even for those, such as the dean of the Beats, Allen Ginsberg, who did not grow up in either place and who lived for the latter part of his life in New York's East Village, not really part of the Lower East Side.

But he, or the masses of American Jews who have participated in the process of enshrining eastern Europe, usually described as a "shtetl" (small town), and the Lower East Side did not have to directly experience either place because the representations of both have played key roles in shaping American Jewish popular culture. They could be found almost anywhere. Their images ran through the imaginative world of American Jews as instant mnemonics of places that everyone knew, but, ultimately, few had lived in.

The American Jewish past, like all eras in the history of the Jewish people, exists as both history and memory. This past, as history, is the subject of scholarly inquiry and the focus of graduate and undergraduate courses, learned journals, and formal conferences—all dedicated to the proposition that the history of the Jewish people in America, like any other, is a measurable and changeable construct that can be known and, over time, known better and differently. American Jewish history's practitioners claim, by virtue of their academic training and emotional distance, the right to interpret the experience of the Jewish people in America.[1]

Yet the past, as memory, exists also, but as a set of unshakable truths that inform American Jewish public understanding. It consists of a series of linked images that have grown organically out of the contemporary cultural needs of that public, however diverse it may be, as it defines and justifies itself and its present condition. Those themes, emphasizing the cultural richness of *the* (singular) immigrant experience, the inevitability and loneliness of success, the altruistic progressive Jewish social vision of the past, and the spiritual price tag attached to mobility, all resound in American Jewish folk memory. They provide the intertwined leitmotiv in American Jews' understanding of where they have been, where they are now, and, possibly, even where they might be heading. This bundle of memories plays a crucial role in the creation of an American Jewish narrative. Memory, after all, as the Polish poet Adam Zagajewski noted, functions as an "indispensable part of creating culture."[2]

The culture that American Jews fashioned for themselves in the decades after World War II was shaped by the aftermath of that war, particularly the knowledge of the destruction of European Jewry. The memories were also shaped by a counterforce, the triumph of American liberalism, as it played itself out in the era of greater civil rights. American Jews experienced few liabilities as a result of being Jews, and they took advantage of the opening up of suburban communities and professional opportunities.

It was in the convergence of these two phenomena that the Lower East Side changed from being a place where many Jews had once lived to become the epicenter of American Jewish memory. The Lower East Side, a swath of lower Manhattan, has assumed that same kind of sacred status in the consciousness of American Jews. It is a place invested with deep memories of a shared past that offers them some ideas about their present.[3]

In the narratives that American Jews tell about their collective past in the United States, the Lower East Side functions not just as a particular neighborhood where many Jews lived for some period of time but as exemplary of *the* Jewish experience in America. Refugees from the shtetl, they came to America and found instead the Lower East Side, a warren of crowded, dirty, and mean streets. In this slum, these impoverished Jews re-created the culture of eastern Europe, thick with the smells, sounds, tastes, and noises of life in the "Old World." But through the miracle of the American dream of mobility, their sons and daughters emerged from the Lower East Side as teachers, lawyers, doctors, movie makers, musicians—aggressive and assertive about their rights as Americans but more ambivalent toward the nature of their Jewish legacy. The memory of the Lower East Side assumed its power not only from the Jewish sojourn there but also from the drama of the exodus from it.

On one level the Lower East Side story as American Jewish memory reflected in microcosm the broad outlines of the metanarrative of the Jewish past. The recurrent themes of oppression, constriction, and danger, on one hand, followed by the expansiveness of liberation, on the other, run through it. In between, Lower East Side memory culture posited that immigrant Jews lived in a liminal state. In a kind of transitional zone, they underwent an ordeal of cultural reeducation as they learned to be free. The Lower East Side served as that metaphoric middle ground where Jews dwelled among themselves while waiting for permission to enter the real America. It served as their narrow bridge between slavery and freedom, between the Egypt of Russia and Poland and the promised land of America.

Significantly, the immigrants themselves, as well as their children and grandchildren, who then became both the historians and the participants in the memory culture, used historical analogies to describe Europe as Egypt (or other sites of Jewish suffering) in distinction to America as a place of freedom, opportunity, and promise. Jews, regardless of generation or nativity, transferred these metaphors to help them understand the momentous events of the late nineteenth and the early twentieth century, the period of the great exodus of 2.5 million Jews from eastern Europe to the United States.

Sometimes they associated eastern Europe with Spain and its grim history of expulsion and Inquisition. Sometimes the persecution in eastern Europe became linked to the very moment when

Jews lost their homeland and national sovereignty, and became a diaspora people. A Mr. Katzenellenbogen, a Canal Street book-seller in the 1890s, explained to Abraham Cahan, then writing for New York's *Commercial Advertiser,* the reasons behind the im-pending fast of Tisha B'Av. "We mourn the loss of our Temple," he noted, referring to the destruction of the great Temples in Jeru-salem in 586 B.C.E. and 70 C.E. "We sit on the ground," he contin-ued, "reciting our tale of woe. Is there anything strange in the way our hearts break at the thought of the atrocities perpetrated on us in Russia, Rumania, Austria?" He then told the reporter, who knew all this quite well, "Well, when we sit down barefooted on the ground to tell the tale of famine and desolation, of the loss of our home, many a worshipper will think of Galicia and perhaps also the riots in Russia which drove him to this land of freedom."[4]

Because the eastern European part of the narrative corres-ponded to Egypt's slavery (as well as other sites of Jewish sorrows), the migration, in American Jewish popular terms, had to be pos-ited as a desperate flight from oppression, persecutions, and pogroms. In Russia, indiscriminately used in American Jewish rhetoric as a stand-in for anyplace in eastern Europe, Jews had been immured in their narrow ghettos, trembling in the face of oppresive czarist pharaohs. They had no option but to escape to freedom.[5]

Anzia Yezierska's "America and I," a short story published in 1923, written for an English reading audience, gave voice to "one of the dumb, voiceless ones. . . . One of the millions of immigrants beating, beating out their hearts at your gates for a breath of un-derstanding." An immigrant herself, who came as a teenager from Plinsk in Russia,[6] Yezierska used biblical terms to contrast the "be-fore" and "after" of her experience:

> Choked for ages in the airless oppression of Russia, the Promised Land rose up—wings for my stifled spirit—sunlight burning through my darkness—freedom singing to me in my prison. . . .
>
> I arrived in America. My young, strong body, my heart and soul pregnant with the unlived lives of generations clamoring for expression.

> What my mother and father and their mother and father never
> had a chance to give out in Russia, I would give out in America.
> The hidden sap of centuries would find release.

America, Yezierska rhapsodized, was "the golden land of flowing
opportunities."[7]

Because of both historical realities and the power of such rhetoric, American Jews, in their popular renditions of the past, have
repeatedly contrasted their migration to America with that of
other immigrants. In the process of positing that contrast, they
strengthened the theme of the Exodus from Egypt and entry into
the promised land.[8] Others, the story went, chose to come to
America for economic reasons; Jews, escapees from persecution,
came in search of religious freedom and personal survival. Others
had a home to go back to; Jews came for good. As such, we can
understand how, in 1951, Oscar Handlin, a child of eastern European Jewish immigrant parents, could write a book about immigrants in general, which clearly did not fit the Jewish model and
entitle it *The Uprooted*. Three years later he wrote a history of American Jews and entitled it, *Adventure in Freedom*.[9]

By understanding their migration as singular and as an escape
from oppression, Jews could actually link themselves to an American motif, that of the pilgrim. Thus one of the earliest excursions
into American Jewish history was Lee M. Friedman's *Pilgrims in a
New Land*.[10] Friedman's use of the pilgrim analogy worked well in
the context of American Jewish writing since the immigration era.
He had most likely never read Anzia Yezierska, since her vast body
of writing was discovered (or rediscovered) only in the 1970s, but
she, too, had used that language. In "America and I," she boldly
declared about America and herself, "And I, the last comer, had
her share to give, small or great, to the making of America, like
those Pilgrims who came in the *Mayflower*."[11]

This understanding of the Jewish past has thoroughly become
the American Jewish narrative and serves as the foundation of collective memory. Yet it defies the meticulous findings of historians
who offer a more complicated and nuanced understanding of why
Jews immigrated to the United States when they did. Historians

have amply documented the complex class relations and religious divisions among Jews in eastern Europe. They have convincingly argued that the immigrants had long been exposed to cities, industry, mass culture, secular ideas, and other elements of modernity well before their arrival in America. Additionally, we have a large corpus of material that demonstrates the economic impetus to the Jewish migration, and, finally, evidence from around the world points to the fact that Jews from eastern Europe went to all sorts of places, not just to America. The power of the "America" idea in this memory culture jars with the fact that most Jews did not leave eastern Europe. Most of them opted for better opportunities in the large cities to be found on their side of the Atlantic, indeed, their side of the Elbe River.[12]

But popular Jewish audiences—consumers of lectures, public programs, films, and novels—continue to insist on the memory of the tradition-bounded shtetl Jews who chose America as they fled pogroms.[13] In the face of a large body of historical evidence to the contrary, Irving Howe, in a 1984 essay, created an archetypal eastern European Jewish immigrant, "your barely literate Jew, with his few scraps of Hebrew and his kitchen Yiddish," who "ran away from pogroms."[14]

The idea of America as the newest promised land and, as such, the sacralization of America, suffused American Jewish culture and extended far beyond the realm of the immigrant eastern European Jews. The Passover Haggadah (the book used at the seder) issued by the Reform movement's Central Conference of American Rabbis in 1923 concluded the ritual event with the singing of "America." A photograph of the statue *Religious Liberty*, dedicated by the Union of American Hebrew Congregations in 1876 as the Jewish contribution to the grand celebration of American independence in Philadelphia, graced the page opposite the text and music to the patriotic hymn. Lest this be considered further evidence of that movement's desire to distance itself from Zionism and the long-standing dream of the Jewish people to see their homeland restored, the Reconstructionists in their 1942 Haggadah also venerated America. In this text, the words to "America" appear on the same page as those of the traditional "L'shanah

Habah b'yerushalayim" (Next year in Jerusalem) and the Zionist anthem, the Hatikvah. Rather than being just another example of Jews identifying with and praying for the good fortune of the country in which they lived, this liturgical twist allowed American Jews a way to link America, their home, with the drama of enslavement, liberation, and revelation that had been marked that very night.[15]

To fully capture this trope, the sacred memory of American Jews needed one more key element. Before the newcomers from eastern Europe could enter America in earnest, they had to experience a kind of journey through the desert in which a new generation, born into American freedom, would learn the rules. Milton Hindus, writing an introductory essay for a Lower East Side anthology of the late 1960s, described the liminality of Jewish life in the neighborhood as "an ordeal, a transition, a painful initiation, a trauma which accompanied passage from the old world *shtetl* to the sense of a privileged new nationality and status which has come to American Jews in the last fifty years or so."[16]

These children would be the ones to actually cross over. While the streets of the Lower East Side in no way resembled the sandy wilderness through which the children of Israel stumbled for forty years, waiting for the waning of the generation that had known slavery, the terms of the American narrative boldly resemble the Jewish rendition of the mythic wandering in the desert. The narrow streets, the crowded tenements, the congested sweatshops played, in the American narrative, the analogous function of that seemingly endless desert. Grinding poverty, rampant illness, industrial accidents, and exploitation by merciless bosses show up repeatedly in the memoirs of life on the Lower East Side. So do the images of desperate parents fretting over the dangers of the city's streets, its lures and temptations lying in wait to ensnare their children. They describe the breakdown of authority, and, depending on who did the telling, they bemoan or celebrate the pitfalls of America for Jewish tradition.

In the Bible the descendants of the former slaves had to prove themselves capable of freedom and had to have the memories of Egypt erased from their consciousness. In the American story they had to go through as profound a transition. They had to become modern and refined, internalizing new ideas about decorum and behavior that would distinguish them from their parents, who, in one way or another, could never really leave the Lower East Side borderland.

Children, the key players in the narrative of the "Lower East Side as desert," got their first glimpses of the real America that awaited them as they sat in the classrooms of public schools, in the hushed stillness of the reading rooms of the neighborhood's libraries, and in the horizon-expanding programs of the settlement houses. They learned about the world they were going to enter when they journeyed out of the Lower East Side to summer camps provided by charitable societies. The young Morris Raphael Cohen, who later, as a professor of philosophy at the City College of New York, would shape the intellectual orientation of thousands of other young Jewish men, wrote at length in his autobiography about the tremendous influence of Thomas Davidson, a teacher at the Lower East Side's Educational Alliance. Davidson arranged for Cohen to attend a summer camp in the Adirondacks, this immigrant's first venture beyond New York City. Here he encountered not only nature and fresh air but also a "breakfast of oatmeal and cream, bacon and eggs and coffee." This obviously nonkosher breakfast "was a novel one to me." The camp, Davidson the teacher, and the Educational Alliance provided models of mainstream American habits and behaviors.[17]

In the retelling of the immigrant Jewish saga of the Lower East Side, the last step on the journey from desert to promised land took place, for boys, when they went uptown to attend City College, a central icon in the story. In Abraham Cahan's fictionalized version of this transformation, *The Rise of David Levinsky*, the book's main character described the public university as "My Temple." "The ghetto," he wrote, "rang with a clamor for knowledge." Working in a cloak-making shop, Levinsky made the acquaintance of two young men, both students at the college, one supported by a father, a presser, and the other by an aunt, a "bunch-maker in a cigar-factory." Listening to them talk, witnessing the struggle of the older generation to educate the younger, "made me feel as though I were bound to that college with the ties of kinship." For

them and for the others, "poor Jews—wage-earners, peddlers, gro-
cers, salesmen, insurance agent—who would beggar themselves to
give their children a liberal education," the attainment of college
status represented the real journey "across the river."[18]

All of these sites helped the immigrant Jews remake themselves
so that they would be worthy of entry into America. The archetypal
story of the process of remaking the children of the immigrants
usually involved certain stock characters. The Old World parents,
who could never really learn the rules, stood for the bonds of the
past. The children, Jewish adventurers, would make the transition
outward. The "German" Jews, condescending and patronizing,
disliked everything about these newcomers. Americanized Jews
derided traditional Judaism, feared radical socialism, worried
about assertive Zionism, and loathed the crudeness of their "Russian" charges. They hoped to hold on to communal power despite
their numerical minority. Few non-Jews made it into Lower East
Side stories, for this is a Jewish narrative. Gentiles appear in the
classic renditions of the saga only when the American children
take their first steps out of the Lower East Side cocoon.

Finally, the Jewish metaphor of Egypt-Russia, desert–Lower East
Side, and promised land–America required one more rhetorical
element to make the analogy work. As the metaphor went, in the
process of making their final transition to the good life, the Jews
inevitably needed to give something up. Admission to America
came at a steep price. This, too, paralleled the metanarrative of
the biblical tale.

The years of wandering in the desert described in Exodus, Levi-
ticus, Numbers, and Deuteronomy, while arduous and full of danger, represented a period of heightened engagement with God
and with the realm of the spiritual. Upon entry into their promised land, however, the Jews lost the keen spiritual edge that had
been theirs in the desert. Once settled amid the prosperity of the
"land flowing with milk and honey," they fought and bickered
among themselves, became too comfortable, lusted after local
gods, and wanted to be like the nations around them. The voice
in Deuteronomy, offering Moses' parting prophecy, admonished
the people to think back to their years of wandering. "Remember

the days of old, consider the years of many generations," he ordered. He reminded the children of Israel who stood poised to cross the Jordan River that "the Lord's portion is his people. . . . He found him [the people Israel] in a desert land, and in the waste, a howling wilderness, he led him about, he instructed him, he kept him as the apple of his eye" (Deut. 32: 7–10).

But then Moses foretold the future in terms that would resound in the post–Lower East Side narratives about the loss of cultural authenticity as the immigrants' children opted for America over Jewishness. "But Jeshurun [Jacob/Israel's third name] grew fat and kicked." God came to despise the wickedness of the people, because "you have forgotten the God that formed you." They were, he thundered, "a perverse generation, children without faith" (Deut. 32:15–20).

So, too, in the hundreds of reminiscences, recollections, and renditions of the Lower East Side, and indeed in the writings of intellectuals and literati: the neighborhood did not just come to stand for what urban historians call "the area of first settlement" for many eastern European Jews in America. Rather, it *was* Jewish cultural authenticity—pure, untarnished Jewish cultural honesty. In their Lower East Side desert immigrant Jews may have been poor, but they were real and lived intensely Jewish lives. And like the children of Israel in the biblical verses, the American children of the eastern European Jewish immigrants, when leaving the neighborhoods, inevitably lost touch with tradition. They, too, would become "a foolish nation," a "nation void of counsel, neither is there any understanding in them."

Since so much of the invention of the Lower East Side developed after the majority of Jews who had ever lived there had moved beyond its borders, it was in their memoir literature that the notion of loss sounded most sharply and ruefully. Harry Golden, publisher, editor, sole writer, and voice of the *Carolina Israelite* from the 1940s until his death in 1981, had grown up on the Lower East Side, having been brought to America from Galicia as a young child in the early years of the century. While he made a notable career for himself as a southern Jew, he participated, through his columns in the *Carolina Israelite* and books such as *Only in America,* in the romanticization of the neighborhood he had left for the very different clime of Charlotte, North Carolina. While the vignettes in that book focused on warm, tenderly remembered anecdotes of the amusing people and situations of his youth, it was in another work that he most perfectly captured the trope of lost authenticity that went in tandem with abandoning the Lower East Side. In his preface to the 1965 reissue of Hutchins Hapgood's 1902 book, *The Spirit of the Ghetto,* the Jewish sage of Charlotte, wrote: "In retrospect, I would say that I am happy to have grown up on the Lower East Side of New York. I believe it was a happier time to have grown to manhood than that in which my three sons grew to manhood. It was more vigorous, it contained a higher sense of involvement, and a wider feeling of hope."[19]

The "in retrospect" suggests that Golden may not have felt so spiritually charged when he lived there; his feelings about the intensity of life were less benign after he fled. But as remembered life, the very challenges of Lower East Side life offered those who had endured them a heightened consciousness. Other memoirs, including many of Golden's journalistic ramblings from below the Mason-Dixon line, depicted the difficulties of the earlier Lower East Side days in the context of heightened senses: smells, tastes, sights, and sounds. Everything stood out more boldly, was felt more sharply.

Emma Beckerman's 1980 memoir of hard times as an immigrant girl on Rivington Street at the turn of the twentieth century easily conflated descriptions of hunger with memories of food. Although she presented herself and her siblings as "often hungry" and her mother as scouring "the neighborhood for day-old bread," she sounded her memories most loudly in the sensuous tropes of plenty. As she recalled, "When I revisit the Lower East Side . . . I can almost smell the conglomeration of garlic, gefilte fish and cabbage." Dedicating the book to her American-born son, she, like Golden, proclaimed, "Of course there were hard times. But looking back . . . I can truthfully say, 'It's a great life.' "[20]

If the Lower East Side narrative conformed to a classic Jewish formulation, it also had a distinctively American tenor. Certainly, the "pilgrim" language connected the Jewish and American ideologies. Furthermore, the terms of Lower East Side rhetoric offered a particular version of the often-repeated American success story demonstrating how, through hard work, a person could go all the way from poverty to plenty.[21] It offered a twentieth-century Jewish rendition of Benjamin Franklin's autobiography: the tale of the young man who bucked tradition and hierarchy, set a series of goals for himself, and with just the right blend of determination, luck, pluck, and sacrifice, remade himself exactly as he, not anyone else, wanted. The Philadelphia printer began his autobiography in terms that would resonate in Lower East Side, American Jewish memoir literature: "Having emerged from the poverty and obscurity in which I was born and bred to a state of affluence and some degree of reputation in the world and having gone so far through life with a considerable share of felicity, the conducting use I made use of, which with the blessing of God so well succeed."[22]

Told either directly or indirectly, in fiction or in tales of "how it really was," the Lower East Side testimonies presented their narrators' experiences as stories of rebirth. The young woman, or man, born in eastern Europe but nurtured in America found herself constricted both by the poverty with which she lived and by her father's (and sometimes, although less often, her mother's) rigid and unyielding traditionalism.

On the Lower East Side of Anzia Yezierska, for example, the fictional daughters of "Old World" parents were reborn as their American selves. In her own life, as in her fiction, Yezierska was determined to shape her options, set priorities, devise a strategy to get there, and become whatever she wanted. Her most widely read work, *Bread Givers* (1925), focused on this self-creation; she subtitled it *A Struggle between a Father of the Old World and a Daughter of the New.*[23] Abraham Cahan's eponymous hero in *The Rise of David Levinsky* traversed the path from Talmud student in Antomir, in the "Northwestern Region, Russia," to a man "worth more than two million dollars and recognized as one of the two or three leading men in the cloak-and-suit trade in the United States." The Lower East Side served as the transitional space between these two selves. There Levinsky learned to shed the trappings of the former to become the latter. He reflected on this, looking backward at the book's begin-ning: "Sometimes, when I think of my past in a superficial, casual way, the metamorphosis I have gone through strikes me as nothing short of a miracle."[24] In terms not so different, Yetta Helen Dine, who came to America from a small town in Kovno in 1890, remem-bered that September 22, the day her ship, the *Rhineland*, docked at Castle Garden happened to be her twenty-fourth birthday. That was "the day of my rebirth and my real birthday. I regret that 24 years—the best part of a life—were wasted," presumably because they had been spent in Lithuania rather than the United States.[25] Morris Raphael Cohen also linked his arrival in America with a met-aphoric moment of self-creation. Not sure about his actual birthday on the Gregorian calendar, he recalled that he had to pick a date: "I chose July 25 because that or some other day in the summer of 1892, my mother, my sister and I reached the harbor of New York and a new chapter of my life began."[26]

While most of the rhetoric of re-creation among eastern Euro-pean Jewish immigrants involved the children who soared beyond their parents' restrictions, sometimes the immigrant parent un-derwent this kind of metamorphosis. In a poem from 1938, Del-more Schwartz allowed his grandfather to experience firsthand the transformative power of America:

> O Nicolas! Alas! Alas!
> My grandfather coughed in your army.
> Hid in a wine-stinking barrel
> For three days in Bucharest,
> Then left for America
> To become a king himself.[27]

While Jewish immigrants told these stories from and about other spots around the United States, such as Mary Antin's Boston or even Sophie Turpin's rural home described in her *Dakota Dias-pora*, more such memoirists found their voice on the Lower East Side than any other place. The other places where those stories were told came to be viewed as interesting because they were *not* the Lower East Side. They achieved their edge from the novelty of being about places other than the Lower East Side, which became the cultural metaphor for any place in America where Jewish traditionalism inevitably clashed with American opportunities. The neighborhood meant the zone of contest between these two forces, where it became clear that the former would triumph and exact a price from the latter.[28]

Even personal narratives of American Jews shaped by other places echo the Lower East Side narrative. These stories of growing up as American Jews and moving out into the wider world take the Lower East Side as the marker of place of origin and as the handy point of reference that all are assumed to understand. In the opening text panels for a retrospective exhibit, *A Voice of Conscience: The Prints of Jack Levine*, at the Brooklyn Museum of Art in 1999, the artist recounted his early life in Boston, where he was born in 1915. "The area," as he described it to the exhibit's curator, "was teeming, full of pawnshops. It was very like Hester Street." The recognizably Jewish phrase "Hester Street" brought to mind a set of pictures, the details of which could then be superimposed upon the idea of "Boston," a less widely recognizable immigrant Jewish space, less linked to fixed images.[29]

The name "Lower East Side" contains meaning that is automatically understood by all as distinctive, replete with a set of icons associated with it, and usually with it alone. Tenements, pushcarts, sweatshops, and synagogues inhabited by old men are the images that come instantly to mind with the evocation of the Lower East Side, along with pungent smells, loud noises, crowded spaces, and good, rich food. Pious elders, rebellious children, passionate socialists, aggressive union women, and supercilious German Jewish uptown philanthropists people the canvas of Lower East Side memory. These icons have become firmly fixed in the American Jewish consciousness as synonymous with *the* American Jewish experience. They have become so thoroughly reified that the neighborhood has assumed the status of American Jews' cultural homeland, which they seek to connect with both physically and metaphysically.[30] The Lower East Side has as such entered the realm of the sacred.

Whereas the word *sacred* usually carries with it connotations of religiosity or a connectedness to some belief in a divine being, its other, and broader, meanings make it an apt concept for the Lower East Side. The *Oxford English Dictionary* defines *sacred* as "dedicated, set apart, exclusively appointed to some person, or some special purpose" as its second usage.[31] Likewise, in Hebrew the word *kadosh*, usually defined as "holy" and having to do with God and to those practices specified in *halakah* (Jewish law), can mean "dedicated" or "distinctive," "separate" or "set apart."

Sacred has meaning beyond the realm of formal, institutionalized religious practice, not just as a matter of dictionary definitions. Scholars of religion have long acknowledged the breadth of the concept and its many manifestations beyond the confines of church or synagogue. Georg Simmel, a German sociologist, described *sacred* as the experiences people encounter in "a certain inner mood," which "stir relations, meanings, sentiments, which of themselves are not yet religion ... [but] they become religion."[32] Likewise, the Romanian-born Mircea Eliade considered any time as potentially sacred, as long as it functioned and was commonly used as wholly different from ordinary time. As long as groups of people mark off moments as fixed, distinct, and meaningful, Eliade considered them worthy, in his intellectual schema, of being designated as sacred.[33]

For a time, place, or object to acquire sacred status, it must become separate from others that initially seemed very much like it. It must traverse a path from ordinariness to distinctiveness, from optional to fixed. It needs to be connected intimately to identity, on either a personal or a communal level.[34]

An example might help to demonstrate this process. Almost all Americans mark off the last Thursday of November as a Thursday unlike all others. They travel, sometimes vast distances, to be with family. They "gather together" to eat a formulaic meal—turkey, stuffing, mashed potatoes, cranberry sauce, pumpkin pie—that varies not a bit from year to year.

But this sacred moment has a history. It went through a historically specific process of moving from the ordinary to the sacred, from being celebrated only by some Americans until the time of the Civil War, when President Lincoln issued an official National Thanksgiving Proclamation. Lincoln was influenced by the ardent campaign of Sara Joseph Hale (also known for composing "Mary Had a Little Lamb"), the editor of *Godey's Lady's Book* who advocated such a day as an addition to the American calendar, a new holiday or, better, holy day. She advocated its universalization as a sacred day by writing: "The *last Thursday in November,* let it be consecrated now to our Father in heaven, for His bounteous blessing bestowed upon us, as the perpetual Day of Thanksgiving for the American people."[35] That is, then, the last Thursday in November became sacralized.

The Lower East Side has also moved along this path. American Jews have constructed it as singular and special. It is paradigmatic of *the* Jewish narrative in America. As such, it has also become sacred in the sense that it is reenacted through ritual, visited as pilgrimage, and invoked as a shorthand way of encapsulating an entire trajectory of Jewish history.[36]

The specialness of the Lower East Side manifested itself throughout American Jewish culture of the post–World War II era. In representations of Jews in America, the Lower East Side served as the standard of Jewish measurement. A 1980s "docudrama" about a young Jewish peddler who learned about America and about himself while on the road bore the title *West of Hester Street,* obviously a big swath of geography.[37]

Irving Howe, the great literary critic who in the 1970s turned to the Lower East Side for his magnum opus on immigrant life in America, and Kenneth Libo, a popular writer, collaborated on two photodocumentary books on the history of Jewish immigration. These lavishly illustrated books made their way to numerous synagogue libraries and American Jewish coffee tables. By their very titles we can see the Lower East Side as normative, and elsewhere as exceptional. *How We Lived: A Documentary History of Immigrant Jews in America, 1880–1930* (1979) focused, not surprisingly, on the Lower East Side. Despite the word *America* in the title, the book captured the sights and words of the Lower East Side only. The Library of Congress cataloged it under the heading and call numbers for "New York," the designation in the title of "America" notwithstanding. Five years later, Howe and Libo turned to the rest of the story. *We Lived There, Too: In Their Own Words and Pictures—Pioneer Jews and the Westward Movement of America, 1630–1930,* informed the incredulous that some Jews had willingly crossed the Hudson.[38]

Late-twentieth-century American Jewish rhetoric as reflected in journalism carries forward the normative nature of the Lower East Side as the marker against which all American Jews must measure themselves. An article from the Jewish Telegraphic Agency that was picked up by Jewish newspapers around the United States and the world, described an effort to save and restore the Breed Street Synagogue in Los Angeles. The article, published in July 1998, explained the importance of this *shul,* its association with some of Hollywood's legendary figures, and its setting in the Boyle Heights neighborhood, "which was dubbed the Lower East Side of Los Angeles." The few written histories of the Jews of Los Angeles do not claim that residents of Boyle Heights in the 1920s, for example, ever compared their neighborhood to the Lower East Side. At its apex in the 1920s, the neighborhood housed ninety-thousand Jews, which would certainly qualify it as a major Jewish enclave that probably did not need to be justified in terms of another Jewish neighborhood a continent away.[39]

Los Angeles Jewry in the 1920s experienced a golden age of cultural productivity. Here immigrant and native-born Jews created a society in a climate notably unlike the ones they had left on the other side of the Atlantic, and the other side of the American continent. They picked up on that physical distance and difference to celebrate the uniqueness of their communities in the diaspora. The Yiddish poet Joseph Katzenogy waxed eloquent about Los Angeles in 1925:

> Far—
>
> from the narrow New York streets, Chicago clouds,
>   Pittsburgh smoke—
> Los Angeles!
> You are intoxicated by the smell of orange blossoms,
> blinded by the towering mountains, refreshed by the
> straight proud palms.[40]

Thus, a Los Angeles Jewish Yiddish-language poet in the 1920s did not feel compelled to single out the Lower East Side from the rest of New York or to celebrate the Edenic qualities of California as opposed to *only* New York. Seventy years later, however, after the construction of the Lower East Side as the central metaphor of American Jewish memory, the wire service article could not help but link Breed Street with the Lower East Side.

Indeed, so sacred is that imagery of the Lower East Side that it actually blurs the line between the tenacity of memory and the writing of history. Historians use the phrase "Lower East Side" as an understood point of reference without exploring exactly what or where it was. They do so for a good reason: more Jews lived in New York City than anywhere else in America. Indeed, more Jews lived there than in any other city in all of Jewish history. The most important port of disembarkation of immigrants from Europe, New York attracted more Jews than any other American city, and it attracted Jews to a degree unmatched by any other immigrant group. Jews, more than most other immigrants, stayed put in New York, and from the 1880s until the 1920s, most settled in the area that came to be known as the Lower East Side. In 1890, close to 75 percent of New Yorkers who listed their mothers' birthplace as somewhere in Russia or Poland—almost all Jews—lived in the three wards that constituted the Lower East Side.[41]

These historians, almost exclusively American Jews themselves, certainly have been justified in focusing on New York and the Lower East Side as the key geographic zone in their attempts to understand American Jewish history. The ways they have focused on it, and the ways in which they articulated their findings, demonstrate the gravity of Lower East Side memory.

A few examples should suffice. In 1954 the United Jewish Federation of Buffalo, like a number of other Jewish communities at that time, commissioned a book to chart the history of the local Jewish community, inspired by the 1954 tercentenary of Jewish settlement in North America. The book, *From Ararat to Suburbia*, published in 1960, offered readers a dense base of information about the history of the Jews in this upstate New York city. Its authors narrated the experience of the Jews who came there, the institutions they built, and their activities as Jews and as citizens of the city. Amid the many specific, localized details of Buffalo Jewish life, the book informed its readers that "the William Street area of that period was, in miniature, every bit as picturesque as the Lower East Side of New York City."[42]

In a history of the Jews of Brownsville, a neighborhood in Brooklyn where Jews made up a larger percentage of the population than they ever did on the Lower East Side, the title of the first chapter is "Brooklyn's 'Lower East Side': Brownsville before the Boys Club."[43] Likewise, a history of the Jews of Denver used words and pictures to prove that even in the Rocky Mountains, where eastern European Jews settled, their communities "soon resembled the lower east side of New York with its many synagogues, small businesses and adherence to an Orthodox Jewish tradition."[44]

The Jews of Oregon: 1850–1950, by Steven Lowenstein, is a well-researched, information-packed history of the Jews of the Pacific Northwest. It convincingly argued that Jews ought to know the history of the Jewish communities in which they live, and that non-Jews ought to know it as well. Lowenstein made a good argument for local history: "It is not only in Israel, in Europe, in the East or Midwest, but in Oregon—this beautiful outpost of the Diaspora— where we have chosen to live our lives." Yet when Lowenstein began his discussion in part 2, "The Coming of the Jews from Eastern Europe," he allowed his future Oregonians a stopover on the Lower East Side before bringing them to their "beautiful outpost of the Diaspora." This book on the Jews of Oregon includes a photograph of Hester Street, with the caption "Hester Street was a ferment of activity. Most immigrants to Oregon who came from Eastern Europe spent their first weeks in America on New York's Lower East Side." This same statement was then repeated on the next page, along with another: "For Jewish immigrants, the Lower East Side had the strangeness of a new country, and yet the familiarity of a teeming Old World *shtetl.*" Lowenstein not only never proved his contention that most future Oregon Jews spent some time in New York but also failed to explain why, when reading a book on Oregon Jews, we need to know that "Lower East Side life was both confusing and intoxicating." If the memory of that brief sojourn informed the kind of community Jews built in the Wilamette River Valley, that would be worth proving, or if the future Jews of Oregon went west because of that confusion and intoxication, the references would seem reasonable.[45]

Actually, the reason for including these references is so centrally embedded in American Jewish consciousness and so connected to the intensity of Lower East Side memory that Lowenstein did not have to explain the references. By telling his readers that these Jews who went to live in Portland, Oregon, had spent time on the Lower East Side, he is indicating that they shared in the normative American Jewish experience. They may have ultimately set up homes on the shores of the Pacific Ocean, but they still had, however briefly, engaged with American Jewry's central sacred space.

Likewise, a recent scholarly history of the Jews of Hartford, Connecticut, *Making a Life, Building a Community*, repeatedly referenced that city's East Side to New York's, presumably to give legitimacy to the Hartford experience.

> As in New York's Lower East Side . . . crowded and
> unsanitary living conditions were the norm.

> On Hartford's East Side, as on New York City's Lower East Side, "dark and airless rooms and corridors and the ever-present sounds of too many people crowded into too little space. . . ."

> On Hartford's East Side, as on the Lower East Side in
> Manhattan, tuberculosis was known as "the Jewish disease."[46]

Here David Dalin and Jonathan Rosenbaum did more than just compare East Sides. By linking the experience of Hartford's eastern European Jews to those who lived on New York's Lower East Side, the writers unintentionally seemed to legitimize their more provincial subjects. Rather than allowing the story of Hartford to speak for itself, as well it could, they validated the ordeal of that city's Jews and their transition to America in Lower East Side terms by informing their readers of its similarity to how it was "on the Lower East Side." That act of validation did not demonstrate any problems with their research or writing, nor did it detract from the value of what they produced. Rather, it proved how firmly the Lower East Side as the icon of memory had been fixed in the consciousness of American Jews.

The Lower East Side has functioned as the most dense geographic space that Jews in America have marked off as *theirs*, as paradigmatic for what it meant to be an American Jew. The Lower East Side as an exemplar of Jewish life in America stands for all the other places where Jews lived, the other large cities—Chicago, Philadelphia, Boston, St. Louis, Cleveland, Baltimore—chief among them. The Lower East Side evokes them, whereas they, in the imagination of Jews and non-Jews, do not evoke it. As an American Jewish paradigm, it is the theme, they the variations.

But the Lower East Side offers America not just a visible and powerful example of "the Jewish experience." It also occupies a zone unto itself. It is the essence of that experience, the metaphor through which Jews have told, and continue to tell, their story. Its artifacts and images have been transformed into icons of the sacred. Photographs, film clips, artistic representations, pilgrimages to it, literary and historical references to it—all point to its singularity. These texts throb with the images of an all-Jewish, eastern European Jewish neighborhood, inhabited by poor refugees from the pogroms who clung to this space and within it shaped a world of their own.

What do we know about the history of the Lower East Side? How much does the memory deviate from the fact of its past?[47] First, in its heyday as an immigrant Jewish neighborhood, it did not have a fixed name, and "Lower East Side" rarely was invoked to refer to it. American observers who came there—journalists, writers, reformers—called it variously the "Jewish Quarter," "downtown, the "Russian Quarter," the "Jewish east side," the "Hebrew Quarter," or, most often, the "ghetto."[48] Likewise, Jewish residents of the neighborhood who were involved in explaining the immigrant Jewish enclave to other Americans, Jewish and non-Jewish, used a variety of terms, including "downtown," "ghetto," and "east side."[49] Even when the adjective *lower* preceded the place-name, it was not capitalized. More often than not, when writers capitalized the

25 Public School 63
26 Music School Settlement
27 Asch Building
28 Astor Library
29 Cooper Union
30 Hebrew Technical School for Boys
31 Labor Temple
32 Rand School
33 Hebrew Charities Building
34 Metropolitan Life Building
35 Madison Square Garden
36 City College

Boundaries of sub-ethnic districts
······· Hungarian
—+— Galician
—○—○— Rumanian
〜〜〜 Levantine
— — — Russian

Shaded blocks indicate Tenth Ward

0   ¼ MILE

THE LOWER EAST SIDE

1 Newspaper Row
2 World Building
3 Chatham Sq. Library
4 Beth Israel Hospital
5 Israel Elchanan Yeshiva
6 Seward Park Library
7 Forward Building on Yiddish Newspaper Row
8 Educational Alliance

9 Henry St. Settlement and Clinton Hall
10 Machzike Talmud Torah
11 Hebrew Sheltering House
12 Hebrew Technical School for Girls
13 Home for Aged
14 Jewish Maternity Hospital
15 Young Men's Benevolent Association
16 Camp Huddleston Hospital Ship School

17. Beth Hamedrash Hagadol
18 Pro-Cathedral Mission
19 University Settlement
20 Grand Theater
21 Yiddish Rialto
22 Thalia Theater
23 People's Bath
24 Police Headquarters

77

Figure 5. Moses Rischin offered this map in his book *The Promised City.* The Lower East Side included the whole area up to Fourteenth Street to the north, and a range of spaces well beyond that were highlighted as part of the space used by residents of the Lower East Side. (Reprinted with permission of Harvard University Press)

KEY TO LOWER
EAST SIDE MAP

1. Lavanburg Homes
2. Bed Linens Market
3. Orchard Street Pushcart
   Market
4. Henry Street Settlement
   Playhouse
5. Amalgamated Dwellings
6. Henry Street Settlement
   (Main House)
7. Educational Alliance
8. Jewish Daily Forward
9. Division Street Shopping
   Center
10. Knickerbocker Village
11. Oldest House in Manhattan
12. Franklin Square
13. Spanish-Portuguese Cemetery
14. Columbus Park
    Mulberry Bend
15. Olliffe Pharmacy
16. Secondhand Clothing
    Market
17. Manhattan Bridge Plaza
18. Bowery Outdoor Jewelry
    Market
19. Mott Street Pushcart Market
20. Police Headquarters
21. "Thieves' Market"
22. Salvation Army Hotel
23. Bowery Mission
24. First Houses
25. Condict Building
26. Old Merchant's House
27. Colonnade Row
28. Statue of Peter Cooper
29. Cooper Union
30. Secondhand Book Market
31. St. Mark's In-The-Bouwerie
32. Jewish Theater District

Figure 6. Map of the Lower East Side included in the *WPA Guide to New York City* (1939). In the text the Lower East Side was subdivided into a number of smaller, more homogeneous neighborhoods than the large urban space depicted in the map.

three words (or two of them), they did so to expose problems and pathologies of the neighborhood. The *New York Tribune* quoted David Blaustein, the director of the neighborhood's Educational Alliance, as saying in August 1903, "It is impossible to understand the Lower East Side or the hostile attitudes of the people there towards American institutions without knowing the conditions from which these people came in eastern Europe."[50] A contributor to the book *The Russian Jew in the United States* (1905) similarly (and erroneously) wrote, "No walls shut in this ghetto, but once within the Jewish quarter, one is as conscious of having entered a distinct section of the city as one would if the passage had been through massive portals, separating this portion of the Lower East Side from the non-Jewish districts of New York."[51]

The lack of a fixed name in the past went along with the lack of a fixed set of historical borders marking off the Lower East Side from the urban spaces around it. The 1911 edition of the *Encyclopaedia Britannica,* which like many contemporary accounts did not use the designation "Lower East Side" at all, distinguished between "the Russian quarter near East Broadway" and a "Hebrew quarter on the Upper Bowery."[52] By bifurcating the Jewish residential space of lower Manhattan, the writer for the *Encyclopaedia Britannica* implied that no single Jewish enclave existed.

Rather, Jews lived over a vast part of downtown Manhattan. They clustered in different areas, creating a series of subsections based primarily on place of origin in Europe.[53] Hungarian Jews opted for the northwest section of the neighborhood just above Houston Street, where many German Jews also lived. Galician Jews clustered in the south, between Houston and Broome. Sephardim, the Levantine Jews who came from Syria, Greece, and Turkey, settled along with Romanian Jews in the area from Chrystie Street to Allen. Russian Jews, numerically dominant, occupied the streets from Grand Street to Monroe.[54] A breezy guide to New York's ethnic enclaves written in 1938 included a Polish district in the author's travels through Jewish New York:

> On the other side of Grand Street and below Avenue A is the Galician and Polish district, with men and women who still believe in miracle rabbis abounding in the neighborhood, the men with

side-locks and long caftans and the women with wigs on their hair. . . . The further up, encompassing the district from Delancey Street to Houston Street and First Street, and westward to Second Avenue is the region of the Rumanian Jews, distinguished from the others by the number of cafes and dancing-places, and also by the number of libraries, one of which, the Rivington Street Branch, has the most complete Rumanian library in the city.[55]

The level of intra-Jewish splintering within *the* neighborhood certainly raises a set of questions about the Lower East Side. Ought it be considered a single neighborhood? Did immigrant Jews actually occupy a series of separate but adjoining neighborhoods? Where and when did "Lower East Siders" conceive of themselves as such?

The history of the Lower East Side not only complicates the remembered past as a place and time where Jews occupied a singular, integrated urban space but also raises questions about exactly how Jewish the area really was. *The WPA Guide to New York City*, published in 1939, alerts us to this issue. It located the Lower East Side (capitalized) on "Fulton St. (South St. to Pearl St.) and Franklin St. (Baxter St. to Broadway) on the south to 14th St. on the north; from the East River west to Pearl St. and Broadway; excluding Chinatown."[56] By drawing the area's boundaries as it did, this book made the Lower East Side something other than a Jewish neighborhood. It actually made that point quite clearly: "The district is best known as a slum, as a community of immigrants, and as a ghetto; yet not all of the district is blight, not all of its people are of foreign stock, and not all are Jewish."[57] The section of the guidebook on the Lower East Side indeed indicated that there existed a subset of "East Side Neighborhoods," including the historically Irish "Old Fourth Ward District," the "Jewish Quarter," "Little Italy and the Bowery," the latter of which included Chinatown, the commercial "Astor Place District," and "Tompkins Square," made up of "Italians, Slavs, and East European Jews."[58]

The broad definition of a multiethnic Lower East Side fit quite well with the writings of Jews and non-Jews who lived in the neighborhood and described the encounters between the various peoples who made it up. Edward Harrigan, an Irish American songwriter, immortalized the Lower East Side in his 1882 song, "McNally's Row of Flats," a hit from his play, *McSorley's Inflation*:

> The great conglomeration of men of every nation,
> A Babylonian tower O, it could not equal this
> Peculiar institution where Brogues without dilation,
> Were rattled off together at McNally's Row of Flats.
> CHORUS:
> It's Ireland and Italy, Jerusalem and Germany,
> Oh Chinamen and Nagers, and a paradise for cats,
> All jumbled up together in snow and rainy weather,
> They represent the tenants in McNally's Row of Flats.

Harrigan once commented that on the Lower East Side he knew, people of many backgrounds lived "sort of thick an' mixed like the innards of a mince pie."[59]

Samuel Ornitz, born on Hester Street in 1890, recorded the ethnic mixing that went on in his Jewish childhood days in his novel *Haunch, Paunch and Jowl* (1923). In the creation of urban popular culture, as described by Ornitz, Jewish and Irish idioms mixed. Sam Rakowsky, a character in the novel, was the musician among the Jewish boys from Ludlow Street. He played "first an Irish reel very zippy, see, and when I am good and warmed up in the middle of the Irish jig, giving the regular Irish steps, I want the music to slip into a Jewish wedding *Kazzatzka* with a barrel of snap . . . [an] Irish-Jewish potpourri."[60] In *Call It Sleep* (1934), Henry Roth's coming-of-age novel set on the Lower East Side, David Schearl, the child through whose eyes life is presented, developed a friendship with a rough Irish youngster, Leo, who exposed the sensitive Jewish boy to Christianity, nonkosher food, and street violence.[61] Finally, an elderly Italian resident of the neighborhood who grew up at 46 Eldridge Street recalled the multiethnic neighborhood of the old days: "The tenants in our building were from Palermo, Naples, Minsk, Bucharest, and Warsaw, with a number of unidentifiables thrown in. How did we communicate? In Yiddish, partly. . . . My father . . . [a] tailor, mastered conversational Yiddish in the needle trades; conversed in Italian with his compatriots; and spoke English at home. My mother [American-born] spoke enough Italian and Yiddish to shop and communicate with in-laws and neighbors."[62]

Given these complications, it might be more appropriate to historicize the Lower East Side as a broad urban borderland, a sprawling zone where pockets of Jewish life functioned alongside areas shaped by other peoples, many of whom were also newcomers to America. Jews moved all over this space, using parts of it for work. Indeed, the garment industry, where about half of them, at one time or another, made a living, tended to be situated outside of the densest sections of Jewish residence. By the first decade of the twentieth century, the garment factories clustered around Madison Square, at Twenty-sixth Street, quite removed from the "Jewish Quarter."[63] Individual biographies of Lower East Side Jews confirmed the historic reality that the men and women of the neighborhood worked at some distance from where they lived. Harry Roskolenko's father left his family's Cherry Street apartment every day to work in a factory in Greenwich Village, to the north and the west. The Triangle Shirtwaist Company, the scene of the deadly fire of May 26, 1911, that killed 146 workers, mostly young women, was located in the Asch Building. This site of industrial exploitation and Lower East Side martyrdom stood two blocks to the east of Washington Square, geographically outside the core of Jewish settlement.[64]

Lower East Side Jews not only ranged over this vast neighborhood to work but also used urban spaces far from where they lived in constructing their political culture in America. They attended lectures and mass meetings at Cooper Union. Their rallies and marches frequently focused on Union Square. Perhaps most important, the jewel in the crown of their expressive culture, the Yiddish theater, sparkled between Houston Street and Fourteenth Street, an area where few of them lived. Indeed, at the time it was occupied by more German Jews than eastern Europeans. The "Jewish Rialto," the theatrical district where Boris Thomashefsky, Ludwig Satz, Jacob Adler, and the rest of the Adler clan (Molly Picon, Bertha Kalich, and Maurice Schwartz) dazzled audiences with the range of their dramatic talents and the breadth of their repertoire, made its home on the Bowery and then up Second Avenue, far from Delancey and Eldridge Streets.[65] Even the famous Café Royale, where Yiddish writers, actors, and critics, along with their adoring public, drank tea and engaged in "vehement arguments . . . for or against a new play, book, or art movement," made its home on Twelfth Street and Second Avenue.[66]

Lower East Siders seemed to have used New York beyond Houston and beyond Fourteenth Street as theirs, maintaining a broad contact with the rest of the city. In 1891, fifty thousand Jews who lived in the lower reaches of the city signed a petition to keep the Metropolitan Museum of Art, on Fifth Avenue in the Eighties, open on Sunday. They visited the Central Park Zoo,[67] and young Jewish men from the neighborhood vied for places at Townsend Harris High School, located on the campus of the City College of New York, by 1907 located on 138th Street.

The Lower East Side as such may have been where hundreds of thousands of Jews lived, but the name tells us little about the breadth of their urban knowledge. That they used the rest of the city with ease and without encountering overt hostility gives a glimpse of these immigrants as American "learners" and a suggestion of the relatively positive reception they found.

Additionally, the Lower East Side was not home only to the poor among the Jewish immigrants.[68] Many became the owners of cigar and garment manufacturing enterprises, small ones that could be classified as sweatshops and larger ones that became the factories of the neighborhood. They bought property in the Lower East Side and owned the tenement buildings where fresh recruits found places to live. Sender Jarmulowsky lived in the neighborhood and served as the first president of the Eldridge Street Synagogue. An eastern European immigrant, he had amassed enough capital to open a bank on Canal Street in 1873. Jarmulowsky's was the place where Jewish and Italian Lower East Siders put their money for safekeeping.[69]

Jarmulowsky may have been one of the wealthiest and most prominent of the immigrant Jews to live on the Lower East Side, but others succeeded economically and remained put for some time. In fact, Andrew Heinze's notable achievement in his book

Adapting to Abundance was to interrogate the image of the eastern European Jews in America as poor laborers, struggling to put bread on their families' tables. Heinze's data pointed to the consumption, on a grand scale, on the Lower East Side of new clothes, good food, pianos, vacations at the Jewish hotels in the Catskills, and other commodities on which the residents spent their disposable income.[70] Louis Freedman, a neighborhood physician who had immigrated from Russia in 1895, lived at 150 Henry Street. Freedman graduated from Cornell University Medical College in 1903 and remained in the neighborhood until 1935, living in the building he owned.[71] Although this was not a wealthy neighborhood, nor did comfortably middle-class Jews or other affluent people predominate, to have lived on the Lower East Side in 1890, 1910, or even 1930 did not ipso facto imply poverty.

The Lower East Side functioned as something much broader and more variegated than the all-Jewish "ghetto" where poor immigrants from eastern Europe clung to their special space, as posited in the sacred memory. Indeed, the Lower East Side had a Jewish history long before the great wave of immigration from eastern Europe began in earnest after 1880. Jews from Bavaria, the Rhineland, and other provinces of what would become a unified Germany in 1871 occupied parts of the Lower East Side since the 1820s. The notorious Chatham Street, heart of America's second-hand clothing trade, home of the much-maligned "slopshops," functioned as a Jewish street for decades before the 1880s. In 1833 a British traveler described with revulsion his visit to Chatham Street, commenting that "the inhabitants of this street are mostly of the tribe of Judah: as anybody may be satisfied by going into their shops as well on account of their dealings, and their long beards which reach to the bottoms of their waists."[72]

In the 1840s, German, Dutch, and Polish Jews lived and worked in shabby stores and home workshops, essentially sweatshops, on Bayard, Mott, Baxter, and Chatham Streets, as well as on Division and Henry. In that decade clusters of Jewish residents, particularly Bohemian and German Jews, could be found on Grand, Ludlow, Attorney, Clinton, Ridge, Pitt, and Rivington Streets: all the streets on which the eastern European Jewish saga played itself out in the sacred stories told about a later age.[73]

This Jewish occupation of the neighborhood could obviously not be described, literally, in Lower East Side terms. In the 1830s, when Jews first began to live on these streets, they occupied the northeastern edge of what then constituted the developed area of Manhattan.[74] More commonly, the area went by the name *Klein-deutschland* (little Germany), because of the hundreds of thousands of German speakers who lived there, both Christians and Jews. Jewish merchants here sold clothing from the street, loudly "pulling in" customers to see the jumble of goods inside.[75] They sold kosher meat, kosher wines, kosher breads, and Jewish ritual objects. Isaac Gellis transferred his kosher sausage-making operation from Berlin to Essex Street by the time of the U.S. Civil War. Gellis and the other Jewish food purveyors from Germany left a powerful legacy to the later Jewish arrivals, the eastern Europeans. These food entrepreneurs transformed the newcomers into the consumers of delicatessen meats, including corned beef, salami, and tongue.[76]

Eddie Cantor, a Lower East Side child born of immigrant parents from eastern Europe, got his first job as a delivery boy for Gellis. Raised by his poor grandmother, he relished the chance to deliver the delicatessen meats to neighborhood shops; in the course of his sampling, he became the self-described "world's supreme delicatessen eater, absorbing more salami, pastrami, bologna, and frankfurters in that short span than most families do in a lifetime."[77] Had the Berliner Isaac Gellis and others like him not set up shop on the Lower East Side, the culinary life of the later neighborhood would have been different indeed.

The German residents of these streets made them Jewish ones. They marked their stores with Jewish symbols and Hebrew words attesting to the *kashruth* (ritual purity) of the foods sold. They built synagogues like Anshe Chesed on Norfolk Street, Rodeph Shalom on Attorney, and Sharey Shamayim, which in 1853 bought Rodeph Sholem's building when that congregation built a new structure on Clinton Street. The Jews who created these institutions decorated their buildings with visual reminders to passersby that Jews worshiped there.[78] Before the Lower East Side got its name and its eastern European Jewish cachet, twelve Jewish men got together in 1843 at Sinsheimer's Saloon on Essex Street and formed the B'nai B'rith, the oldest continuing Jewish organization in modern history.[79]

Before the tidal wave of impoverished Jews arrived from eastern Europe in the 1880s, the Jewish residents of this neighborhood—the "Germans"—ran over eighty charitable associations to feed their hungry, support their widows and orphans, provide *gemillas chesed* (free-interest loans) to those without means, dispense coal in the winter to the poor, and provide free *matzo* at Passover.[80] As such the German Jews who lived on the very streets that became sacralized as the eastern European heartland in America also could claim a place in that sacred narrative.

To complicate the history of the neighborhood even further, eastern European Jews actually lived on the Lower East Side well before 1880. Jews hailing from the Polish region of Suwalk, others from Posen, a Polish province annexed by Prussia, as well as Jews from various parts of Lithuania and western Russia had been living on the Lower East Side starting in the late 1840s.[81] The first "Russian" Jewish congregation, Beth Hamedrash Hagadol, had been organized in 1852 in a "garret of No. 83 Bayard Street."[82] In the 1850s the congregation boasted a *bes medrash* (study house) where, as Judah David Eisenstein, one of its early members, recalled, one could "find Jews engaged in study. . . . It has many books, as in the great House of Study in Poland."[83] Rabbi Pesach Rosenthal, an immigrant from Poland, opened a school, a Talmud Torah, in 1857 in the neighborhood. Yiddish served as the language of instruction, and the curriculum never swerved from that used at the time in the land of his birth. His son Isidor took over the school in 1861, and by 1876 it was teaching children at 27 East Broadway.[84]

By the time the large-scale eastern European Jewish migration began, eastern European Jews already lived in New York, indeed on the Lower East Side. They lived alongside other Jewish immigrants from Bohemia, Hungary, and Germany. Together these earlier denizens of lower Manhattan had created a Jewish presence and a Jewish infrastructure, which the newcomers inherited and then used to fulfill their own needs.

Finally, for all the invocation of the Lower East Side in both scholarly and popular texts, it functioned as a Jewish residential sieve. Jews entered it, but more left. In 1892, 75 percent of the city's Jews lived in lower Manhattan. But by 1903, although the rate of immigration of eastern European Jews grew, the percentage of Jews who lived on the Lower East Side had declined to 50 percent of New York City's Jews, and by 1916, to 23 percent. By 1905, two-thirds of the East Side Jews had left the neighborhood's environs for Washington Heights and Harlem in Manhattan, for parts of the lower Bronx, and for Brooklyn, particularly Williamsburg and Brownsville.[85]

The historical irony here is that Brownsville was actually more thoroughly Jewish, at least in terms of proportions, than the Lower East Side ever was. In 1923 the Bureau of Jewish Social Research estimated that Jews made up 95 percent of Brownsville's residents, a level of Jewish concentration never approximated by the Lower East Side.[86] Yet the Lower East Side has come to be a repository of American Jewish memories on a grand scale. Brownsville, by contrast, has not emerged in the American Jewish memory culture as a meaningful place from which to shape subsequent identity.[87]

But what Brownsville or Harlem lacked was a vast verbal and photographic paper trail. Few observers went to Brownsville to document, describe, and discover it. The Lower East Side, on the other hand, attracted outsiders galore. It beckoned Jews and non-Jews, who looked around, wrote, and published. Hutchins Hapgood, one of them, understood that he was part of a Lower East Side phenomenon. "Well-to-do persons," he wrote, including himself, "visit the ghetto . . . from motives of curiosity or philanthropy." In the wake of these visits they left a vast corpus of writings to tell later generations about it. Brownsville attracted far fewer observers and spawned far less in the way of a historic record.[88]

All of this historical information stands to one side; the memory of it occupies a much larger and powerful zone on the other. That culture of memory includes no references to a past before 1880.

It contains no snapshots of German Jews, other than haughty outsiders who wanted to make the eastern European immigrants into
respectable Americans. It allows only for the poor among the eastern Europeans, and it needs to make them the sole inhabitants of
a tightly bound singular space. It needs to contain these iconic
elements precisely because as a mnemonic it serves powerful cultural needs, based on the shaping of identity and the preservation
of group loyalty.

No other ethnic group in America, with the exception of the
African-American construction of Harlem, has so thoroughly understood, imagined, and represented itself through a particular
chunk of space. The phrases "Lower East Side" and "Harlem" do
not need ethnic adjectives to precede them and identify the group
that occupied the space. The "Chinatowns" or "Little Italies,"
"Greektowns" or "Polonias" where these groups experienced their
first encounters with America have been found in any large city
with a substantial Chinese, Italian, Greek, or Polish population.[89]
None were specific to, or framed completely around, a single
neighborhood in a single city. Boston's North End, an Italian
neighborhood since the end of the nineteenth century, cannot
claim any primacy over New York's Little Italy, or Philadelphia's,
Baltimore's, San Francisco's, or Chicago's, for that matter. Neither
San Francisco's nor New York's Chinatown can encapsulate the
experience of all Chinese immigrants to America, nor does one
of them speak for the other. St. Louis, Milwaukee, Cincinnati, Buffalo, and Chicago all housed massive German communities, but
none dominated over the rest. Was New York the capital of Irish
America, or was Boston or Chicago? These other ethnic enclaves
shared with each other the right to tell the story of their people
in America. None served as the primary vehicles through which
the saga of those groups came to be understood and represented
by other Americans.

But the Lower East Side could, and did, do that for America's
Jews. In the context of the long Jewish history of diaspora, the
Lower East Side also has a singular prominence. No other city
in the Jewish dispersion, and surely no other neighborhood, has
resonated as widely in Jewish popular consciousness as New York's

Lower East Side. No Jewish neighborhood in Warsaw, Lodz, Vilna, Odessa, Berlin, Budapest, or London has approached the Lower East Side in terms of its mythic memorial tenacity. Certainly, each city had its supporters and advocates, and each claimed a distinctive Jewish culture. None of those other Jewish cities, however, exemplified "the Jewish experience" in Poland, Lithuania, Russia, Germany, Hungary, or England, as the Lower East Side has been the epitome of the Jewish experience in America. Vilna Jews, for example, dubbed their city the "Jerusalem of Lithuania," but Vilna could not be said to have embodied what it meant to be a Lithuanian Jew, a particularly problematic geographic term, given the history of shifting borders in that region. Jews in Bialystok, Kovno, Pinsk, Minsk, Grodno, and the numerous other Lithuanian Jewish communities did not necessarily defer to their Vilna coreligionists as somehow more exemplary of the essence of being a Litvak, a Lithuanian Jew.[90]

But for American Jews, the vast majority of whom derived from the immigrants of eastern Europe, the Lower East Side came to be the place about which they told their stories, where they located the narratives that explained who they were, where they had come from, and how they got there. In the books they wrote, the films they made, the songs they composed, and in a wide array of texts for children and adults, for themselves and for others, the Lower East Side loomed large as the setting for memories.

CHAPTER TWO

The Texts of Memory:

Representations of the

Lower East Side

Born on the wilds of Delancey Street

Home of gefilte fish and kosher meat.

Handy wid a knife, O herzach tzi [listen],

He flicked him a chicken when he was only three.

Duvid, Duvid Crockett,

King of Delancey Street.   —MICKEY KATZ, *"Duvid Crockett"*

IN THE 1950s Mickey Katz, a
musician and comic, parodied "The Ballad of Davy Crockett," the
enormously popular theme song from the television saga of the
American frontiersman. Like much of Katz's repertoire going
back to his early radio broadcasts in Cleveland, this Yiddish-En-
glish mélange derived its humor from the art of lowbrow cross-
over. Katz made a career of concocting Yiddish-Irish, Yiddish-cow-
boy, Yiddish-Scottish, and Yiddish-Chinese fusions, which
incongruously merged the language of the Jews of eastern Europe
with images, words, and often melodies associated with very different places and cultures.[1] In this particular Katz linguistic mixture,
the Lower East Side setting for the very Jewish actions of Duvid
Crockett, as opposed to his American counterpart, shaped the hi-
larity of the disjunction. After all, the "wilds of Delancey Street"

replaced the "wilds of Tennessee," and "Home of gefilte fish and kosher meat" balanced off with "Greenest state in the Land of the Free."[2] Whereas the original ballad, memorized and sung at that time by millions of American children, often wearing coonskin caps, celebrated Davey's childhood feat of "killing him a bar" at age three, the Jewish Duvid demonstrated his prowess by plucking chicken feathers. Would the same parody have worked particularly well had Duvid been wielding his poultry knife on Woodland Avenue in Cleveland, Katz's birthplace, home to a large Jewish immigrant population at the turn of the century, with its very own cadre of chicken "flickers"?[3]

In Katz's ballad, Delancey Street represented the heart of authentic Jewish culture in America. So, too, on October 24, 1991, as millions of Americans turned their television sets to their local Fox Network affiliate to enjoy their weekly encounter with *The Simpsons*, the paradigmatic dysfunctional cartoon family of the decade, they could engage with the idea that the Lower East Side meant, in and of itself, Jewish traditionalism. In that week's episode, entitled "Like Father, Like Clown," Lisa and Bart Simpson, the all-American kids from Springfield, try to shake their hero, Krusty the Clown, out of a severe depression. Krusty has fallen into a mood as blue as Marge Simpson's impossible hairdo. The clown's personal crisis has jeopardized his brilliant television career, and the Simpson kids, loyal Krusty fans, want to help him.

Krusty, it turns out, was Jewish, and his real name was Hershel Krustofsky. He felt deep anguish at the ruptured relationship between himself and his father, Rabbi Krustofsky, descended from a long line of rabbis. Rabbi Krustofsky objected bitterly to his son's career as a clown and disowned him for not carrying on the family's long rabbinic tradition.

Krusty reveals this background to Lisa and Bart, explaining, "I was born on the Lower East Side of Springfield." Lisa and Bart then serve as the mediators between Krusty and his Orthodox father, trying to convince the rigid traditionalist that Krusty could be both a good Jew and a clown.

In this cartoon parody of *The Jazz Singer,* the 1927 movie that also centered on a Lower East Side setting, Lisa and Bart engage

Figure 7. Rabbi Krustofsky, his errant son, Krusty, with Lisa and Bart. This episode of *The Simpsons*, "Like Father, Like Clown," showed how the Lower East Side had come to be universally understood as the epicenter of the American Jewish experience.

with Rabbi Krustofsky on his own terms. They comb various rabbinic sources to prove to the recalcitrant Lower East Side rabbi that humor—the son's chosen career—is a worthy calling.

Without a doubt, no other space could have been invoked by Krusty, and the cartoon's creators, than this one. No other space would have served as well to clue the audience in to the Jewish content and the depth of Krusty's travail. No other neighborhood would have demonstrated the gap between the density of his Jewish upbringing and the distance he had traveled since being banished from his father's home.[4]

If the creators of *The Simpsons* pointed to the Lower East Side as the source of Krusty's Jewishness, "The Source for Everything Jewish" has taken Judaica into the 1990s world of catalog shopping. Subtitled "Hamakor Judaica, Inc." (*Hamakor* means "the source"), this brightly illustrated catalog allows shoppers to order Jewish ritual objects: *mezuzot* (markers for the doorposts of a Jewish home), *tallitot* (fringed prayer shawls), *tzedkah* (charity boxes), spice boxes, and special braided candles used for the *habdalah* ceremony to mark the end of the Sabbath, and wine goblets, candlesticks, challah covers, and platters to welcome it.

Among the ritual objects, "The Source for Everything Jewish" offers many *chanukkiot*, the nine-branched candelabra, centerpiece of the home celebration of Hanukkah, in a dazzling array of colors, sizes, shapes, and materials. On the cover of the summer 1997 edition, and repeated once inside, was "The New World" *chanukkiah*, a rendition of the Lower East Side, "hand-painted, hand-cast polystone blend with brass vessels." For $150 one could then bless the arrival of the Hanukkah festival, praising God for miracles that took place "for our ancestors, in those days" with an American variation of the Jewish sacred.

The caption underneath the picture of the chanukkiah linked this traditional sacred object to the sacred on American soil:

> "The New World" Chanukkiah by Maude Weisser. Enchanting creation—a typical street of New York's Lower East Side around the turn of the century—rendered with attention to the tiniest detail. In addition to the tenements, shops and pushcarts, the *chanukkiah*

Figure 8. Artist Maude Weisser created "The New World" *Chanukkiah*, a ritual object for use at Hanukkah. She used Lower East Side buildings to serve as the candleholders and by doing so demonstrated the neighborhood's sanctity. (Reprinted with permission of Aleph Judaica, distributors for Maude Weisser. Photographer Omer Davidson)

> depicts the Etz Chaim Anshei Wolozin Synagogue and the Yiddish Art Theater. The Immigrant Receiving Station, Ellis Island, is the *shammash* [the "helper" candle, which is used to light all the others]. This artistic tribute to the Jewish past will be treasured for generations to come.[5]

Here a sanitized Lower East Side served as the context for memory. No garbage cluttered the chanukkiah's stylized street, and a peaceful Lower East Side provided the site for the sacred. The twinned legacies of the Lower East Side, religious piety, represented by the synagogue, and artistic creativity, as signified by the Yiddish Art Theater, easily shared a common space.

These three artifacts—the Mickey Katz ballad, Krusty's confession of his Lower East Side upbringing, and the Hanukkah menorah—used the Lower East Side as the marker of an authentic Jewish culture. The invocation of the Lower East Side allowed their creators and consumers to locate the Jewish experience in Ameri-

Figure 9. Students at Northeastern University in Boston, Massachusetts, could feast on delicatessen items from "Leo's Delancey St. Deli" in their student union. (Photographer Shira Diner)

can space. The artifacts also served as touchstones of invented memory.

By the middle of the twentieth century, and even more so by the century's end, the name "Lower East Side" had become so securely tied to the American concept of "Jewish" that creators of texts and artifacts, like these, and the audiences who engaged with them, understood that they functioned as synonyms for each other. "Lower East Side" meant Jewish, and Jewish could be best represented and assimilated through the words and pictures associated with the Lower East Side.

Texts that effortlessly blended the concepts of Jewish and Lower East Side ran the gamut of cultural expressions. This mnemonic fusion informed the work of writers of fiction and autobiography, advertisers, ceramicists, filmmakers, museum curators, comedians, and parody artists. Jewish educators used it to instill in young

American Jews a sense of connection with their historic roots. It expressed itself in products intended for specifically Jewish audiences and those geared to wider, more heterogenous American ones, traversing the zones of "high" and "popular" culture, and as such offering a unifying theme to the cultural output of post–World War II American Jewry.

These items were produced all over America. Their creators did not necessarily have a personal connection to New York or to the Lower East Side. The consumers of these artifacts likewise were spread across the United States and had no need to actually have been there. The veneration of a particular moment in the American Jewish past, the immigration of the eastern European Jews in the decades between 1880 and 1920, also played itself out on the contemporary Lower East Side and served as the basis for museum projects, historic restorations, and organized walking tours of the neighborhood. Vastly changed from the space which the eastern European Jews confronted, the neighborhood became a memorial to itself, and in the process it took on a new life.

Authenticity served as a key concept in the sacralization of the Lower East Side. That which existed outside the Lower East Side was inherently less Jewish. The institutions of the Lower East Side, on the other hand, inhered with true Jewishness. By situating a text—novel, film, advertisement—in the Lower East Side, its creator could claim an organic connection to the undiluted essence of Jewish culture in America, not watered down by American compromises. An artifact's Lower East Side setting carried a mythic certification of its Jewishness. This concern with authenticity unites the earliest of these texts, produced in the immediate aftermath of World War II, and those still being created a half century later as Jewish communal leaders struggle over the fate of American Judaism, the meaning of the concept "the Jewish people," and the prospects for its continuity.

Ironically, in the half century of Lower East Side memory, the neighborhood has become more deeply associated with religious traditionalism. The further from the immigrant era we scan, the more intensely have texts been created to draw upon and reinforce Lower East Side memories. The further from the immigrant era, the more the texts of memory depict the neighborhood as a place of Jewish religious piety, of traditional practice, and of deep observance.[6]

ROMANCING THE PAST

In 1951 the Lower East Side broke into the mainstream of American culture. That year Follett Publishing Company, a New York trade house, published Sydney Taylor's *All-of-a-Kind Family*, the first commercially published, widely distributed children's book with a Jewish subject. The book also had the distinction of providing the first postwar mass-market depiction of the Lower East Side. Nearly fifty years later, it, as well as the later volumes in the series, remains in print and is still stocked on the shelves of public libraries and general bookstores as well as Jewish ones.

All-of-a-Kind Family received rave reviews and won Follett's three-thousand-dollar prize as the outstanding book for children in 1951.[7] *Publishers Weekly* speculated that the judges decided to choose this book "not only on the [basis of the] story but also on the fact that it would portray New York's teeming East Side, an unusual setting for a juvenile, to children throughout the country."[8] Advertisements noted that the book's drama centered on "five little girls who live with their parents in a four-room apartment in New York's lower East Side."[9] *All-of-a-Kind Family* received the accolades of the Jewish world as well. The book won the first Isaac Siegal Memorial Award for Jewish children's books, bestowed by the Jewish Book Council of the Jewish Welfare Board. This book, and those that followed—*More of All-of-a-Kind Family* (1954) and *All-of-A-Kind Family Uptown* (1958) essentially made up the entire corpus of children literature in the 1950s that identified the lives of American Jews as fit reading material for American children.[10]

The Lower East Side setting did not play an incidental role in the book's warm reception and its achievement of canonical status. Nor did the author consider the setting as a mere vehicle to tell a family story. The lives of these girls developed as they did precisely because they lived on the Lower East Side, a throbbing, bustling place. The centrality of place in the book, in turn, helped establish the Lower East Side's as American Jewry's sacred center.

Published at a moment when American Jews were moving to the suburbs of the nation's largest cities, this book for the first time in the history of American publishing presented ordinary American Jews to their non-Jewish neighbors.[11] A "heartwarming bit of Americana. Delightful," commented *Library Journal*.[12] Describing *All-of-a-Kind Family* as "Americana" allowed the experience of Jews to be enshrined in the rhetoric of American national culture, like Laura Ingalls Wilder's *Little House on the Prairie*[13] or Esther Forbes's *Johnny Tremaine*,[14] which themselves placed the experiences of children in America's sacred soil and sacred time.[15] The author was born in 1904 on the Lower East Side, the back of the dust jacket revealed, and had created the story of this immigrant Jewish family to recapture the texture of life in the "old" neighborhood for her own daughter. The adventures of Ella, Henny, Sarah, Charlotte, and Gertie—"Mama's girls"—reflected the stories that Taylor's parents had told of their immigrant childhoods earlier in the century.

Like the girls in the book, Taylor came from a family of five girls, and she initially wrote these stories just for her daughter. When her husband read about a contest sponsored by Follett, he submitted the manuscript without her permission. Taylor won, and the book launched her career.[16]

Taylor had moved beyond the Lower East Side. American-born, American-educated, the product of cleaner, quieter neighborhoods, she was an actress and a playwright and had also spent time as a dancer in Martha Graham's company. She had traveled far from the Lower East Side of her parents.[17]

In *All-of-a-Kind Family*, however, we hear the voice of longing for a space where everyone helped everyone else; where warmth, religious ritual, home, love, noisy streets, and a throbbing public culture made life for these Jewish girls seamless and laden with meaning. Families got along, and those families were large, noisy, and demonstrative. Neighbors cared about each other and shared generously. The senses operated at a sharper level, and even the food tasted better than in the suburbanizing world where Taylor's readers found themselves.

Taylor herself noted in an interview years later that she had only one child, her daughter, Jo.

> When she was a little girl she would say: Mother, I hate going to bed. It's so lonesome. Won't you stay awhile?
>
> I would look around the room with its solitary bed, and my mind would go back to my own childhood. Once again I would be living in the flat on New York's lower East Side where five little girls shared one bedroom—and never minded bedtime. Snuggled in our beds we would talk and giggle and plan tomorrow's fun and mischief.[18]

She could not have presented the contrast more clearly: the warmth and the shared lives of the Lower East Side with the privacy of affluence. The remembered Lower East Side stood for the jumble of family and fun, of camaraderie and togetherness, in sharp contrast to the loneliness of success.

The narrative line and rhetorical style of *All-of-a-Kind Family* attested to the emerging sanctity of the Lower East Side and the particular ways in which American Jews after World War II remembered it. First, Taylor contrasted the "meanness" of the neighborhood's physical appearance with the sweetness of its people—all immigrant Jews—and their intense relationships with each other:

> The East Side was not pretty. There was no grass. Grass couldn't very well grow on slate sidewalks or in cobblestoned gutters. There were no flowers except those one saw in the shops of the few florists. There were no tall trees lining the streets. There were tall gas lampposts instead. There was no running brook in which children might splash on hot summer days. But there was the East River. Its waters stretched out wide and darkly green, and it smelt of fish, ships, and garbage.[19]

Unlike suburbs, which boasted lawns and wide-open spaces, the place where "Mama's girls" lived was one where personal relationships, rather than landscape, defined values.

Figure 10. The outdoor commercial life of the Lower East Side gave Sydney Taylor's *All-of-a-Kind Family* its distinctive vibrance and drama. (Reprinted by permission of GRM Associates, Inc., Agents for the Estate of Ralph Taylor, from the
book *All-of-a-Kind Family* by Sydney Taylor. Copyright © 1951 by Follett Publishing
Company; copyright renewed 1979 by Ralph Taylor.)

In this neighborhood, Jews lived in a universe of almost total
Jewishness. With the exception of Miss Allen, the librarian, the
mysterious but handsome Charlie, who worked with Papa in his
junk shop and turned out to be Miss Allen's boyfriend, and the
one reference to "Joe, a swarthy Italian" ragpicker, everyone and
everything here was Jewish. "Only one tongue," Taylor asserted,
could be heard in the noisy marketplace. "Yiddish. It was like a
foreign land right in the midst of America. In this foreign land, it
was Mama's children who were the foreigners since they alone
conversed in an alien tongue—English."

The world of that marketplace, of loud peddlers, of obtrusive
hucksters who hawked and screamed and shouted out their wares,
offered a portrait of life unlike that which children born right
after World War II, the book's original readers, would ever know,
particularly if they joined the stream of migrants to the outlying
areas of the cities and to suburbia, touted by developers for the
quietness of private space and the green stretches of lawn. In this
marketplace, the heart of the Lower East Side, Taylor took her
readers on a sensory journey to a realm of distinctive sounds,
smells, tastes, and sights:

Heaped high with merchandise, they [pushcarts] stretched in endless lines up and down the main streets. . . . They were edged up close to the curb and wedged together so tightly that one could not cross anywhere except at the corners. The pushcart peddlers, usually bearded men in long overcoats or old women in heavy sweaters and shawls, outdid each other in their loud cries to the passers-by.[20]

The sweet potato man stopped before her [Ella] and pulled open one of the drawers of his oven. There arose on the air such a delicious smell that Ella smacked her lips expectantly. Inside she saw the plump sweet potatoes in their gray jackets. . . . For her penny, Ella got a large half and as she bit into it, she wondered why sweet potato baked at home never tasted half so good.[21]

(In a subsequent volume when the family moved to the Bronx, Mama comforts her daughters by telling them, "We'll still be able to buy *bagel* and lox for Sunday morning breakfast"[22]—an amusing anachronism, since no accounts of *real* life on the Lower East Side ever mention lox as a commonly eaten food, or Sunday mornings as a day that merited a special breakfast ritual, or lox and bagels as a particular combination.)

In at least *this* Jewish home of the Lower East Side, traditional practices, holidays and Sabbaths in particular, caused no one embarrassment. In no place did Mama, Papa, and the girls (and, by the last chapter of the first book, little brother Charlie) suffer any personal inconveniences in order to fulfill ritual practice, nor did the demands of acceptance into the American mainstream rub up against the inherited, cherished ways of marking off time or eating. The girls' Aunt Lena, in *More All-of-a-Kind Family*, observed the commandment of immersing herself in a *mikvah* (ritual bath) before her wedding. Although Taylor did not explain Lena's act in sexual terms, she, unlike almost all other Jewish writers of the era, including rabbis writing for adults, included this element of the Judaic repertoire in her depiction of immigrant life.[23]

Taylor portrayed an imagined cultural moment in which no conflict separated home and street. The central public institution for this family was the public library, where the girls made a weekly

Figure 11. The little girls of Taylor's books lived intensely Jewish lives, never disturbed by debate over tradition and the restrictions it placed on them. (Reprinted by permission of GRM Associates, Inc., Agents for the Estate of Ralph Taylor, from the book *All-of-a-Kind Family* by Sydney Taylor. Copyright © 1951 by Follett Publishing Company; copyright renewed 1979 by Ralph Taylor.)

pilgrimage, fittingly, as they prepared for the Sabbath. "No, not Sarah, nor any of the girls could forget that Friday was library day," Taylor told her readers on the book's first page. Avid readers, the girls connected to the American world primarily through the library, where they went after school every Friday afternoon to stock up with armloads of books.[24]

The joys of Sabbath suffused the family's apartment, without any intrusions from the outside world: "At home, the kitchen was warm with the smell of fresh-baked white bread. The room sparkled with cleanliness. The table, which wore only an oilcloth covering all through the week, now had on a snowy white tablecloth. . . . They were just in time to see Mama saying the prayer over the candles. . . . A lovely feeling of peace and contentment seemed to flow out from Mama. . . . Thus was the Sabbath ushered in."[25] After the inevitably tasty meal, everyone sat around the table, with the Sabbath candles flickering, reading: "the children with their books, Mama with her magazine, and Papa with his Jewish newspaper. . . . So they would continue reading until the candles burnt low. Then they would . . . go to bed. . . . There could be no light struck on the Sabbath. That was the law."[26]

Finally, on Taylor's Lower East Side, American patriotism cozily existed side by side with Jewish life, uncontested by conflicting demands. So, the Fourth of July came to the Lower East Side: "The streets were full of excitement. Everybody was expressing their joy in freedom today. From tenement house windows and from store fronts flew American flags. . . . The air was filled with the clang of cowbells and the blasts of horns." Mama prepared a special meal for the Fourth, as befitted this sacred moment. "What a wonderful meal it was! . . . Mama took the kugel out of the oven and bore it triumphantly to the table. It looked very festive in all its crusty brown deliciousness on Mama's best company platter." Mama's special Fourth of July meal had as its centerpiece a kugel, a dish that surely graced her Sabbath table as well.[27]

So, this early artifact of the memory of the Lower East Side, written by a Jewish woman a generation removed from it, offered post–World War II readers a glimpse of a world where food tasted better, where grass and trees did not make the good life possible, where families could be observant Jews and enthusiastic Americans at one and the same time. Taylor's Lower East Side, an almost hermetically sealed world of Jewishness and love, existed without contest over culture or generational conflict.

However, conflict deeply informed three earlier Lower East Side texts that were "rediscovered" and reissued in the postwar period: Abraham Cahan's *The Rise of David Levinsky*, Henry Roth's *Call It Sleep*, and Anzia Yezierska's *Bread Givers*. Published originally in 1917, 1934, and 1925, respectively, these tense novels about the discord of immigrant Jewish life on the Lower East Side reached new audiences in turn by 1960, 1962, and then 1975. They achieved a canonical status after their reissues, becoming standard fare for college literature and ethnic studies courses. Scholars around the world turned to them for access to what they defined as the authentic voices of the immigrant era of the late nineteenth and early twentieth centuries.[28] They also ushered Americans, particularly the grandchildren and great-grandchildren of eastern European Jewish immigrants, "back" to the Lower East Side.

All these novels, as well as a number of other works written during the heyday of the Lower East Side as an immigrant Jewish neighborhood, had a common fate, of sorts. Published, reviewed, and read at a time when immigrant Jews were defined as a problem and when American Jews pondered the fate of their poor, newly arrived coreligionists, the books then fell into obscurity. They ceased to be actively discussed, since the condition of the Jews had ceased to be an American concern. Notably they were revived, republished, and reread in the emerging culture of Lower East Side memories.

These novels, as well as other texts written about the east European Jewish immigration to America, shared a common fate. Written, reviewed, and discussed during the years of immigration, these works attested to the degree to which Jewish immigrants were considered to be both a novelty and a problem. As the immigrant era came to an end, as Jews entered increasingly into the middle class, and as they ceased to be a problem, these works lost their readership. But when Lower East Side memory culture surfaced after World War II and when it became particularly powerful in the 1960s as an element in American Jewish culture, these works achieved a new lease on life as they provided voice and texture to the place now defined as the heart of the American Jewish historical experience.

All these novels, written for general as opposed to Jewish readers particularly, dealt in uncompromising terms with class, gender, and religious conflict. Two involved coming-of-age stories that demonstrated repeatedly the chasm between the youth, who intimately knew the American streets, and their parents, who could never achieve that knowledge. (The Cahan novel posed the crisis somewhat differently in that the young David came to America alone, and in essence the parent-child conflict over Jewishness took place within himself.) In all, the Lower East Side served as the powerful locus of conflict, maturation, and the inevitability of the generational gulf.[29]

The three books likewise had a similar history. They received various levels of positive acclaim, but then were truly lost. Since being reissued in the post-1960s era, they have entered into the realm of the canon.

Call It Sleep, described by the literary critic Leslie Fiedler as "the best single book by a Jew about Jewishness written by an American,"[30] underwent the most dramatic example of this trajectory. First published in 1934 when the author was twenty-eight years old,[31] *Call It Sleep* focused on a young child, David Schearl, who came to America with his mother to join his father, who had preceded them there. It depicted a bleak life of poverty, violence, and family discord, embedded in the noise, dirt, foul smells, and vermin of the neighborhood.

Critics greeted the novel favorably, lauding its literary strength, the power of its language, and the tension in its structure. Likened to James T. Farrell's *Studs Lonigan*, it emerged on the mid-1930s American literary landscape both as *the* Jewish proletarian novel of the decade and as a deep, complex novel laced with Freudian insight, akin to the writings of James Joyce, particularly *Portrait of the Artist as a Young Man*.[32] It went into an immediate second printing and then died.[33]

After the mid-1930s, *Call It Sleep* faded into obscurity. According to one literary scholar in a postscript to the 1962 paperback reissue, "Until recently, no one I met, American or British, seemed to have heard of it, much less to have read it." Before the 1960 reissue, the novel figured in literary criticism only twice, and then as an interesting text that, despite its merit, had no audience to speak of. When, in 1956, the literary scholar Walter Rideout included—and praised it—in his study *The Radical Novel in the United States, 1900–1954: Some Interrelations of Literature and Society*, he discussed it as a book that no one else would have been familiar with.[34] Both Alfred Kazin and Leslie Fiedler cited it in a 1956 symposium, appropriately entitled "Neglected Books," in the *American Scholar*.[35]

In 1960, a small publishing house, Cooper Press, saw fit to reissue the Roth novel in hardback, and two years later a bigger concern, Avon, purchased the paperback rights, due in part to the efforts of literary agent Harold Ribalow. Within two years the book had gone through twenty editions, and nearly nine hundred thousand copies had made their way into circulation.[36] It brought the Lower East Side into the American literary landscape. Repeatedly reissued with new introductions, it became the focus of international critical inquiry.[37]

In the same year that *Call It Sleep* got its new lease on life, so, too, did Abraham Cahan's *The Rise of David Levinsky*, reissued by Harper Brothers with an elegant introduction by John Higham, an eminent scholar of both immigration and American intellectual history. Initially Cahan had tinkered with the basic idea for his novel in a multipart series in 1913 in *McClure's Magazine*, entitled "The Autobiography of an American Jew." Four years later the fully developed novel, *The Rise of David Levinsky*, appeared. Initially it enjoyed only modest success, even in the face of the quite positive reviews it earned in such publications as the *New Republic*, which hailed it as "one of the most impressive novels produced in America in many a day."[38] Cahan had hoped for literary acclaim among American readers, but despite the close relationship between him and the author William Dean Howells, *Levinsky* did less well in terms of sales and literary fame than Cahan expected.

Higham rightly concluded in his essay that the book, which "has received more respect than attention," did not fit the Zeitgeist of American Jews before the 1960s, and therefore it had fallen into disuse. The book, he noted, had made upwardly mobile Jews uncomfortable. Its portrait of the "Jewish East Side" (Higham, like many early commentators, did not use the name "Lower East Side") did not shy away from the unflattering and the coarse. "Readers," Higham noted, presumably for the most part Jews, "thought he had perversely documented all the anti-Semitic stereotypes." They, as they were "escaping from confinement" in their "immigrant ghettoes," found the novel embarrassing. They preferred texts that had "decontaminate[d] Jewish life from the color and flavor of the Ghetto."[39]

More important, however, *The Rise of David Levinsky* did not endure. After its brief surfacing, it drowned in obscurity. It was reissued once in 1928, as "a cheap edition," but by 1943, "the book went out of print."[40] In 1952 critic Isaac Rosenfeld published a piece in *Commentary* testifying to the seeming irrelevance of *David Levinsky* and the Lower East Side genre: "I had long avoided *The Rise of David Levinsky* because I imagined it was a badly written account of immigrants and sweatshops in a genre which—though this novel had practically established it—was intolerably stale by now."[41] Rosenfeld, who died a few years after writing these words, ones that reflected a deep disinterest in the immigration experience and by extension the Lower East Side as "stale" subjects for engaging literature, could not have known that these topics—immigrants and sweatshops—would resurface in the next decade and beyond as central metaphors of American Jewish memory.

Since the novel's reissue and the emergence of the Lower East Side as a central focus of historical interest, numerous historians have drawn from Cahan's life and his observations in *David Levinsky* to describe the nature of that community and to document its life and demise.[42] They have taken Cahan and his fictional immigrant, Levinsky, to be the paradigmatic and defining characters of the Lower East Side, which in turn defined the immigration experience of the Jews to America.[43]

Anzia Yezierska's *Bread Givers* (1925) received wide acclaim in its initial incarnation, although, like *The Rise of Levinsky* and *Call It Sleep,* it then went into a tailspin of neglect. In the 1920s this book and Yezierska's other works, such as *Hungry Hearts,* garnered stellar reviews in major American publications. The reviewer for *International Book Review* in 1925 compared Yezierska to no less than Henry James and Tolstoy, while Samson Raphaelson (author of the short story "The Day of Atonement," on which *The Jazz Singer* was based) declared that "Miss Yezierska has accomplished for the Yiddish what John Synge has done for the Gaelic," oblivious to the fact that *Bread Givers* had been written in English.[44] In general, critics hailed the book as realistic and authentic, offering readers an "almost barbaric tapestry of the east side . . . raw, uncontrollable poetry."[45] (*Hungry Hearts,* published five years earlier, had been reviewed in the *Nation* alongside D. H. Lawrence's *Women in Love* and Knut Hamsun's *Hunger.*[46] It caught the attention of Samuel Goldwyn, who purchased the rights to the book, transformed it into a movie in 1922, and briefly brought Yezierska out of the Lower East Side to the sunshine of California.)[47]

In the 1920s, Yezierska mingled with George Bernard Shaw, Gertrude Stein, and the cream of American and European literary society.[48] But by the 1930s, her career devolved from fame to obscurity, and her work, including *Bread Givers*, went out of press and merited no notice from literary scholars or historians.

But that all changed in a new cultural era. In 1975, with the rise of the women's movement, the efforts of feminists to reclaim a women's past and culture, and the flowering of a specifically Jewish feminist movement, *Bread Givers* and Yezierska emerged from the shadows, and, in a way, so did the Lower East Side. The rediscovery of *Bread Givers* was due in large part to the efforts of labor historian Alice Kessler Harris, who in the early 1970s was writing about Jewish women's lives on the Lower East Side in the context of their trade union activism.[49] Kessler Harris played a pivotal role in Persea Press's 1975 reissue of the book. In her introductory remarks, the historian thanked a number of individuals who had played a role "in rescuing this novel from the world of 'out-of-print' books." Since then, *Bread Givers* has been in print continuously and never far from the reading public. It finds its way into general bookstores, Jewish bookstores, synagogue libraries, and the required reading lists of college courses.

The three books described here—so unlike *All-of-a-Kind Family*, with its depictions of family warmth, love of Jewish ritual, and deep harmonious community bonding—presented grim portraits of Lower East Side life. Poverty and prostitution show up here. Gangsters, criminal violence, husbands and wives who shout at each other and who treat their children with brutality seem to bear little resemblance to Mama and Papa and their girls. Crass materialists devolved out of Old World Talmud scholars.

But as with the children's books, *The Rise of David Levinsky*, *Call It Sleep*, and *Bread Givers* could not have been written about other places. For all their anger and disgust at aspects of immigrant Jewish life in America, they posited the Lower East Side as the incarnation of Jewishness, the intensity of life, and the essence of authenticity.

Sara Smolinsky, the heroine of *Bread Givers*, despised everything about the neighborhood, whose narrowness is encapsulated in her feelings about her father, a cruel man who spent his time, energy, and very limited money on himself. As the representative of Judaism, Sara's father, with his disregard for his wife and daughters, his blend of self-centered concern about money and "fanatical adherence to his traditions," made Sara question her relation to that tradition. Yet every time Sara left the Lower East Side, she found herself inexorably drawn back to it, just as ultimately she could not abandon her father. In the novel's final scene, as she confronted her father on his death bed in his Lower East Side tenement apartment, Sara "walked on. But I felt a shadow there, still over me. It wasn't just my father, but the generations who made my father whose weight was still upon me."[50]

Place also shaped David Levinsky's life and Cahan's narrative. The entire "I Discover America" section of the book played itself out in "the heart of the Jewish East Side." A place of scurrying and bustle, of old-timers who derided the greenhorns, and the greenhorns who initially tried to retain tradition, Levinsky's East Side thrived on the endless contradictions within its boundaries. It was on the Lower East Side that Levinsky lost his soul. As the neighborhood and the city forced him to accommodate to modernity, he made a bargain that success should come at any price. By the book's end, when the unbelievably successful cloak maker returned to the streets of his youth, he felt sadness, not triumph:

> One day I paused in front an old East Side restaurant that I had often passed in my days of need and despair. The feeling of desolation and envy with which I used to peek in its windows came back to me. . . . On another occasion I came across a Canal Street merchant of whom I used to buy goods for my pushcart. I said to myself: "There was a time when I used to implore that man for ten dollars' worth of goods. . . . Now he would be happy to shake hands with me." . . . And yet in all such instances I feel a peculiar yearning for the very days when the doors of that restaurant were closed to me and when the Canal Street merchant was a magnate of commerce in my estimation. Somehow encounters of this kind leave me dejected.[51]

In *Call It Sleep*, place shaped David Schearl's life and Roth's narrative as well. In an unusual twist, the Schearl family first lived in Brooklyn, but a quarter of the way into the book, he and his parents moved to the Lower East Side, a "world as different from Brownsville as quiet from turmoil."[52] Roth offered little in the way of Brownsville street life to explain the boy and his family, and the action of the early part of the book took place largely within the confines of the apartment. On the other hand, the Lower East Side as lived out-of-doors space shaped the boy's development, and the neighborhood functioned as a key element in the narrative.

If the polyglot Lower East Side seemed different from almost exclusively Jewish Brownsville, it stood even more radically apart from the non-Jewish sections of America. On an excursion uptown to the Metropolitan Museum of Art with his aunt, a "greenhorn" who followed David and his mother to America, he witnessed that world through a Lower East Side lens. "The further they got from Third Avenue," Roth narrated, "the more aloof grew the houses, the more silent the street. David began to feel uneasy at his aunt's loud voice and Yiddish speech." To David's aunt the most obvious difference between real life, that is, the Lower East Side, and Fifth Avenue involved the absence of children. "Not a single child on the street. Children, I see, are not in style in this portion of America," she commented.[53]

But the streets of Roth's Lower East Side teemed with children, good ones, bad ones, noisy ones, studious ones, but children everywhere. They, and the crowds of adults shouting, pushing, running, selling, buying, became the central element in the Lower East Side landscape of memory. People rather than buildings or nature endowed the Lower East Side with its distinctive quality. As such Roth, through David's aunt, early expressed a key element in the memory of the Lower East Side, the image of masses of people moving about at a frenetic pace.[54]

Such rhetoric about the Lower East Side as quintessentially Jewish, decidedly not American, throbbing with life, people, and conflict, informed these novels, which were canonized in the 1960s and 1970s. Their very history of loss and retrieval functioned as a ritual act and, as with the Lower East Side narrative itself, had clear parallels in the history of Jewish sacred texts, namely, the finding of hidden books like the Dead Sea Scrolls and the discovery of the Cairo *genizah* (a trove of hidden books). Once found, these texts became objects of both intense study and deep veneration, in part because of their histories.

The canonization of these "classic" Lower East Side novels did not, however, preclude the production of new fiction that foregrounded the neighborhood and its people. The late 1970s saw the emergence of a particular genre within American popular literature, the Lower East Side romance novel. Novels such as Belva Plain's *Evergreen* (1978),[55] Gloria Goldreich's *Leah's Journey* (1978),[56] Meredith Tax's politically charged *Rivington Street* (1982) and its sequel, *Union Square* (1988),[57] and Janet Robertson's *Journey Home* (1990)[58] all conformed to the formula of the highly popular style of romance fiction and simultaneously reflected peculiarly Jewish and decidedly Lower East Side memories.

Like the corpus of romance novels that take up whole sections of American bookstores, all of the Lower East Side romance novels were written by women authors and tell their stories through the voices of female protagonists.[59] Like the genre as a whole, its Jewish variant explored women's emotions set against some very specific turbulent location.

However much the Lower East Side romances conform to the genre, they appealed to Jewish audiences in particular ways. Goldreich won the National Jewish Book Award for Fiction for *Leah's Journey*, a sure sign of the novel's endorsement by Jewish literary tastemakers. These books appeared in Judaica gift shops, synagogue libraries, and Jewish book fairs, bearing witness to at least the tastemakers' assumptions that Jewish audiences would receive such books warmly.

Publishers must have sensed a fertile market for this type of book. In 1994 Zebra Books, a major romance house, advertised three Jewish books at the end of Emily Maxwell's *An Easter Disguise* ("A daring masquerade could bring her ruin . . . or romance"). One, *Heritage*, involved the Holocaust, but the other two, *The Lion's Way* and *Tiger's Heart*, used the Lower East Side as the locus for

love and adventure. A brief description of *Tiger's Heart* linked the
rhetoric of romance writing and Jewish history:

> A family held together by tradition—and torn apart by love! As
> beautiful . . . as the natural gem she was named for, Pearl Resnick
> always stood out in the crowded world of New York's Lower East
> Side. And as she blossomed into womanhood, she caught the eye
> of more than one man—but she vowed to make a better life for
> herself. In a journey that would take her from the squalor of a
> ghetto to the elegance of Central Park West, Pearl triumphs over
> the challenges of life—until she must face the cruel twisted fate of
> passion and the betrayal of her own heart![60]

These Lower East Side books shared certain characteristics with
each other and with their non-Jewish romance counterparts, the
ubiquitous "bodice rippers." Place mattered a great deal. The
drama could not have occurred just anywhere, and the feel of the
setting crucially informed the characters' behavior. They derived
their motivation and intensity from the very essence of the Lower
East Side, whose noisy streets and constricted apartments, the intensity of relationships, shaped their lives and their fantasies.
When they moved to other places, the quality of their lives altered
dramatically. The sights, sounds, and smells of the remembered
Lower East Side endowed these books with the authenticity so necessary to the romance genre in general, and to Lower East Side
texts in particular.

The Lower East Side romances depended on early and repeated
descriptions of place to draw readers into the intimacies of the
characters' lived world. To feel for the heroine in the romance
genre requires that the reader be in her world. Goldreich and
Plain placed their characters in tenements on Hester Street, while
Tax used the Levys' Rivington Street address as her book's title,
and Robertson's Klugerman family made its home on Orchard
Street. Indeed, Robertson included the specific house number,
40 Orchard Street, leading us right up the stairs into the dark,
problematic space the characters occupied.

The characters of romance novels expressed the realities of the
world around them through their senses. Thus Belva Plain's Anna

of *Evergreen* experienced the five-story tenement on Hester Street as crowded and noisy. "The stench surged from the street door . . . cooking grease; onions; an overflowing toilet . . . the sickening steam of pressing irons; a noxious drenching of tobacco from the front apartment where the cigar-makers lived." Leah Goldfeder began her American journey in a bleak apartment on that same street, where "the narrow panes . . . were covered with soot minutes after they had been scrubbed," while the "stairway smelled of ammonia and urine." Conditions were horrible, and Meredith Tax's Hannah and her family lived in a "dark hole." "Where was the sun? How could it get in? And where were the trees?" Hannah's husband asked, humiliated by his failure to support his family in the American style he had expected. Through the narrator's voice we learn that on the Lower East Side, "colors glowed more garishly, dirt was greasier, people grew bigger, and all the latent exaggerations in their characters flowered. Hannah heard her own voice come out louder than before."[61]

As with all romance novels, these books hinged on a plot of forbidden sex between the heroine and a dashing man, often in contrast to a steady but boring husband. The inner worlds of the Lower East Side heroines involved the turmoil of secret lovers, either past or present. Leah's affair with the union organizer Eli Feinstein, for example, reverberated with passion, as opposed to the heavy silences between her and her husband. "We never pretended to love. Never," she convinced herself. Anna of *Evergreen* chose to marry Joseph Friedman, steady and reliable, when she found herself pregnant with a child fathered by Paul, the dashing but callous son of the wealthy uptown, German Jewish family she had worked for as a domestic servant. Sarah Klugerman, in *Journey Home*, carried a deep, dark secret, and despite her *shitel* (the head covering worn by married Orthodox women), she was a woman with a past. In that past she had an illicit affair. She fulfilled her halakic ritual duties of immersing herself in the mikvah, but at times, when her husband came to her bed, "she thought of David Nathan and wondered."[62] Her need to confess that affair informed the book's basic plot.

Although these Jewish tales conformed to the basic romance outline, they should not be seen as mere imitations. Their authors did not just replace the Scottish Highlands with Hester Street's *chazzer mark* (the so-called pig market, a sarcastic comment, implying that one could buy anything on Hester Street except for pork). As pieces of fiction they balanced the romance formula with the post–World War II American Jewish narrative. With the exception of *Journey Home*, all these books began in eastern Europe. (In *Journey Home*, Sarah went back to Hungary to see her dying mother and got caught up in the horrors of World War I, thus still allowing the author to pose the contrast between America and "back home.") They all rely on the pogrom story to bring the family to America, and they all focus on the challenges to tradition posed by American realities. Leah, of *Leah's Journey*, confessed that in the course of beginning her affair with the handsome, fiery labor organizer, she also began to eat nonkosher food. After a passionate night in bed, Leah and Eli went off to eat. "It was the second time," she recounted to herself, "in as many days that she had eaten meat that was not kosher. But now, in this holiday interlude in her life, all things were permitted just as all things had been forbidden."[63]

The novels all focused on the details of Jewish life, highlighting the home rituals and focusing on those involving Sabbath preparations and cooking, highlighting female-based activities. The heroines, before or after their affairs, braid challah and light candles. They cook traditional meals of soup, gefilte fish, kugel, roasted chicken, and compote. Indeed, the details of food, depicted so sensually that the reader might whiff the aromas and hear the sizzling in the pans, defined these romance novels as particularly Jewish. In the more general books of this genre, heroines *never* engage in such corporeal acts as eating. Remembering food also functioned as a particularly salient element of most Lower East Side narratives, and as a fundamental element in American Jewish memory culture.[64]

These post–World War II Jewish novels contrasted America and its possibilities with the violence and destruction of eastern Europe. The pogrom scenes play a crucial role in establishing the reason for migration and in heightening the vast distance between America and "back there." Thus in the aftermath of the pogrom in "Proskurov, in the Ukraine," which opens *Rivington Street*, we see the horror through the eyes of a little child:

> Lev was only five. When he saw what the soldiers were doing, he hid in a hole under the stairs, stuffing his shirt in his mouth, covering his eyes.
>
> Mama was still lying where they had left her, her clothes ripped off, blood dried, horror frozen on her face. She was cold and had begun to smell. Tentatively he [Lev] touched her cheek. A tear rolled down his face. . . . They had ripped off her skirt, and an envelope had fallen out of the torn pocket, onto the floor. He squinted and picked it up. That was it. The letter from their cousin in New York, and the picture of her family.[65]

The frequency of rape in the Russian episodes of the Lower East Side romances moved these books further away from the conventional romance genre, which assiduously avoids this disturbing subject. But Lower East Side novels must have rape or its specter as the peculiarly women's take on the exodus from Russia. The emphasis on rape established for the women, both protagonists and readers, the horrors of Europe as the place that must be fled. The relationship between eastern Europe and America could have not been more obvious. Jews migrated to America because of pogroms. America loomed in their consciousness as the beacon of hope and salvation; eastern Europe signified murder, rape, violence. This formulaic understanding of Jewish immigration ran through *all* the Lower East Side romances, as well as the entire sweep of post–World War II American Jewish culture.

Thus America functioned as a hope and a dream, in contrast to the evils of eastern Europe. Belva Plain's Anna remembered about her migration: "Keen American air. Beautiful America, more wonderful, painful, generous, difficult and kind than she could have dreamed when she had been a child and longed so much to see it."[66] Even the most politically leftist of the books, Meredith Tax's *Rivington Street*, could not avoid the theme of ultimate success, the leitmotiv of American Jewish history. Although the book's dust jacket touted it as not like the American Jewish success story ("*Riv-ington Street* is the story of the Jews who didn't move to the suburbs or strike it rich"), it still allowed one of the Levy girls to become a world-renowned clothing designer and another to mimic the Rose Pastor Stokes story of the Lower East Side radical young woman who married the gentile American millionaire.[67]

Mobility and the achievement of their material dreams drove the novels' heroines and their men. As Anna's cousin told her when she first arrived in America from the countryside of Russia— symbolized by the evergreen—"It is not beautiful here, God knows. . . . But one has a future here."[68] That future, its expecta-tion and fulfillment, provided another distinctively Jewish ele-ment to the romance fiction. Goldreich structured the chapters of *Leah's Journey* to chart Leah's physical and economic mobility. The chapters and the heroine go from "Russia, 1919" to "Lower East Side, 1925," "Brighton Beach, 1933," and "Scarsdale, 1939." (A final section, "Home, 1956," took place in Israel, at the fictional Kibbutz Shaarai HaNegev. In the book's brief epilogue, Leah re-turned to Russia, only to find her village obliterated. She learned, as "gentle ghosts travelled at her side," that Russia could no longer figure in her memory as back home.)[69]

In *Evergreen*, Anna and Joseph moved uptown and finally out to tonier and tonier suburbs with their increasing wealth. We know, however, from the beginning of their moves to comfort and afflu-ence, that all will not be well, and emotional trouble will overtake them as they get farther away from the Lower East Side. Success had been their goal, comfort their dream, but that trajectory as depicted in these Jewish novels did not come without a sense of loss. In *Evergreen* and *Leah's Journey*, once the families have left the Lower East Side, we no longer read about Jewish ritual obser-vances other than funerals. No more Sabbath dinners or flickering candles. No more descriptions of food preparation, hearty meals, and good fellowship. Indeed, the juxtaposition of the Lower East Side, as life lived intensely and fully, with the loneliness and steril-ity of success brought both of these novels to a close. In both nov-els, wealth may have brought material comfort, but it also brought suicides, intermarriages, conversions to Christianity, lovelessness, and loneliness.

Joseph's mother in *Evergreen* (like Henry Roth's real mother) probably knew this would happen. "More than once," Plain informed the readers, "he [Joseph] had urged her to sell the store and move uptown to the Heights [Washington Heights]. But she would not. She had made one great move in her lifetime, across the ocean, had put down tentative roots on Ludlow Street and that was enough."[70]

But staying put had not figured into their calculus. The reader cannot ultimately be sure who made the better decision. Anna and Joseph became very wealthy, but the quality of their lives deteriorated, and their children and grandchildren lived lives disconnected from the past and from Jewishness.

Evergreen ended with Anna's grandson bringing out a tape recorder to take down her life story. Anna looked at her very American grandson and mused: "He has my father's pale eyes . . . he moves like him, clumsily. How can he understand what life was like for his great-grandfather, maker of boots and harness? For him it's a story, picturesque and touching."[71] Anna knew better. Leah, too, understood the losses that came with success. If the Lower East Side had overwhelmed these women with its smells, noises, and the press of people crowding in on them from every direction, success brought emptiness. The bittersweet endings of Lower East Side romance novels moved these books further out of the romance category, as perfected by the Harlequin and Silhouette publishers, and made them a distinct Jewish genre. More than anything, readers of the immensely popular books demanded a happy ending, but Lower East Side tales involved as much loss as gain, and the endings could not avoid mixing the happy with the sad.[72]

This theme of Lower East Side memory—people everywhere, densely packed, but life lived to its fullest—provided the leitmotiv of yet another formative element in the sacralization of the Lower East Side, the popular Jewish Museum exhibit *Portal to America*, of 1966. It, like the exhibit catalog of the same name published in

1967, took the Jewish public by storm, and drew large, enthusiastic audiences. Estimated at over 150,000 visitors, the crowds poured into the Jewish Museum by virtue of the Lower East Side's salience in the search for an American Jewish "usable past."

The show's curator, art historian Allon Schoener, noted that the Jewish Museum had been interested in staging such an exhibit for a while, but not until the mid-1960s did the time seem propitious, and no one had stepped forward to curate it until he did.[73]

In the show's catalog Schoener clearly linked his professional interest in exhibiting the Lower East Side with his own reservoir of memory. He noted that despite his lack of expertise in the field of American Jewish history, the idea of such an exhibit moved him. It "provided me with the opportunity to discover my heritage." A tool in that reconstruction of memory, the Lower East Side moved Schoener, educated at Yale, and stirred a sense of the past that he had not known before. "Born and raised in Cleveland," he reported, "I never knew the Lower East Side until I went to college. When I came to New Haven, I found myself roaming around Delancey Street and Second Avenue eating food that my mother never cooked. . . . By the time I started to look, it was gone."[74] By dedicating the book "to my father, who was a Lower East Side boy, and to my mother, who, as I did, learned about the Lower East Side from my father," Schoener connected the physical neighborhood's images and words with a lost Jewish world, which he could experience only several steps removed from some assumed past reality.

In this, Schoener seemed to differ little from the thousands of people who streamed into the Jewish Museum to see *Portal to America.*" According to literary scholar Milton Hindus (whose book of 1969, *The Jewish East Side,* drew its inspiration from the museum exhibit), the crowds came to celebrate how far they had traveled from their years, literally or figuratively, in the neighborhood. "The majority," he speculated, "consisted of suburbanites, who were descendants of the immigrants pictured in the exhibit." These Jewish residents of neighborhoods with green lawns and garages and private homes separated by wide spaces saw the sad-looking faces in the photographs, the jumbled streets, the dreary tenements, and were "moved to self-congratulations on their es-

cape."[75] Hindus actually had no evidence for this assertion. The
people could just as logically have been moved by a sense of loss.
They might have wondered, when looking at the pictures and
hearing the sounds, if they had lost as much as they had gained.

What did they see and hear at the exhibit? They could pack into
one room and listen to the actor Zero Mostel, America's "Tevya,"
star of the still-running *Fiddler on the Roof*, reading and commenting on snippets from the *bintel brief*, the advice column of the *Forverts*, America's largest-circulation Yiddish newspaper, published
on East Broadway. There they saw the paintings of John Sloan,
Chaim Gross, and Max Weber, early-twentieth-century artists who
depicted the jumbled intensity of the Lower East Side on canvas.
They scanned blowups of posters for plays staged in the neighborhood's Yiddish theaters and perused mammoth reproductions of
the covers of Yiddish sheet music scores, written in America and
published by the neighborhood's flourishing presses. Gigantic
maps of the neighborhood covered the exhibition space, with the
key spots of Lower East life marked off.[76]

But mostly they saw photographs. Vastly enlarged, these images
dominated the walls of the Jewish Museum. Viewers looked at
street scenes and the indoor tenement scenes. They saw the photographic record of ordinary people in the marketplace and in their
schools, working, recreating, enjoying themselves, and mourning.
Some caught women and men bent over sewing machines in their
sweatshops; others caught packs of children giddy at play. In one,
a woman carried a bundle of rags on her head; in another, a
woman toted a bale of kindling wood. Jews in the *Portal to America*
exhibit were shown in prayer and in sacred study. They sat at their
Sabbath tables, and the meanness of their physical surroundings
contrasted with the sanctity of the ritual moment.

Since the Jewish Museum exhibit, these images, taken by notable photographers such as Lewis Hine and Jacob Riis or by "un-
known" others have often been reproduced elsewhere. They have
become some of the most powerful icons of Lower East Side memory. Their very use as an illustration links any text to the Jewish
past in America.[77] So much did these Lower East Side works endow
an artifact with the imprimatur of Jewish authenticity that when

Mr. L, a family-style restaurant in upper northwest Washington, D.C., wanted to market itself as a Jewish-style delicatessen in the late 1970s and early 1980s, it festooned its walls with photographs by Lewis Hine and Jacob Riis—some of the same ones that *Portal to America* had transformed into icons.

Mr. L offered people well within the Beltway a chance to enter the world of the Lower East Side. A standard "kosher-style" eatery, it offered a menu that effortlessly combined corned beef, pastrami, chopped liver, lox, bagel and cream cheese, blintzes, and other standard fare of American Jewish cuisine with ham and cheese, shrimp salad, bacon and eggs—nonkosher and clearly not part of the Jewish repertoire. After a few years of serving this type of fare, the restaurant added a range of Chinese dishes and changed its name to Mr. L and Son.[78]

On the walls of Mr. L and its successor hung those black-and-white photographs, some of which first appeared in *How the Other Half Lives* (1890), a book by Riis, a Danish-born photographer and reformer. The photographs had been intended to expose the wretchedness of poverty and the human toll of economic exploitation on the Lower East Side. To Riis, "Jewtown," as he called the Lower East Side, unquestionably bore the impress of its Jewish residents: "No need of asking here where we are. The jargon of the streets, the signs of the sidewalk, the manner and the dress of the people, their unmistakable physiognomy, betray their race at every step."[79]

Was Mr. L a Jewish restaurant? Its eclectic menu, its nonkosher offerings, and its presence in a non-Jewish neighborhood did not suggest a particularly authentic Jewish establishment. Unlike the streets of "Jewtown," which anyone and everyone recognized as Jewish, Mr. L had to prove its Jewishness. The photograph of the deep, brooding, dark eyes on the face of a hungry man who could never have afforded a meal at Mr. L, and probably would not have been willing to eat "kosher style"; the picture of a mother, father, and children bowed low over the table of their tenement apartment sewing garments; the image of a young woman rushing down the street with a mountain of clothes on her head as she went

Figure 12. Mr. L., a restaurant in Washington, D.C., relied in part on photographs by Jacob Riis to give the eatery a Jewish flavor. (Museum of the City of New York)

either to or from the contractor who would pay her a pittance for her miserable labors; and that of a dark, crowded basement *kheder* (a religious school for small children; literally, a room) marked this as a "Jewish" space for the patrons, among whom, most likely, non-Jews outnumbered Jews. Diners could read the photographs as texts of the Lower East Side, and Lower East Side meant Jewish.

The restaurant critic for the *Washington Post* sang the praises of Mr. L and concluded by noting, "Beer and wine are available, but so are egg creams and Dr. Brown's Celery Tonic—both as important to the deli atmosphere as the few Old World/New World photographs lining the wall." She got it wrong if she thought that the photographs had been taken in the Old World, if by that she meant Europe. But she got it right if she considered the Lower East Side, the actual setting of the photographs, American Jews'

Figure 13. The images created by the social reformer Riis were not intended to market Jewish authenticity, but they came to be used as such
by the latter decades of the twentieth century. (Museum of the City of
New York)

"Old World." That was indeed what the neighborhood had become for their culture of memory. A foray to Mr. L meant a chance
to touch down on an imagined sacred space of American Jews and,
through the medium of photographs and food, inhabit, however
briefly and vicariously, that most Jewish of places.[80]

    In the 1970s, Hollywood also discovered the Lower East Side as
a place of Jewish memory, although this was not Hollywood's first
encounter with the neighborhood. In the era of silent films, which
obviously coincided with the high point of Jewish life on the Lower
East Side, a whole series of films placed their drama in "the
ghetto," with its distinctive environment and its Jewish people. *A
Child of the Ghetto* (1910), *The Ghetto Seamstress* (1910), *The Heart of
a Jewess* (1921), *Humoresque* (1920), and, most important, *The Jazz*

Figure 14. Jacob Riis captured the image of a poor Jewish man preparing to greet the Sabbath in his tenement apartment. This picture graced the walls of the nonkosher delicatessen on upper Connecticut Avenue in the District of Columbia. (Photofest)

Singer (1927) displayed scenes of the Lower East Side amid melodramatic personal stories, juxtaposing its constrictions, both physical and emotional, with the expansive opportunities of American life.[81] A whole genre of Yiddish films made in the twilight years of the immigrant generation derived their dramatic punch from Lower East Side settings, which represented a past, already gone. Typical of the genre, *Uncle Moses* (1930) and *Tsvey Shvester* (Two sisters; 1938) played out the two faces of the Lower East Side: the place of narrowness, sorrow, and exploitation, as well as the place of togetherness, solidarity, and authentic Jewish life.[82]

The 1970s cinematic discovery of the historic Lower East Side took a decidedly more complicated yet positive turn,[83] in the sense that the neighborhood served as a place full of possibilities,

Figure 15. Joan Micklin Silver brought Abraham Cahan's short story "Yekl," with its Lower East Side setting, to American movie theaters in the 1970s. (Photofest)

brimming with life.[84] In 1974 Joan Micklin Silver, whose parents had immigrated from Europe and settled in Kansas City and Omaha, where she grew up, directed a film version of the Abraham Cahan short story "Yekl, a Tale of the Ghetto" (1896). She changed the title to *Hester Street*, however, making the Jewishness of the film unmistakable. After all, the name "Yekl," a Yiddish nickname for Ya'akov, would have meant little to American audiences, and "A Tale of the Ghetto" on the theater marquee could imply anywhere (and given the uses of the word *ghetto* in post–World War II America, viewers might assume this to be a film about African-American life). "Hester Street" labeled it firmly as New York and Jewish. (Hester Street seems to have been a particularly attractive and densely Jewish marker for those who played with Lower East Side memory. Steven Spielberg's *An American Tail*, a cartoon of

Figure 16. Stephen Spielberg's *An American Tail* was also a Lower East Side tale. Fieval Mouskewitz swung amid the Lower East Side's laundry to find his parents, from whom he had been separated during the voyage in steerage from Russia to America. (Photogest)

1986, used Hester Street as the place where the Mouskewitz family settled after leaving pogrom-plagued Russia. Their lovable little rodent son Feivel, separated from his family during the harrowing voyage in steerage, reunited with them on this most memorable and Jewish of streets.)

Hester Street, as a film, and Hester Street as the place where the traditional bewigged Gitl, seemingly naive, joined her "yan-keefied" Yekl, now Jake, certainly operated as a site of conflict. On this street, she who represented tradition came up against him, with his lusting for all that was new and American, including his new name, his shaved face, his love of dancing classes, and his extramarital liaison with a girlfriend, Mamie. But on this Hester

Street, tradition did not necessarily have to lose out completely to modernity. In the end the loser, Jake, now entrapped by the fancier and Americanized Mamie, must pay the price for wanting too much of the new. Gitl, freed of her philandering Yekl, will marry the scholarly, bearded, and thoroughly traditional Bernstein. She will open a store and support him, much as she might have had they met in Lithuania. But innovation has crept in to even Gitl's tradition-bound world of Hester Street. In the movie's penultimate scene, when she is asked the name of her son, whom she had always referred to as "Yossel," she answered proudly, "Joey."

The 1970s embrace of difference and the emphasis on resisting homogenization transformed the celluloid Lower East Side from a place where Jewish and American stood as polar opposites as they had in earlier films. Movement from the former to the latter during the age of the silent movies required a wholesale transformation of self, and the Jewish had to go. In Joan Micklin Silver's Lower East Side, women, and men presumably, could pick and choose among those elements of Jewish and American culture, and they had the power to decide what to accept and what to reject.

So, too, Kenneth Roseman, a rabbi at the Reform Temple Beth El in Madison, Wisconsin, used the idea of human agency to produce an American Jewish history "choose-your-own-adventure" book with a Lower East Side setting, *The Melting Pot: An Adventure in New York*. Published in 1984, it joined an endless stream of children's adventure books of this type.[85] In each one, set as they might be in ancient Egypt, outer space, the land of the dinosaurs, pre-Columbian Mexico, and so forth, the youthful reader follows a prescribed, standard text until some point where she must make a decision. "If," as Rabbi Roseman noted, "you decide one way, the instructions tell you to turn to page 8; if you elect the other option, you will go to page 9. Almost every page thereafter asks you to make a choice. . . . There are many different stories in this book."[86]

The two choices that readers of *The Melting Pot* could never make were first, to stay put in Kapulia, a Russian, shtetl (naturally) near Minsk, or, second, to take their first American footsteps anyplace other than the Lower East Side. Readers had to go there first, to join "hundreds of thousands of immigrant Jews like your-

The Melting Pot
An Adventure in New York

by Kenneth Roseman

Figure 17. A Jewish "choose-your-own-adventure" book challenged young Jewish readers to make important choices. All of those choices, however, began in the Lower East Side, the site of their founding narrative. (Permission granted, Union of American Hebrew Congregations)

self." Only after they had engaged with America through the Lower East Side could they actually choose their own adventure. According to this text of remembered Jewish life, all choice grew out of the details of the Jewish experience on the Lower East Side. Readers could, for example, pick work, deciding to be sewing machine operators, butchers, or pushcart vendors. Did they want to join a labor union or sidle up to Tammany Hall? Would they observe the Sabbath or violate it? Should the Lower East Side adventurer go to college or buy a deli? Should the deli be kosher, or should it serve *treife* (forbidden) food? Perhaps some readers became Zionist and moved to Palestine. Others might become Communists and, inspired by the excitement of the Bolshevik revolution, return to Russia. How about moving across the Hudson to Hoboken, or uptown to Harlem? Remain observant? Go to the Jewish Theological Seminary and get involved with Conservative Judaism, or perhaps opt for Reform? More important than the choices that readers could make, *The Melting Pot* offered yet another insight into the central place that the Lower East Side occupies in American Jewish memory. In this book, all of the key developments of American, and indeed world, Jewish history emanated from a jumble of streets, south of Fourteenth Street and north of Fulton, nestled between Broadway and the East River.

Jewish choices also informed yet another Lower East Side text. This one, a ritualized reenactment of the Lower East Side, had its origins in Palmer, Massachusetts, then traveled to Los Angeles, and from there to Eagle River, Wisconsin, and by the end of the 1990s still is being performed back in California, in the lush climate of Ojai.

In 1976 Philip Warmflash, a rabbinical student at the Jewish Theological Seminary, had the responsibility of creating some engaging programs for a winter program at the Conservative movement's Camp Ramah in the Berkshires. He wanted something that linked Jewish life with the bicentennial of that year, and in the library, came upon the catalog for *Portal to America*. Out of the staff deliberation and research came a simulation game—a staple of Jewish summer camps—on how the Jews got "here," not the Berkshires, not Boston, but America, which obviously had to mean New York, and, if New York, then obviously the Lower East Side. This became "Lower East Side Games."

Campers reenacted the arrival in America. They had their papers inspected and their names changed, and they were forced to learn American table manners. In the simulated English classes (where the campers actually learned a little Yiddish), these late-twentieth-century American kids, dressed in faux immigrant garb, tried to experience the ambience of the Lower East Side. Staff members lugged pushcarts around the room, and campers could earn "money" by mastering American skills (etiquette, English) and "mitzvah" points (a mitzvah is a behavior commanded by Jewish law) for doing something defined as "Jewish."[87]

By the early 1980s, Warmflash, a newly minted rabbi, went to Los Angeles to assume the directorship of L.A. Hebrew High School. His opus, created for a Massachusetts winter, easily made the move to California with him. Here again, Jewish teenagers performed their story, the Lower East Side one, as a fun tool to shape Jewish identity. The staff of Camp Ramah in Ojai, California, adopted the game, which since 1987 has been a staple of the camp's summer programming. Sometimes they call it "Ellis Island," other times "Lower East Side." Either way, the camp directors have constructed this performance of the immigration story as a program to combine fun, education, and inspiration.

The campers disembark beneath the palm trees at a mock immigrant receiving station in New York Harbor, where some are detained, some rejected; some have their long, Yiddish last names abbreviated and Americanized, but all eventually end up in a fictionalized Lower East.

Here again, once deposited upon the sidewalks of New York, as in *The Melting Pot*, the real choices get made. The camp has been divided physically into a series of "stations," each one representing elements in the history of Jewish immigration to the United States and the history of Lower East Side life. Campers/new immigrants can opt for a sweatshop job or can try to eke out a living from a pushcart. They can attend a class at the Educational Alliance, participate in a political meeting, or get involved in founding a labor union. They might learn English and American etiquette as upper-class German Jews attempt to civilize them. Amid all these choices, Lower East Side "characters," such as matchmakers and knish vendors, talking with Yiddish accents, roam around the camp attempting to simulate the noisy, people-filled streets amid the semitropical setting of southern California. Finally, beneath an image of the Statue of Liberty, Camp Ramah has also sought to engage the campers in a reenactment of the immigrants' religious life. The kids get a chance to *daven* (pray) in the mode that might have been typical of the eastern European Jewish immigrants.[88]

This kind of memory culture, going strong near the beginning of the twenty-first century, which centered the immigrant Jewish experience in America on the Lower East Side, had been building since the end of World War II. It made quantum leaps after the tumultuous 1960s, with its revolution in American identity politics and the emergence of a new Jewish cultural assertiveness in the larger public sphere. Irving Howe's masterpiece of memory, *The World of Our Fathers*, defined the Lower East Side's sanctity like nothing before or after.[89] Howe's book stands as the densest statement of that mnemonic culture and as the canonical work that represented the American Jewish sacralization of the Lower East Side.

Howe's journey toward his personal "reconquest of Jewishness"[90] began slowly in the aftermath of the war, and his own tortured recognition of his utter indifference to the slaughter of six million Jews in Europe. Born Irving Horenstein, he spent much of his youth and early career distancing himself from anything Jewish, in particular what he perceived as the limited vistas and narrow parochialism of his East Bronx Jewish upbringing.[91] His engagement with Jewish culture, specifically in its secular Yiddish variant, first manifested itself in his three-volume collaboration with Yiddish poet Eliezer Greenberg, producing *A Treasury of Yiddish Stories* (1954), *A Treasury of Yiddish Poetry* (1969), and *Voices from the Yiddish* (1972).[92] In these books Howe and Greenberg compiled a canon of Yiddish literary culture, what Howe's biographer has dubbed a "substitute Torah" for secular Jews like himself.[93]

In whatever order Howe might have ranked the significance of his own voluminous output, *World of Our Fathers*, published in the year of America's bicentennial, catapulted him to fame. Growing out of his interest in Yiddish literature, his involvement with his father as he lay dying, and his bitter disillusionment with the New Left, *World of Our Fathers* put the name "Lower East Side" into the mainstream of American rhetoric and allowed the children of those fathers (and mothers) to be able to claim a public history of their own. The sociologist Nathan Glazer, one of Howe's classmates from City College, has written that "Irving Howe would bring *us* [emphasis added] the classic study of the Lower East Side, *World of Our Fathers*." That is, Howe's book became a canonical text, a legacy for American Jews.[94]

Without a doubt, Howe's book took the world of Lower East Side memories out of the confines of the American Jewish world and into that of the larger culture. *World of Our Fathers* catapulted onto the *New York Times* best-seller list. Howe appeared on television talk shows and became a sought-after speaker at Jewish events. He spoke at synagogues, Jewish community centers, Jewish book fairs, and communal gatherings. One Jewish community group staged a Lower East Side pageant, a re-creation of "the world of our fathers," to accompany his talk.[95]

Reviewers for Jewish publications attested to the deep chord of memory struck by *World of Our Fathers*. Bonnie Lyons, writing for *Congress Monthly*, saw personal connections between Howe's narrative, her own story, and the future of the next generation, as Jews. "What Howe has done is to rescue the immigrant Jews from oblivion—and many of us from ignorance and forgetfulness. For my daughter who never had the chance to really know my grandmother he has performed a *mitzvah*."[96] In his review in *Hadassah Magazine*, Victor Bernstein segued easily from summarizing Howe's opus to retrieving his own memories:

> Mr. Howe's invaluable statistics are in support . . . of my memory. . . . Much of Mr. Howe's material will be familiar to those readers who were born before World War I. Anyone whose life was touched, even obliquely, by the noise, the smells, the intellectual

ferment, the chaotic street life, the crowded tenements of the Lower East Side of those days can never forget them.[97]

In his autobiography, *A Margin of Hope*, Howe both deprecated his own "fifteen minutes" of fame and probed what the book meant to American Jews:

> A good many people, most of them probably Jewish, hurried out to buy it . . . I suspect, not by any authentic desire to "find their roots" (they hardly had to wait for me, if that was what they wanted), but by a readiness to say farewell in a last fond gesture. *World of Our Fathers* enabled them to cast an affectionate backward glance at the world of their fathers before turning their backs upon it forever and moving on, as they had to, to a world their fathers would neither have accepted nor understood. My book was not a beginning, it was still another step to the end.[98]

Howe's observation hit the mark in the sense that his book did not represent the beginning of anything: Lower East Side memory culture had been set on its track well before this book and this author became familiar names to Jewish audiences. He did, however, give a great boost to the public veneration of the neighborhood, which, in quiet ways, had been percolating in American Jewish culture for two decades.

In the decades since the publication of *World of Our Fathers*, the volume of artifacts drawing on the memory of the Lower East Side has continued to grow. The neighborhood has become even more firmly entrenched in American Jewish collective narratives, and the retelling of its supposed golden age is the device used by American Jews to locate and display their memories. Miriam Sagan's *Tracing Our Jewish Roots* (1993) used sepia-toned photographs and cartoons to lead American Jewish children through a journey in Jewish history to help them find their collective origins. To locate the source of one's Jewish roots, the book made clear, one had to begin in the "Shtetl, a Jewish Village," in order to get to "Jewish Life, Today." Needless to say, the book spent more time on the Lower East Side, a place that "belonged to the children," than anywhere else. Indeed, it told the American story from no other place.[99]

The 1998 winner of the Association of Jewish Libraries Sydney Taylor Book Award, named, obviously, for the author of *All-of-a-Kind Family*, was Elsa Okon Rael's *When Zaydeh Danced on Eldridge Street*. The book's promotional material situated the narrative on "The Lower East Side of New York City," a place that "crackles with life as *Zeesie* . . . learns the significance of the Torah." Rael had published *What Zeesie Saw on Delancey Street* the year before, and that book had been chosen by the American Library Association for a Notable Book Award.[100] Eldridge and Delancey, like Hester, functioned then, as the century was drawing to its close, as the setting for childrens' books, written with both Jewish and non-Jewish youngsters in mind.

So, too, actor-singer Dale Davidson performs a Lower East Side immigrant Jewish woman as part of the American Vaudeville Theater. Set on the Lower East Side at the beginning of the century, and performed there in the spring of 1999 at 167 Ludlow Street, the act uses the neighborhood on two levels: historic setting and contemporary performance setting. Davidson's fictional character (whom she modeled on her Polish-born, Brooklyn grandmother) sings "Di Grine Kuzine," a popular Yiddish song of the early twentieth century, and teaches the audience Yiddish words. She informed the late-twentieth-century children and adults who watched her act about the historic moment and place in which her performance has been set, "everybody here on the Lower East Side speaks Yiddish," as she pretends to be stepping out for a visit to the local Yiddish theater. The California-raised Davidson, whose mother was born in Germany, escaping in 1940 from the Nazis, and whose American-born father spoke no Yiddish with her, felt herself drawn by the idea of New York, Yiddish culture, and the Lower East Side. Doing the performance allowed her to "feel . . . connected in a backwards way" to a world she never lived in, that her family had no connection to, but yet which informed her identity deeply.[101]

RELICS OF THE PAST:

THE SHAPING OF

THE PRESENT

All these texts, spanning *All-of-a-Kind Family* and Camp Ramah's staging of a Lower East Side day, venerated a moment in the past. They assumed a bygone era that had been, but was no more, although it possessed the power to shape collective identity. But not all textualizing of the Lower East Side depended upon the trope of a past, once there, now gone. Rather part of the salience of the Lower East Side as a site for Jewish memory grew out of the fact that Jews continued to live in parts of the neighborhood, in smaller numbers, than in 1900 or 1910. But they, their shops, and some religious institutions could still be seen in the final decades of the twentieth century. They could be engaged with, and as such a more vibrant, thriving past could be imagined. It was this residue of past glory that inspired Allon Schoener on his gastronomic forays from Yale to Delancey Street. Seeing, hearing, and tasting the Lower East Side, even in its attenuated form, seemed to be enough for a range of rememberers to feel an engagement with the sacred and to sense a connection between present and mythic past.

The Jewish Catalog, one of the key documents to emerge from the Jewish counterculture of the 1960s participated in the discovery of the Lower East Side as still-lived Jewish space. The book expressed the mood of a particular segment of American Jewry, young people based heavily on college campuses who disparaged what they saw as mainstream American Jewry's shallow compromises with bourgeois culture. Deeply influenced by the youth-oriented cultural ferment of their era, they fused the antiestablishment tones and terms of their generation onto their Jewish lives, expressing admiration for what they saw as the incivility of the authentic, at the same time that they felt empowered to create new experimental forms of self-expression. Simultaneously they revived such moribund cultural forms as klezmer music and rhapsodized over Hasidic *nigunim* (melodies). Yet they experimented with new forms, creating *havurot* (prayer fellowship groups), which functioned without rabbis, where worshipers took off their shoes, sat on the floor, and women got their first chance to emerge out of their inferior—indeed invisible—status in public ritual.[102]

For "*Catalog* Jews," the past of the Lower East Side and its continuing life as home to poor, relatively traditional, definitely not suburban Jews proved to be a gold mine of inspiration. The remnant of Jewish life set in the heavily Asian and Hispanic Lower East Side served as a token recalling an earlier, golden age of unabashed Jewish traditionalism.

Thus the writers of the *Catalog* accepted the idea of the Lower East Side as American Jewry's sacred place, a place of real rather than derivative Jewishness. It served as the place where a Jew could engage with authentic Judaism. By going to the Lower East Side, a suburban Jew could sensually imbibe the residue of a more traditional past.

Not surprisingly, much of the *Catalog* text about the Lower East Side involved the consumption of Jewishness. The neighborhood became the premier place to "buy" Jewish traditionalism. For example, if a reader wanted to buy a *lulav* and *etrog* (the palm, myrtle, and willow branches woven together, along with the citron, used for the holiday of Sukkoth), the *Catalog* suggested "the market area of the Lower East Side." "Advantages" to shopping there for these ritual objects, listed by the *Catalog*, included the chance to bargain with "what seem to be hundreds of street vendors," "the huge, almost unending selection and price range," and, most important, "the incomparable flavor of the area." The *Catalog* did offer a cautionary note for its most acculturated readers, those so Americanized that they now could operate only in suburban shopping centers: "If you are not a bold bargainer you may get taken."[103] Shopping as such on the Lower East Side brought American Jews into a realm of Jewish commercial negotiation utterly different than the familiar and standardized patterns.

Likewise, when it came to helping its readers find Yiddish books, the *Catalog* quickly commented on good buying opportunities in Chicago, Detroit, and a few other large cities. But, "then there's the Lower East Side . . . a visit to which calls for the time-tested

Jewish skills of haggling and striking a bargain with the book-
seller." No doubt unselfconscious of the construction of this sen-
tence, the writer for the *Catalog* implied that the Lower East Side
was more Jewish and adhered more closely to the Jewish peoples'
"time-tested" patterns. Most American Jews, it implied, had become so removed from their own traditions, including commercial ones, that they needed the *Catalog* to guide them on relearn-
ing their Jewish culture, which actually served as the raison d'être
of the *Catalog* enterprise.[104]

The *Catalog* went even further in linking the Lower East Side,
the sacred, and shopping for Judaica as it advised its readers on
how to prepare for the High Holy Days. For those in the market
for a shofar, the ram's horn used to sound Jews to worship on
Rosh Hashanah (Jewish New Year's), two places, according to the
Catalog, offered real possibilities: "First, it helps a lot to be in close
proximity to either Jerusalem or (not to mention the two in the
same breath) New York. If you are so situated, head for Meah
Shearim [an ultra-Orthodox neighborhood in Jerusalem] or its
diasporic equivalent, the Lower East Side." After giving instructions to potential shofar shoppers on how to dress appropriately
(men, covered heads; women, covered heads if married and long
skirts, and blouses with sleeves, regardless of marital status) for
the Lower East Side, the *Catalog* then acknowledged the realities
of American Jewish geography: "Jews live almost everywhere, and
you, dear reader, might be reading this in Butte, Montana, Don-
aldsville, Louisiana, or some other exotic place west of the Hudson." The *Catalog*'s sage advice: "Don't give up." Try some "*local*
Jewish bookstore, if such exists. . . . And remember, if all else fails,
you can always make your own."[105]

Although we cannot know how Jews living in Butte, Don-
aldsville, or other spots outside New York responded to having
their diasporic homes labeled "exotic places," we do have one text
of this era to demonstrate the power of the Lower East Side, as
remembered and lived, in shaping Jewish identity in the 1970s. In
1982 Paul Cowan, a reporter for the *Village Voice*, wrote a moving
memoir, *An Orphan in History: Retrieving a Jewish Legacy*.[106] This
book traced the journey "home" of a young man who grew up

knowing he was Jewish but having no connection to that knowledge. The product of an Episcopalian boarding school, the son of two successful, assimilated parents who celebrated Christmas, put up a tree, and served a traditional ham to complement the Yuletide festivities, he had been raised to think of himself only as an American. The journey Cowan stumbled into was a journey back to a Judaism that had never been his.

In this highly self-reflective book, the Lower East Side symbolized what beckoned Cowan toward the act of retrieval. Indeed, he described the Lower East Side as "the one place in America that had seemed to ease my loneliness."[107] The Lower East Side, for Cowan, served as a place for pilgrimage, the source for the retrieval of lost legacies, and the site for identity formation.

The journey back to his Jewish home by necessity began with a long, introspective description of his childhood and young adulthood bereft of Jewishness. But early on in his narrative, Cowan dropped a hint that indeed he had, someplace in his background, a point of reference to that lost Jewish identity that over time would serve as the lodestone for return.

We learn that the Cowan family, which never lived as Jews, did in fact touch down on a regular basis on Jewish space:

> On Sundays, when I was a boy, he [his father, Lou Cowan] would often take the entire family down to the Lower East Side, which was still a predominantly Jewish neighborhood. Our ostensible mission would be to buy some bagels and lox and challah. But we could have gone around the corner to do that. He would spend delighted hours lingering on those crowded, noisy streets, exploring the small stores, watching the transactions, usually in Yiddish, between the shoppers and the storeowners, who wore yarmulkes and stroked long gray beards as they talked. Back then I thought my father liked the neighborhood because it was quaint, or because he had an insatiable curiosity for new faces, new ideas. It never crossed my mind that the place might evoke memories for him.[108]

The author's father had never lived on the Lower East Side (he grew up in Chicago). But the New York neighborhood could still evoke "memories" of a shared, common immigrant Jewish past in America.

By stepping onto the streets of the Lower East Side, Lou Cowan connected to all that was Jewish and all that he had given up.

As Paul Cowan moved along his seemingly inevitable journey toward Jewishness, he experienced his rebirth (he even played with a new name, "Saul Cohen"), his epiphany, on the Lower East Side. He showed up there ostensibly in his professional capacity as a *Village Voice* reporter doing a story on poverty among the neighborhood's elderly Jews, and then a piece on artisans. These stories called him. He found himself drawn to and then transformed by both the topics and, even more so, the neighborhood. "I felt," he recalled, "an unexpected attraction to their world."[109] The rest of the book finds the increasingly Jewish-conscious and observant Cowan embarking on multiple stages of a pilgrimage to his final transformation into a new person, defined sharply by his Jewishness. He contrasted his parents' surrender of Jewishness for America with the poverty-stricken, observant women and men of the Lower East Side who had refused to enter into the pact with America that his parents—and, in a milder way, most American Jews—had. "Sometimes," Cowan mused, "elderly Jews . . . preferred the threatening streets of the Lower East Side to the goyish [non-Jewish] suburbs where their children lived. . . . Modern American neighborhoods left them feeling depressed and disoriented."[110]

For Cowan, then, the Lower East Side represented authenticity. It stood for community in the densest meaning of the term, a world shaped by deeply felt and continuously enacted commitments between people. Rabbi Singer, Cowan's Orthodox guide to both Judaism and the Lower East Side, fretted all the time about the Jews in the neighborhood—their health, their safety, their very existence. Their needs *were* his. As Cowan portrayed Rabbi Singer, the poverty of the Jews of the Lower East Side informed his every waking hour. Helping them embodied Jewishness. "His Judaism," Cowan felt, "with its ethical and ritual demands, reached from the majesty of Sinai to the lower depths of the Lower East Side."[111]

Finally, to Cowan, as to so many others who remembered the neighborhood, the Lower East Side stood for a public space stripped of concern for bourgeois respectability. Here people shouted, yelled, cried, gesticulated, and did not worry if their behavior jarred with American definitions of civility. The Lower East Side represented the polar opposite of the paradigm of Jewish modernization that has been the basis for much historical scholarship.[112]

Emancipation had demanded of the Jews that they act, at least in public, in polite, unobtrusive ways, that they adopt for common space a persona of respectability. The poet of the *haskalah* (the Jewish Enlightenment), Russian-born Yehuda Leib Gordon, said it best in his poem "Awake My People" (1863): "Be a man abroad and a Jew in your tent, / A brother to your countrymen and a servant to your king."[113] What Paul Cowan loved about the Lower East Side actually was the defiant attitude of its people, their unwillingness to be "a man abroad" and to save their Jewishness for the privacy of their "tents." He found the neighborhood and its people "rough-edged, slightly crack-brained, Old World,"[114] a far cry from Choate, Harvard, and the other spaces Jews like Cowan had occupied, where they had to put on masks to hide their Jewishness.

To Cowan the Lower East Side offered a place to evade the pressures of assimilation. In its authenticity, it stood for all that was Jewish. Its Jewishness could be expressive, emotional, unassimilated, and even unassimilable.

These same themes and images of a lived-in Lower East Side as the site of memory and identity informed two movies of the 1980s, *Crossing Delancey* and *The Jazz Singer.* Although the two films made opposite statements about Jewishness, choices, and memory, they both used the Lower East Side as the place where Jewish identity dramas could be most sharply defined.

In *Crossing Delancey* (1988), Joan Micklin Silver not only returned to the streets of the Lower East Side as a setting for a Jewish film of life in America but also—much like Paul Cowan—offered the Lower East Side as the place where a Jew could be a Jew, without the hollowness of life beyond its sacred borders. In this film a young woman, Isabelle Grossman, eager to make it professionally and romantically in the sophisticated literary circles of "uptown," found true love and personal meaning in the world of her grandmother, a resident of the Lower East Side. Her grandmother, Ida Cantor, a warm, intense woman with a thick accent redolent of

Figure 18. For her second Lower East Side movie, Joan Micklin Silver in the 1980s made the neighborhood a continuing source of identity formation. *Crossing Delancey* involved the process of reconnecting to that which was authentic and essential. (Photofest)

Figure 19. *Crossing Delancey* fit well into an American Jewish culture that highlighted the Lower East Side as the premier setting for examining Jewish identity in America. (Photofest).

the cadences of the immigrant generation and a table that always appeared covered with abundant food, manipulated the fates to bring her straying, anomic granddaughter together with an Essex Street pickle merchant. Unlike the fake sophistication and meaninglessness of her literary friends, the Lower East Side and its people, particularly, Sam Posner, came off as blunt, honest, and real. He, the grandmother, and the Lower East Side stood on one side of a cultural divide; the bookstore where Izzy worked, the urbane poet whom she yearned for, and the world of uptown represented the other. At one point Izzy, struggling between her cosmopolitan self and the world of the Lower East Side, put it bluntly to Sam, the pickle man: "I don't live down here. . . . I live uptown, a million miles from here." *Crossing Delancey* insisted that cultural authenticity could be retrieved. Izzy could cross back over Delancey Street.

Neil Diamond's poorly reviewed remake of *The Jazz Singer* (1980) also needed the Lower East Side, at least as conceived by the film's director, Richard Fleischer, to mark off traditional Judaism from the rest of America. Indeed, the history of the three versions of *The Jazz Singer*—made originally in 1927, then remade in 1952, and again in 1980—offers a view on the many meanings of the Lower East Side.

The first filming of the well-known story (inspiration for *The Simpsons* episode "Like Father, Like Clown") sprang from a short story written by an undergraduate student at the University of Illinois, Samson Raphaelson, who published his tale, "The Day of Atonement," in *Everybody's Magazine* in 1922.[115] Raphaelson introduced the Lower East Side immediately in his story, making Jakie, the protagonist, the son of "old Cantor Rabinowitz, of the Hester Street Synagogue."

Raphaelson linked Jakie, his powerful singing voice, and his face to the unbroken chain of Jewish history: "Those dark eyes of his might have been the ecstatic eyes of a poet in the days when the Chosen People lived sedately in the land of Canaan. They might have been prophetic eyes, stern and stirring . . . when Jerusalem, 'knew not its God.' They might have been deep wells of lamentation even one generation ago had his lyric voice been born to cry the sorrows of Israel in a Russian synagogue."[116] But America tested the strength of those bonds. Raphaelson immediately set this mighty chain, which extended from the land of Canaan to the sorrow of Russia, against Jakie's present: "But he lived in New York, and his slender, well-set-up figure was draped in perfectly fitting suits of Anglo-Saxon severity, and his dark eyes in his thin, handsome face were restless, cynical and without joy."

The basic outlines of "The Day of Atonement," and the various movie incarnations (and stage and television variants as well), are well known.[117] The young American man craved a different and broader world than the limited sphere of cantorial music and traditional Jewish culture. He aspired to a career in "show business," be it "jazz" or rock music, and to a life of American freedoms. He must defy his father, a cantor, the descendant of a long line of cantors. At the end of the drama, after the errant son returned home, but not for good, to sing the Yom Kippur liturgy of "Kol Nidre," some kind of reconciliation took place.

The 1927 version, like Raphaelson's story, derived some of its sense of the "before" and the "after" from its Lower East Side setting. The swirling street scenes, the cramped interiors of tenements, and the darkness of the old-style synagogue played a crucial role in establishing the quality of life in the neighborhood, and the contrast between it and the world that "the jazz singer" found on the outside. The screenplay for the Al Jolson vehicle made the physical setting immediately prominent as a spatial context: "It is a typical East Side business street at the height of the day's activities, a street that is lined with pushcarts, sidewalk vendors and little stores, with its milling shoppers, its petty marketing arguments, its unkempt kids playing in the street heedless of consequences."[118] Notably, however, when the jazz-singing son and the father the *hazzan* (cantor) clashed, they did so over Judaism and not the neighborhood. The father's anguish came not from the son leaving the Lower East Side but from his abandoning Jewish life.

When director Michael Curtiz chose to remake the film in 1952, with Danny Thomas in the role of the rebellious son, it—accurately—moved the locus out of the Lower East Side, and even New

Figure 20. The 1927 version of *The Jazz Singer* began in the "ghetto." Place was not particularly important as a father and son struggled over how to live and how to make music. (Photofest)

York. Now the family fight over music, career, and tradition played itself out in an affluent suburb of Philadelphia.[119] Like America's Jews of the 1950s, Cantor Rabinowitz moved to the suburbs.

In an American Jewish cultural milieu of the 1980s, however, when a venerated Lower East Side occupied its premier address as the cradle of Jewish identity, *The Jazz Singer* had to move back downtown. To portray the conflict between American independence and Jewish parochialism anyplace else would not have worked, since by then the Lower East Side had emerged as the essence of Jewish authenticity, and California as the embodiment of American options.

Diamond, as Jess Robinovitch, and Laurence Olivier, who played his father, the old *hazzan* (cantor), officiate at the Eldridge Street Synagogue. Although the film is set in the present, as opposed to some moment earlier in the century, they lived, along

Figure 21. The drama of *The Jazz Singer* of 1927 did not need the neighborhood to make its point. (Photofest)

with Jess's young wife, Rivka, in a dimly lit tenement apartment. The old cantor and the young wife wanted to bring Jess back to the Lower East Side after he flew off to California to follow his dream to become a rock star. "It's where we belong. It's what we are," the older man thundered to Jess, as they confronted each other in the sunlit beachfront apartment on the shores of the Pacific, a stark contrast to the almost total darkness of the Lower East Side rooms they occupied on the other coast. "You want to drag me back to Eldridge Street," Jess complained to Rivka, who also made the journey out to California to wean him from his dream of stardom. The neighborhood served as Judaism in this film.

From the point of view of any kind of accuracy, almost nothing about the 1980 version of *The Jazz Singer* worked. By the time this movie was made, the Eldridge Street Synagogue, once the jewel

Figure 22. Neil Diamond's 1980 version of *The Jazz Singer* made space central. In a culture that viewed the Lower East Side as sacred, the story shifted to a generational argument about geographic place as well as tradition. (Photofest)

of Lower East Side houses of worship, had decayed. The skeletal congregation of largely poor, elderly Jews had been banished to the first-floor study room; the majestic sanctuary upstairs was given over to the elements. Most Lower East Side Jews, not just those who made up the bare minyan at Eldridge Street, tended to be old and impoverished. Even Orthodox Jews of New York, as well as others across America, had moved to suburbs, enjoying almost universal affluence.

Yet the Eldridge Street Synagogue of *The Jazz Singer* boasted a thriving congregation with enough members to pack the large sanctuary to overflowing and to put on an elaborate party, replete with a klezmer band, to honor Cantor Robinovitch. It had a Hebrew school, where Rivka taught mixed classes of boys and girls. The boys, who wore sweatshirts and knitted skullcaps, symbols of modern Orthodoxy, sang songs in Israeli-accented Hebrew. Even the bearded, old-style rabbi buzzed around the social hall humming the peppy tune of "Hinei Mah Tov," a staple song of Jewish summer camps. In one scene Jess and a boy he was tutoring for his bar mitzvah practiced at the piano. After the young "man" had successfully sung the same "Hinei Mah Tov," the student asked Jess, the cantor-in-training, "Why do I have to sing this at my bar mitzvah?" Good question, given that the song and its melody would not even be intoned at a bar mitzvah in the most innovative Reform congregation in the suburbs, let alone in this Orthodox institution.

The 1980 metamorphosis of *The Jazz Singer* wanted to make a late-twentieth-century point about family, Jewishness, America, and the possibilities of harmonizing them with personal choices. In order for the movie's makers to pose the problems, and then dramatize the reconciliations most vividly, they had to make Jess and the conditions of his early life as "Jewish" as possible. The family name became, for example, more Yiddish than in the earlier versions. In the 1922 short story and the films of 1927 and 1952, "Rabinowitz" sufficed; by 1980, the name had reverted to "Robinovitch," presumably to indicate the extreme traditionalism of Jess's world.

Most significantly, the family had to move back to the Lower East Side from the suburbs of 1952. That move proved an ineffective setting for the film because it jarred too radically with Jewish demographic patterns to seem plausible. But it demonstrated the emergence of the Lower East Side as an American Jewish icon in the latter decades of the twentieth century. To make a movie in the late 1970s, for release in 1980, about Jewish traditionalism in America, and leave out the Lower East Side would have meant ignoring the most potent symbol of authenticity, by then firmly fixed in the American and American Jewish consciousness as its epitome.

By a nice quirk of fate, the creators of *The Jazz Singer* of 1980 chose the Eldridge Street Synagogue, formally known as Kehal Adath Yeshurun Anshe Lubtz, as the setting for conflict and reconciliation between Jess and his father, between personal choice and Jewish tradition. (The filmmakers shot the exterior of the Eldridge Street Synagogue, but given the building's near-total decay on the inside, they had to film interior scenes elsewhere.) The building itself became an element in the sacralization of the Lower East Side in the 1980s and 1990s. A site of renewal, restoration, and pilgrimage, the Eldridge Street Synagogue played a prominent role in symbolizing the neighborhood's sanctity to American Jews.

Located at 12–16 Eldridge Street and dedicated in 1887, the building was the first Synagogue constructed by eastern European immigrant Jews on the Lower East Side, although this Russian congregation had in fact been functioning in New York, in other homes, since 1852.

Until the 1890s, East European congregations either used former churches or rented halls or made do with the recycled buildings of the better-off Jewish congregations, the "Germans" who had moved uptown. By the early 1880s, the membership of the synagogue Kehal Adath Yeshurun Anshe Lubtz boasted several wealthy members, such as banker Sander Jarmoluwsky, who decided to build a mighty edifice. They had enough capital to finance an imposing structure that mixed Moorish, Gothic, and Romanesque styles, complete with a dramatic rose window that dominated the streetscape.[120]

Completed in 1887, the Eldridge Street Synagogue never ceased to function as a synagogue. While the Jewish population of the neighborhood dwindled over the course of the twentieth century and the size of the congregation thinned, a slim handful of members held out and continued to occupy it, even if by the 1950s they closed up most of the building and confined their activities to a small, street-level room, originally the congregation's *bes medrash* (study room).

Unable to fill the sanctuary any longer, and unable to pay heating bills, the few remaining worshipers abandoned the main sanctuary, with its soaring columns, stained glass windows, and ornate Victorian brasswork. The building seemed bound to share the fate of the hundreds of other Lower East Side synagogues. Many were sold to other religious groups, mostly Christian or Buddhist, whose members made up the neighborhood's newest immigrants, while others were abandoned to decay. In 1979, the year before Neil Diamond put on a white *kittel* (a cantor's robe used on Yom

Did this synagogue help shape your life?

Figure 23. Promotional material for the restoration project at the Eldridge Street Synagogue emphasized the share that *all* American Jews had in the Lower East Side. (Courtesy of the Eldridge Street Project, Inc.)

Kippur) to sing "Kol Nidre" on film for the vast assembled throng in the movie's Eldridge Street Synagogue, a guidebook to the Jewish Lower East Side noted, "Although the building, housing a tiny congregation, may achieve landmark status, . . . it is in perilous condition."[121]

In an almost apocryphal rescue tale, in 1986, one hundred years after the synagogue's dedication, local Jewish residents, New York urban historians, and architectural preservationists rallied to rescue the building from decay, creating a nonprofit conservancy to restore it to its former glory and for use as an educational and cultural resource. Many of those promoting the restoration saw the synagogue as a symbol of traditional religious piety and the primacy of public worship as a central motif in immigrant life. In introductory remarks to one of the earliest of the Lower East Side photography books, *The Synagogues of New York's Lower East Side*, Gerald Wolfe noted (in sharp counterpoint to Irving Howe), "Nowhere else in America can one find a greater collection of magnificent synagogues in one neighborhood."[122]

The backers of the Eldridge Street Project, who sought widespread financial support, conceived of their effort as a *national* one, and the synagogue as an institution meaningful to all American Jews. The massive publicity effort launched across America

played on the poignancy of this particular historical story, the congregation that would not die. It announced to all the country's
Jews that they had a share in the Lower East Side narrative. "Did
this synagogue," the promotional brochure of the early 1990s
asked, "help shape your life?" Jews, regardless of where in Europe
their family came from, regardless of where in America they had
settled, were reminded that the Lower East Side had been the
cradle of their American experience. By a nice twist, according to
Amy Waterman, executive director of the Eldridge Street Project,
actor Neil Diamond sent a one-thousand-dollar contribution in
response to this campaign.[123]

Visitors, far beyond the number that the building and staff
could accommodate, began flocking to the Eldridge Street Synagogue from all over the United States and the world. On Lower
East Side walking tours, Jews engaged with the past and stepped
into the hushed darkness of the synagogue, where they could both
see the disrepair of the present and imagine the majesty of the
past. While the laborious restoration goes on, volunteers stream
to the building, wanting to take part in bringing the past back to
life. The creators of the Eldridge Street restoration effort announced a "Clean and Shine" day in 1991. Catered by Zabar's,
one of New York's signature upscale eateries, the restoration day
attracted hundreds, far beyond the number that could squeeze
into the newly stabilized but still precarious space.[124]

In particular, many Jewish teenagers from suburban communities have designated the restoration project as their special "community service" effort.[125] According to the promotional literature,
suburban Jewish youth groups, including youngsters about to have
their bar and bat mitzvah celebrations, have come down to the
Lower East Side and "polished brass, swept floors and waxed
wood. It was a wonderful experience." One brochure described a
teenage Jewish girl from New Rochelle who spent a day working
to restore the sacred space to its previous beauty, "and as the day
drew to a close, the girl's grandfather told the group that on that
very same day 95 years before, his own father had first set foot in
America."[126]

Figure 24. Exterior of the Eldridge Street Synagogue. (Michael Horowitz. Courtesy of the Eldridge Street Project, Inc.)

Figure 25. Detail, interior, of the Eldridge Street Synagogue. (Wijnanda Deroo. Courtesy of the Eldridge Street Project, Inc.)

The Eldridge Street Synagogue, by Jewish tradition, always was sacred. After all, it had been dedicated as a holy place for religious services. The restoration in essence gave it a double sanctity, one by virtue of its dedication in 1887, the other by virtue of American Jewry's need to have a physical embodiment of its founding narrative. The sacred became more, and differently, sacred.

But other Lower East Side places also became sacred, even those that had been ordinary and mundane and that previously had never been bestowed with religious dedication.[127] In 1988 Ruth Abram and Anita Jacobson transformed an 1863 tenement building at 97 Orchard Street into the Lower East Side Tenement Museum. Over almost eight decades, thousands of families had made their homes in the apartment house at 97 Orchard Street. Many had not only lived in its dark, small rooms but worked there as well, sewing and taking in boarders. Each apartment amounted to only 325 square feet, and at times up to fifteen people lived in a single unit. In 1932, city housing laws required the owner to either bring the building up to code or vacate. The owner chose the latter, keeping the ground-level commercial establishments open but sealing up the upper "residential" floors. When Abram and Jacobson bought the building in order to create this shrine to the immigration experience, they unsealed a time capsule, a space frozen in time. According to urban historian Kenneth Jackson, the building survived as "a rare example of a structure that predated virtually every housing law in the United States."[128]

The museum, like the Eldridge Street Synagogue, has become a major tourist site. Visitors can come in, smell the accumulated mustiness of almost 150 years, walk up the narrow flight of stairs. They can see the apartments and hear the stories of the actual people who lived there—stories of poverty, illness, death, and desertion, as well as life, pleasure, neighborliness, and celebration. They can see for themselves the single toilet shared by everyone on the floor (the toilet and running water were not installed until 1905, four years after the city mandated such amenities). They can feel the cramped discomfort of the minuscule rooms in which entire families ate, slept, and worked.

The creators of the Lower East Side Tenement Museum, themselves Jewish, did not design it as a specifically Jewish site, despite the fact that its events are prominently advertised in New York Jewish periodicals. The museum has emphasized the multiethnic history of the building and the neighborhood. Its charter declared its intention to "promote tolerance and historical perspective through the presentation and interpretation of the variety of immigrant experience on Manhattan's Lower East Side, a gateway to America."[129] One of the apartments, restored in 1998, housed the Baldizzis, an Italian Catholic family that lived at 97 Orchard Street

Figure 26. The Lower East Side Tenement Museum has become a magnet for Jewish tour groups seeking to touch down—momentarily—with the neighborhood's memories. (Courtesy of the Lower East Side Tenement Museum)

Figure 27. A restored apartment of the tenement at 97 Orchard Street. (Courtesy of the Lower East Side Tenement Museum)

until 1932. In 1999 the museum plans to start work on an Irish family that also lived in the building.[130]

Nor did the Lower East Side Tenement Museum specifically conceive of itself as a shrine to the great eastern European Jewish immigration of the post-1880 era. The first apartment to be restored, that of the Gumpertz family, further complicates the terms of Lower East Side sacralization. The Jewish Gumpertz family hailed from Germany. Their story does not play a role in the neighborhood's now traditional narrative, which has been repeatedly framed as the story of the eastern European Jews. But, in fact, the Gumpertzes endured all of the traumas associated with the plight of the later immigrants, those who have claimed this space. One day in 1874, Julius Gumpertz left for work and he never came back. Whether he died or deserted his family made no difference. His wife and daughters had to fend for themselves in the urban marketplace. They turned to their one marketable skill—sewing—and transformed their apartment at 97 Orchard into a tailoring establishment.

The staff of the Tenement Museum has endeavored to tell a historically accurate story: the Lower East Side never existed as just a Jewish neighborhood, and of the Jews who lived there, not all came from eastern Europe. Although many who lived there during the period 1880–1930 happened to be Jews from eastern Europe, Jews from central Europe and non-Jews also called Rivington, Delancey, Pike, Allen, Hester, and Orchard Streets home.

But the Jewishness of the building and its residents emerges despite the efforts of the staff to present the historically more accurate tale of what happened within its walls. Ruth Abram recognized that visitors came to the museum to retrieve their own links to the past. She shared that:

> one of the most moving experiences for me is to see the tenement with someone who's a grandparent or a great-grandparent with their grandchildren or great-grandchildren and hear them tell the simplest stories and realize that this is the first time they've ever been able to say this. They've never had a place to stand and say to their offspring, "This is who we are." Because they can't say that in the mansions and they can't say that in the log cabins.[131]

Jewish tours of the Lower East Side visit the Tenement Museum, just as they make the pilgrimage to the Eldridge Street Synagogue. Indeed, tours organized by synagogues, Jewish community centers, and other Jewish groups from around the country dominate the prearranged visits to the museum. The largest number of "off-the-street" visitors also happen to be Jews, women and men whose families came to America in the post-1880 wave from eastern Europe. They come to experience for a moment "what it was like" and, no doubt, also to allow them to offer a sigh of relief that they have "made it," and can go down the tenement stairs and leave for airier, more commodious homes.[132]

The visited Lower East Side must be old. Old implies authenticity, and there is no need to visit the Lower East Side to see the new and to engage with contemporary buildings, institutions, or cultural expressions. For that, there is all the rest of America. But a visit to the Lower East Side for American Jews provides a vicarious, temporary link to a sacred time in a sacred place. Visitors seem to want to feel that they are reliving the world of their mothers and fathers. That is, after all, the reason for the visit.

The food of the Lower East Side provides a powerful and well-developed mechanism by which this going back in time takes place. For decades New York Jews who moved out of the Lower East Side to other boroughs or other parts of Manhattan continued to shop for food in the old neighborhood. This was particularly the case when they stocked up on holiday-specific, ritually mandated foods, like comestibles for Passover, kosher wine, and other sacred fare. Late-twentieth-century visitors to the neighborhood have continued this tradition simply by including a meal at Ratner's dairy restaurant on Delancey Street, opened in the first decade of the twentieth century, or at Yonah Schimmel's Knishery ("The Original") on Houston Street, which has been dishing out its food since 1910, on their Lower East Side tours.

Even new food establishments on the Lower East Side have capitalized on the longing for the past and for the desire of visitors to feel, even if momentarily, that they are engaging with places hallowed by the neighborhood's history of lived eastern European Jewish life in America. None does this with greater élan and humor than Sammy's Roumanian Steak House, which, despite its shabby exterior, the yellowing newspapers on its walls, and its less than clean interior, has a vintage no further back than 1974. Sammy's, on Chrystie Street, just north of Delancey, trades on the past and visitors' yearning to be part of it, at least for as long as it takes to eat (in nonkosher form) chopped liver, sliced brains, boiled chicken livers and unborn eggs, beef flanken, kishke, or *karntatzlach* (Romanian spiced sausage). Tourists seem to be willing to ignore the jumbled decrepitude around them. Indeed, they tolerate at Sammy's precisely what would drive them away from other places.

The menu beckons to the Lower East Side time traveler, suggesting that she "Turn Back the Clock." The inside of the menu directly addresses the patron's sense of a past retrievable through food, albeit only for the hours it takes to consume the fat-laden, cholesterol- and calorie-rich meal: "Dear Friend: I would like to invite you to turn back the clock to a simpler time . . . a time when your mama served up an appertiser [*sic*] of grated horseradish and chopped onions laced with chicken fat . . . when potatoes were laced with greeven [cracklings made of chicken skin and fat, with garlic, and onions] . . . when chicken soup came with kreplach [dough with meat inside] noodles and a little cooked chicken egg. . . . Nu? So, you remember? So, tell me! How long has it been since you've enjoyed such a home cooked meal?" One section of the menu includes "Sammy's Dictionary of Basic Yiddish," which continues the parody, the signature of the place. *Mishpochen*, a poor transliteration of the Hebrew/Yiddish word for "family," is translated as "troublemakers"; as *zadeh*, a grandfather, becomes "grandchild's piggy bank"; *farblundjet*, or lost, here is humorously defined as "a kosher butcher in Ireland"; and a *goy*, a non-Jew, is "one who buys retail."

A visit to Sammy's for dinner conjoins parody, nostalgia, and a brief encounter with the imagined words and tastes of the eastern European Jewish world of the Lower East Side. Inside Sammy's the descendants of the immigrants become the insiders, the bearers of a kind of in-group knowledge, special to them, and them alone. Food, served as a joke, and language, presented as humor, become at Sammy's powerful vehicles of furthering identity through the imagined past of the Lower East Side. On the restaurant's walls the owners have taped up letters from Jewish tour groups, from rabbis of suburban Reform congregations who brought bar and bat mitzvah classes to taste authenticity, as well as notes from patrons, grateful for the food, the humor, and the chance to be part of the neighborhood's sanctity—evidence that Sammy's does more than appeal just to low-brow, low-class taste. It serves as one more vehicle in the process of remembering and performing the Lower East Side story.[133]

This, too, might describe the complex sentiments that American Jews bring to a final element in the Lower East Side sacralization, touring the neighborhood. Like much of the memory culture surrounding the Lower East Side, touring began in a small way in the decades after World War II and emerged since the late 1960s as a powerful element in American Jewish culture. In the late 1950s and early 1960s, the American Jewish Historical Society organized occasional tours of sites of interest to its members in New York. In a description, for example, of a November 1961 "Walk into the Past," the *AJHS Recorder* never invoked the name "Lower East Side" to pinpoint where Dr. Hyman Grinstein, a professor at Yeshiva University, took the 150 people who had signed up for a historic Jewish tour. Rather, the article described the group's visit to the place where the first synagogue in North America had stood (the Mill Street site of Congregation Shearith Israel); the old Jewish burial ground at Broad and Whitehall Streets; and Fraunces Tavern, where Phila Franks (a member of one of the oldest Jewish families in America, going back to pre–Revolutionary War years, and also the central player in one of the first intermarriage scandals in American Jewish history) had lived. The article included the following caption: "In the lower photo, the tour party is gathered at a corner in present Chinatown, following its walk through *a* [emphasis added] section of the city that was the first Jewish ghetto occupied by Jews from Eastern Europe." What stands out in this seemingly straight reportage of a "bright sunny November Sunday" is, first, the lack of specificity in naming the place. Second, the use of *a* rather than *the* points to a kind of historic accuracy that later venerators of the Lower East Side would miss. Thousands of Jews came from eastern Europe and went directly to sections of Brooklyn, Harlem, and Washington Heights. Obviously many, indeed more, went to the Lower East Side for some period of time, but this did not necessarily make the neighborhood *the* central locus of Jewish life in New York.[134]

Yet by the end of the 1960s, the Lower East Side tour became part of the American Jewish memory landscape. Some of the earliest tours pinpointing the Lower East Side as *the* site to visit grew out of the same Jewish counterculture that had propelled *The Jewish Catalog* into existence. In the late 1960s, Jewish political activists brought to the Jewish community the same kind of "antiestablishment" critique that they brought to American politics in general. The Jewish activists accused the mainstream organizations, especially the Federations, of ignoring the pockets of poverty among elderly Jews in particular. While eventually many of these insurgents, like those involved with New York's Project Ezra, ended up working within the Federation structure, they initially lambasted the community groups for failing to recognize that not all Jews had shared in postwar affluence. In Project Ezra, activists, many of them students, worked with poor older Jews on the Lower East Side to organize tours of the neighborhood, "to give uptown and suburban Jews a feeling for the section's rich history and present problems."[135]

Since then, the Lower East Side tour experience has taken off dramatically. Jewish community groups and schools have organized "pilgrimages" to the Lower East Side—bus and walking tours of the neighborhood—with the mandatory stop at Ratner's dairy restaurant (kosher) at 138 Delancey Street or Katz's Delicatessen (not kosher) at 205 East Houston. The number of tours grew large enough to warrant the publication of Oscar Israelowitz's *Lower East Side Guide* and Ruth Limmer's *Six Heritage Tours of the Lower East Side: A Walking Guide* to help individuals navigate their way around the neighborhood's streets. *The Third Jewish Catalog* also offered maps, pointers on how and where to walk, and, of course, how and where to shop.[136] It offered nine pages of information on how to do your own Lower East Side tour.[137]

Entrepreneurs of various kinds have devised ways not only to sell the Lower East Side but also to invest their sales with the power of historical memory. In the late 1990s, for example, Lower East Side merchants and politicians banded together to stage a yearly Lower East Side Festival. Replete with the carnivalesque, the festival mixed up the games associated with sideshows and boardwalks with historical walking tours, "ethnic food," "hundreds of vendors," as well as clowns, balloon sculptors, and musical performances. The logo for the Lower East Side Festival included a Statue of Liberty with the words: "Lower East Side Festival Gateway to the American Dream."[138]

The success of Seth Kamil's Big Onion Tours, a citywide enterprise founded on Christmas Day 1991, has derived in large measure from the appetite of American Jews to engage with their sacred space. The company owes its origin to Kamil's interest in

studying American Jewish history and his desire to get to know the
Lower East Side as a scholar in training (he was a history graduate
student at Columbia University) and as the grandson of an immigrant who had belonged for over eighty years to the First Romanian Synagogue at 89 Rivington Street.[139] Big Onion offers all
kinds of tours, taking visitors to the Bowery, Gramercy Park, Harlem, Greenwich Village, and other neighborhoods. It also offers
tours based on taste and personal identity, such as "Before Stone-
wall: A Gay and Lesbian History Tour" and "Multi-ethnic Eating"
tours. Likewise, Big Onion has developed specialized Jewish tours:
"The East Village: The Jewish Rialto," "Colonial Jewish New York,"
and "Di Goldene Medina: Jewish Ellis Island," a kosher version of
the "Multi-ethnic Eating Tour." But the single most popular offering has proved to be "The Jewish Lower East Side."

Like the Lower East Side Tenement Museum, Big Onion tours
has taken on, without design, a Jewish aura. Among those who
flock to any of the Big Onion tours, Jews predominate. On the
tours of Jewish sites, Jews overwhelmingly predominate, to the
point of transforming these neighborhood walks into Jewish rituals. Big Onion leads about four hundred organized tours a year
of the Lower East Side alone, and of those no more than "two to
three dozen" are made up of non-Jews. One of the biggest and
most successful annual events of Big Onion Tours is its Jewish family tour of the Lower East Side scheduled on Christmas Day, a day
when many American Jews feel their outsiderness with a particular
sharpness.[140] In a kind of insider discourse, Kamil points out at the
end of the Christmas Day tour the location of "the nearest Chinese
restaurant and the nearest movie theater," two almost ritualistic
ways in which post–World War II Jews have marked December 25.
Indeed, so Jewishly do Jewish tourists feel about their excursions
around the Lower East Side that they, according to Kamil, resent
non-Jewish tour leaders. They "shut down when they learn that
the guide is not Jewish," he noted. "They want the authentic experience," and going through *their* sacred space with a non-Jewish
guide does not work. It strips away the illusion of authenticity.[141]

Jewish groups come from all over America to engage with the
space. Congregation Tifereth Israel (Columbus, Ohio) and Kehil-
lah Chadasha (Washington, D.C., area) have contracted with Big

Onion, as have Temple Israel (Memphis, Tennessee), Peninsula Temple Sholom (Burlingame, California), and the District of Columbia Jewish Community Center.[142] While different age-groups tend to express different kinds of engagements with the neighborhood, they roundly comment, in the visitor's book and in their discussions with docents, that the Lower East Side "feels like home."[143]

Different ideologies shape different tours. Synagogue groups take the religious route, making the trip to Eldridge Street as the high point of the pilgrimage and the Lower East Side as a site of piety. They tell a story of how the immigrants came to America to worship freely. Other tours emphasize the Lower East Side as the cradle of Jewish radicalism and the neighborhood as a place where left-wing ideologies flourished.

The idea of visiting the Lower East Side and drawing upon it as a well-spring of Jewish identity was used by different groups of Jews, each reflecting on the space through their particular lenses. Actual tours and published guides to getting around the neighborhood were custom-tailored to fit any ideology. In 1986, for example, Sarah Schulman, a feminist activist, offered readers of the anthology, *The Tribes of Dina*,[144] directions for a self-guided feminist tour. Readers of "When We Were Very Young: A Walking Tour through Radical Jewish Women's History on the Lower East Side, 1879–1919" were led from Union Square at 14th and Broadway, site of many demonstrations, on the north down to the Forward Building on East Broadway. Each site—Café Metropole on Second Avenue and Ninth Street, Greene and Washington Streets; The Triangle Factory, Eldridge and Rivington; University Settlement House, Grand and Ludlow; P.S. 75, Home of the Women's Literary Club– was explained through the details of women's history. Regardless of how Schulman defined the neighborhood's geographic space, she was very clear as to what parts of its history resonated to her imagined readers. This tour did not suggest that potential walkers stop at the Bialystoker Shul, the Eldridge Synagogue, or the Norfolk Street Shul, just as synagogue-led forays had no need to visit the places where Emma Goldman once lived, or Allen Street, the center of prostitution in the early part of the twentieth century.

Bruce Kayton's Radical Walking Tours offered visitors a chance to traverse the streets of the "LOWER EAST SIDE I!!! RADICAL JEWS." On this particular tour, held on October 10, 1999, walkers could engage with the places once inhabited by such heroes of the past as "Julius and Ethel Rosenberg, Abraham Cahan, . . . Sidney Hillman."[145] Both the religious Lower East Side and the radical Lower East Side allowed adherents to touch down on sacred space. What differed was the focus of the sanctity.

The statement that the Lower East Side "feels like home," voiced in the closing decade of the twentieth century by Jews from California, Tennessee, Washington, D.C., or New York's Upper West Side who took the time out of their ordinary lives to trudge through the streets of an unfamiliar neighborhood looking for Jewish markers of a bygone era and evidence of continued Jewish life in the present, connects them to Paul Cowan, Irving Howe, Joan Micklin Silver, the creators of *The Simpsons*, Maude Weisser and her "New World" chanukkiah, and all those whose words and artifacts employed the sacred specialness of the Lower East Side. While Lower East Side memory created multiple neighborhoods—the radical one, the religious one, the one of warmth and love, the one of alienation and flight—they all imbued the neighborhood with the mantle of authenticity and used it as *the* marker against which to measure all that would follow.

American Jews, both those who yearned for a secular Yiddish culture and those who longed for deeper religious engagement, remembered the Lower East Side, a welter of streets in Manhattan, as a singular space in their history. They made it sacred by invoking it as *the* place on American soil through which they have told their story and by which they made contact with their past. Having invoked it, American Jews made it possible for the Lower East Side to achieve an independent life, beyond what it ever really was.

The sacralization of the Lower East Side did not just happen. Like any cultural phenomenon, it was a product of a particular time and place. The Lower East Side as the embodiment of the American Jewish story and the shrine of its memory took its shape from the stresses and opportunities available to American Jews in the decades following World War II. The actual details of its history when many immigrant Jews did live there, made possible its later transformation into an icon of memory. The particular history of the city of New York in the era of immigration further laid the groundwork for the eventual sacralization of the Lower East Side. The details of Jewish history, the destruction of European Jewry in the 1930s and 1940s, and the expansive openness of postwar America to the children of the immigrants further served as an impetus to the metamorphosis of a set of urban streets into a shrine of memory.

CHAPTER   THREE

The Wellsprings
of Memory

If you live in New York or any other big city, you are Jewish.
It doesn't matter even if you're Catholic; if you live in New York, you're
Jewish. If you live in Butte, Montana, you're going to be goyish
even if you're Jewish. —LENNY BRUCE

IN THIS now-legendary routine, Lenny Bruce, the master of "sick" comedy, sought to distinguish between "Jewish" and "goyish." He typologized foods, body parts, words, celebrity figures, and even other ethnic groups in these two camps. When it came to the spatial divide, he offered two ideas. On the one hand, "any other big city" fell into the Jewish orbit, loosely. But, on the other, New York stood in a class by itself. There, even Catholics (later in the same "shpritz" he threw in Blacks, Italians, and "Irishmen who have rejected their religion"), by virtue of their immersion in New York culture, could move out of the category "goyish."

Bruce died of a drug overdose in 1966, just as Lower East Side memory culture came to be American Jews' spatial icon. What he might have done with that neighborhood in the aftermath of the *Portal to America* exhibit, Irving Howe's *World of Our Fathers*, and the plethora of other Lower East Side symbols, we can only imagine. But as New York emerged in American popular culture as twinned to the word *Jew,* so the Lower East Side came to serve as the emblem of New York in the memory culture of American Jews.

How did this neighborhood emerge as the emblem of American Jewish history? How did this particular rendition of that history, with the Lower East Side as its epicenter, win out over all others and become *the* vehicle through which American Jews presented themselves? The Lower East Side would surely have been guaranteed an important place in American Jewish history and culture by the fact that so many Jews lived there, so many texts shaping their culture emanated from its environs, and so many outsiders went there to observe it. It would no doubt have ranked alongside Babylon, Granada, Venice, Vilna, and Warsaw—major centers of Jewish life in their own times.

The neighborhood's ability to inspire might have happened anyhow just because of its physical location and the visual power of its setting. After all, what other immigrant Jewish neighborhood stood in the shadow of the Statue of Liberty? That symbol, which came to be defined by the millions of immigrants as the symbol not of Franco-American friendship, or even American political liberty, as it had been conceived of by its creator and backers, but of the very act of immigration, could be seen from Lower Manhattan, including from those very streets where the eastern European immigrants made their homes.[1]

But a set of tectonic shifts occurred in Jewish history in the aftermath of World War II, elevating the Lower East Side to iconic status. The transformations in American Jewish life, the suburbanization of the 1950s and the efflorescence of ethnic identity in the 1960s, then secured its role as the powerful metaphor of the American Jewish experience.

These cataclysmic shifts did take place in the history of the Jewish people, and they transformed American Jewish consciousness. In that transformation a warren of streets in lower Manhattan, where many Jews had once lived and where some of them produced an impressive repertoire of books, newspapers, plays, and other works, transcended importance to achieve centrality. The neighborhood jumped from mere significance to the sacred. Because of the events that took place in and around the lives of American Jews after the 1930s and 1940s, the Lower East Side not only got its name, in capital letters, but also received its iconic status.

Sacred memories of a peoples' collective past do not spring up without some kind of factual basis. Memory, "the capacity for conserving certain information,"[2] depends on the accuracy of that "certain information." What obviously might be open to question is how much of that information is "real" and how much has been embellished by the passage of time and the context of remembering. With perhaps the exception of the nefarious uses of history as propaganda churned out by totalitarian regimes and their mastery of using the "Big Lie," memories' roots spring out of the soil of reality.

Historical memory is not falsehood or fabrication. Rather, it functions as the set of stories that a people tell themselves, and others, to explain who they are, where they came from, and the places they have been. Pierre Nora defined collective memory as "what remains of the past in the lived reality of groups, *or what these groups make of the past* [emphasis added]."[3] Although these stories derive their power in part from their mooring in reality, the more they are told, the more fixed they become. They metamorphose from being just pieces of information about the past into memory when, in Nora's words, they become an element in "the lived reality of groups." Ordinary information about the past enters the sacred space of memory when a people need it for their present circumstance and bundle together those pieces of information into a tightly woven tapestry that constitutes their narrative.

Therefore, context is everything. Only under the right circumstances can random facts about the past become memories, and the accumulated data about days long gone enter into the realm of accepted truth, rarely questioned. At the right moment in time, under the right conditions, ordinary places become transformed into spaces throbbing with meaning.[4] The sacralization of the Lower East Side derived both from its actual history and from the subsequent experiences of the Jews, together propelling the transformation of the ordinary into the sacred.

A Place in History

Despite the complexity of the history of the Lower East Side, the fact remains that more Jews lived in the lower regions of New York City from the 1880s through the 1920s than in any other place in America at any time before or after. That simple fact certainly helped secure the neighborhood's iconic status, although mere numbers do not ipso facto guarantee a place or event inclusion in the realm of the sacred. In fact, the memory of the *Mayflower*-Plymouth story as America's founding myth grew out of the image of the small but hardy band who braved the elements in their small outpost on the shores of the Atlantic, persevered, and then, much reduced in number after a harrowing winter, gave thanks. In that case, the tiny number of Pilgrims played a key role in the sacralization process. The minuscule handful, the brave minority, became the symbols of a remembered past.

Likewise, the story of the Jews' resettlement of their homeland in Palestine in the late nineteenth and early twentieth century has been primarily represented through the inspiring pictures and words of a tiny group, the *halutzim*. These attractive pioneers, both women and men, with hoes slung on one shoulder, rifles on the other, strode out to plant fields, drain swamps, and in the process to conquer the land. Unlike the vast majority of other Jews who sat passively in their diaspora homes waiting for conditions to get better, in the narrative of memory, this small group took their destinies in their own hands, built the land as they rebuilt themselves, and captured first places as icons of a mythologized past.[5]

Unlike those other icons of memory, the Lower East Side benefited from numbers, from being the largest Jewish community in America in the late nineteenth and early twentieth century. For a brief but defining moment, the Lower East Side, housed New York City's, and America's, largest Jewish community. In this place Jews outnumbered non-Jews. For a group ever mindful of its small numbers, the narrative of a place where the numbers, at one time, added up on their side made that place quite special.

Certainly the statistics confirmed the obvious point. An enormous number of Jews came through the port of New York, and most stayed there. Between 1885 and 1899, 417,010 Jewish immigrants were estimated to have disembarked in New York, already America's busiest immigrant receiving depot. Philadelphia also served as a major receiver of immigrants, Jewish and others, and in those same years, 36,390 Jews landed there. Baltimore, the other "great" Atlantic coast city where immigrants landed, received 20,410 Jewish newcomers. Fourteen years later the proportion remained the same. Of Jews coming to the United States in 1913, 76,944 set foot in New York City, 7,919 in Philadelphia, and 5,743 in Baltimore. These numbers were estimates and do not tell us how many Jews stayed for how long in any of those cities, but they provide a rough index by which to begin thinking of immigrant Jewish statistics.[6] As the twentieth century dawned, the *American Jewish Yearbook* estimated that 1,058,135 Jews lived in America. Nearly 400,000 of them made their homes in New York State, which meant New York City, minus a few thousand in Albany, Buffalo, Rochester, Syracuse, and a handful of other small towns.[7]

Most New York City Jews chose Manhattan. In 1892, 75 percent of New York's Jews lived in the most southerly regions of the city, as defined by the Seventh, Tenth, and Thirteenth Wards. At the peak of Jewish residence in Manhattan, in 1910, over 500,000 Jews lived in the streets that would come to be called the Lower East Side.[8] To make the numbers even richer, according to the 1911 *Encyclopaedia Britannica*'s entry on New York City, Jews constituted over one-quarter of Manhattan's residents.[9]

Comparing the Jewish population of the Lower East Side with other Jewish enclaves in America provides a sense of proportion. Chicago and Philadelphia tied for the distinction of being America's next largest Jewish community. The *total* Jewish population in each city in 1907, American-born and immigrant, newcomer and old-timer combined, numbered only 100,000. In other words, five times as many Jews lived on the Lower East Side as in all of Chicago or Philadelphia. The city with the next-largest Jewish concentration, Boston, was home to a mere 60,000 Jews in 1907.[10] The sheer number of Jews in New York—and, among them those who lived,

or had lived, on the Lower East Side—made up a staggering proportion of all American Jews.

In addition to the simple numbers and percentages of Jews in
lower Manhattan and in New York as a whole, the memory of the
Lower East Side derived much of its power from the physical concentration of Jews on those streets. This certainly did make the
Lower East Side unique among American Jewish communities.
Jews solidly packed immigrant neighborhoods in other places, including Chicago, Baltimore, Boston, Cleveland, and Philadelphia,
the other major communities. In smaller places as well, immigrant
Jews flocked to the same neighborhoods, chose the same streets,
and fashioned their homes, shops, and institutions around an
identifiable space. Eastern European Jews who came to Washington, D.C., to flood the city's small business sector, clustered in and
around Half Street, SE. They, too, had a "ghetto," even though
the nation's capital was not a port of entry, Jews made up a small
fraction of the city's population, and no Jews lived in tenements.[11]
Even the minuscule Jewish enclave in Johnstown, Pennsylvania,
could boast a thick eastern European Jewish concentration hug-
ging the Orthodox synagogues and the stores in which they all
labored.[12]

But New York *was* different, and housing played a key role in
shaping that difference. Jews on the Lower East Side, mostly immigrants and their children, lived in densely packed apartment
buildings. More people occupied less space in New York City than
anywhere else in America. The tenement building, defined by the
city's 1867 Tenement House Law, may not have been anything
more than a single dwelling containing multiple units,[13] but as a
housing type it dramatically shaped the Lower East Side and the
construction of its memory.

By all accounts, more people crowded into fewer square feet
of living space on the Lower East Side than in other New York
neighborhoods, let alone any in Buffalo or Portland. Manhattan's
unique population density affected all who lived there, not just
Jews, and it affected the evolution of the memory culture. A
greater number of people in New York, the poorest among them
in particular, lived in large, multifamily dwelling places than any-

where else in America. In 1890, 43 percent of New York's residents lived in apartment buildings, as opposed to about 20 percent of Chicagoans. One urban historian, in a study of national housing patterns, has indeed commented on the fact that the Lower East Side is the "most frequently cited" urban neighborhood "because of its imagerial power." Yet, he cautioned, that corpus of citation should be considered problematic. New York and its "Lower East Side" were "an aberration that, in scale at least, was not replicated anywhere in the country."[14]

In the other Jewish immigrant communities, areas of first settlement, newcomers, like their sisters and brothers in New York, also lived in low-cost, relatively substandard housing that they aspired to leave. But those shabby, poorly lit, badly outfitted structures, lacking much in the way of sanitation and light, housed vastly fewer people, Jews or others.

Chicago's Maxwell Street neighborhood supported a teeming, solidly eastern European Jewish population. Its poor housing stock caused reformers to consider it a slum, but its typical dwelling units rose two stories high, or three at the most. A reporter for the *Chicago Tribune* in 1891 took a trip to the Near West Side and described in detail the area inhabited by those "with Semitic features," where one could "hear nothing but the Hebrew patois of Russian Poland." The denizens of the area lived "in a restricted boundary, in narrow streets, ill-ventilated tenements *and rickety cottages* [emphasis added]."[15] Charles Zueblin of the University of Chicago offered a more factual approach to his description of the housing conditions of the immigrant Jews of Chicago in the compendium *Hull House Maps and Papers*: "Among the dwelling-houses of the ghetto are found three types which curse the Chicago workingman—the small, low, one or two story 'pioneer' wooden shanty, erected before the street was grade, . . . the brick tenement of three and four stories, . . . and the deadly rear tenement."[16] Chicago was a huge city. It housed a massive eastern European immigrant Jewish population, and in most ways it resembled New York's Lower East Side. But it took second place when it came to density, and its residents had access to somewhat more living space and somewhat greater options for privacy and indoor room.

Other places offered even more space and packed fewer folks into less cramped quarters. In Hartford, Connecticut, for example, immigrant Jews settled on the east side, in "rows of two- and three-story" structures.[17] Washington, D.C., differed dramatically. In its Half Street ghetto, most Jews lived above and behind their small stores in buildings of one or two stories. So, too, in Johnstown. Even Brownsville, the Brooklyn neighborhood where many Lower East Siders fled, and which by the 1920s came to be defined as a slum, consisted of two-family houses, one- and two-story structures with shops at the ground level, where the proprietors and their families lived as well, and relatively small tenements of at most three stories, as compared with the large ones on the other side of the East River.[18]

Thus the Lower East Side differed from other American "ghettos" by virtue of the hefty aggregation of people living in its buildings and using its streets. Jacob Riis compared the Lower East Side unfavorably, when it came to housing conditions and levels of human crowding, to "Old London" and even China, calculating it to be "the most densely populated district in all the world."[19]

In the Lower East Side's tight spaces, *all* of life took place. The scarcity of indoor space pushed people out of doors, creating a public sphere for seemingly private behaviors. Journalistic reportage, memoirs, and fictional treatments of Lower East Side life depicted whole families sleeping on the rooftops during the heat of the summer, young people courting on the streets, parents disciplining their children on the stoops and fire escapes, for all to hear and see.

Although they did not know it, these new immigrants and their children had created a kind of zone that social and cultural historians have come to view as highly productive of cultural creativity, a zone that blurred the public and the private and erased the line between the binary opposites of what gets done inside, away from the eyes of strangers, and what others can see. These people lived in a "disordered city," as described, almost yearningly, by historian and sociologist Richard Sennett, which "forced men to deal with each other." Sennett, writing in utopian terms about the erosion of "public culture" in an era of suburban affluence and highly privatized life, extolled the implications of a place where "conflict is permitted in the public sphere." He speculated that, in that kind of place, where "unsightly activities like stores and entertainments" blur with domestic and family life, people develop consciousness of place and engagement with each other.[20]

Sennett's broad-brush ideas about cities and civilization merge with literary and memoir texts of Lower East Side life. The young protagonist of *Call It Sleep* moved from Brownsville to the Lower East Side when his father took a job delivering milk. From his childish perspective, he had come to a very different kind of world, "as different from Brownsville as quiet from turmoil." As he saw it: "Here in 9th Street it wasn't the sun that swamped one as one left the doorway, it was sound—an avalanche of sound. There were countless children, there were countless baby carriages, there were countless mothers. And to the screams, rebukes and bickering of these, a seemingly endless file of hucksters joined their bawling cries."[21]

Anzia Yezierska, a product of the Lower East Side, also focused on this public-private blurring and her own inner developments: "Hester Street roared like a carnival. . . . Women with market baskets jammed against each other at the pushcarts, their eyes bright with the zest of bargain hunting. . . . I had been part of this scene—I had looked on hundreds of times when I was in it. Now I saw it with new eyes. Strange how one can love and hate the noise, the dirt."

In her stories, neighbors know each other's business and intrude upon each other's affairs. She opened her autobiography, *Red Ribbons on a White Horse,* with just such a fusion of inner and outer, self and other. Sitting alone in her basement apartment in a rooming house on Hester Street in 1920, Yezierska remembered herself alone, "thankful for this short reprieve from my landlady." Then in burst "Mrs. Katz with her baby in her arms, Mrs. Rubin drying her wet hands on her apron, and Zalmon Shlomoh, the fish peddler . . . into my room, pushing forward a Western Union messenger who handed me a yellow envelope. '*Oi-oi-weh!*

A telegram!' Mrs. Rubin wailed. 'Somebody died?' " As Yezierska opened the telegram, the assembled group, which obviously needed to know her business, kept shouting, " 'Who died?' "[22]

The degree to which immigrant Jewish life in New York played itself out in the streets and other nondomestic spaces undermined the idea of "public" and "private" as opposites. Immigrants living in the teeming tenements blurred these two categories and lived on both the outside and the inside, in part because they had so little inside space. This, in turn, shaped the nature of public behavior.

The Yiddish theater, which came into existence within the borders—broadly drawn—of the Lower East Side in the 1880s, further demonstrated the erasure of public-private distinctions. Given how much of what happened on the stage dealt with immigrants and their troubles, it not surprisingly attracted entire families—babies, children, adults, teenagers—who brought their dinners and talked volubly during the plays. Mothers nursed their babies while actors talked directly to the crowd. The audience shouted and screamed at the characters on the stage, imbuing the characters with an aura of reality. During a performance of the very popular *Yiddishe King Lear*, a man in the audience was overcome with pity for the suffering father, played by Jacob Adler. "Leave those rotten children," the theater patron shouted as he rushed to the stage, and "come home with me. My wife is a good cook; she'll fix you up."[23]

The fusion of public and private typified nineteenth- and early-twentieth-century urban culture. Indeed, the very idea that they existed as clearly definable opposites was alien to that era. The city neighborhoods of the poor and the working class, in particular, as analyzed by historians and described by contemporary observers, wiped away the inside-outside and public-private distinctions that informed middle-class aspirations for the snug security of suburban neighborhoods, evident in American life from the middle of the nineteenth century onward.[24] As such, neither Jews nor their enclaves, in New York or elsewhere, stood out as unique. The extent to which that mixture was seen and described as the most distinctive characteristic of the Jewish immigrant enclave of New

York, however, stood out as notable. In the discourse about the Lower East Side, Jews "in" the neighborhood (that is, those who lived there), Jews "from" the neighborhood (those who had lived there and left), and Jews "outside" the neighborhood (those who never had lived there) all commented on the overlap and confusion. That, in turn, came to be "the problem" of the Lower East Side. As for those who lived on the Lower East Side, and presumably those who left but had experienced American Jewish life there as young people, the concentration, variety, and sheer numbers of Jews there allowed for high levels of institutional specialization and, as such, for the creation of institutions that spoke to their constituents' sensibilities.

In studies of small-town Jews, and by New York standards most places fell into the "small-town" category, congregations made up of a handful of Jews from Bavaria, others from Bohemia, along with Poles, Hungarians, Lithuanians, and Russians, had few options other than to find a common denominator that could serve as the basis for institutional life. They had to find something unobjectionable in the liturgy and in ritual practice, for example, which they could agree on, and use this to create congregations. In many of the hundreds of smaller Jewish communities around America, Jews drifted toward moderate Reform Judaism not because of ideology but because they actually had no choice. Their small numbers made it impossible to hold out for a critical number of their "own kind" if they preferred something else, something more familiar from "back home."[25]

Ewa Morawska, in her study of the Jews of Johnstown, Pennsylvania, a small Jewish settlement in the anthracite coalfields, arrived at the opposite conclusion, but one that still proved the significance of community size in shaping Jewish institutions. In Johnstown the skeletal size of the Jewish population retarded change. The Jews of this tiny community clung to the three Orthodox congregations. They created no secular Jewish organizations or extra-synagogal institutions that fulfilled religious functions outside the orbit of the congregations. According to Morawska, "There were not enough Jews in the area, nor was there enough steady money," to expand and diversify the Jewish institutional infrastructure.[26]

Not so in New York, in general, and especially on the densely packed streets of the Lower East Side. Here belief, predilection, sensibility, taste, and preference *could* be catered to. Enough Jews from literally hundreds of European towns and cities lived close enough together to form a dazzling array of congregations: *anshes*, *hevras* and *minyanim* (the last three terms, meaning "men of," "society of," and simply "prayer quorums," refer to various levels of informal worship groups). In 1910 the *Hebrew Standard* estimated that over six hundred congregations drew members on the Lower East Side, which did not include the large number of informal minyanim that eluded the eye of the reporter who made the count.[27] Similarly, in 1892 Jews formed themselves into eighty-seven separate *landsmanshaftn*, mutual assistance organizations made up of people from the same towns in Europe, on the Lower East Side and by 1910, over two thousand.[28] Undoubtedly, some incalculable number of the worshipers and members of these societies lived elsewhere in New York, but they had to travel "back," literally and figuratively, to the Lower East Side to the meeting rooms and buildings. According to historian Daniel Soyer, most of New York's *landsmanshaftn* maintained their offices, as well as those of their cemeteries, on the Lower East Side. New York Jews, regardless of where they lived, therefore had a constant reason to go there.[29]

Likewise, the hundreds of other institutions—schools, labor groups, Zionist societies, socialist clubs, theaters, restaurants, cafés—that appealed to some particular swath of New York Jewry catered to the Lower East Siders and continued to draw women and men even after they had left the area. Additionally, Jews who had never lived on the Lower East Side but had set up their first American homes in Brownsville or Harlem also partook of Lower East Side institutions—associational, culinary, recreational, religious, or the like. These institutions served to solidify the Lower East Side's reputation as the source for everything Jewish in New York and, by extension, America.

The thousands of formalized institutions allowed ideology and loyalty to entities smaller than "the Jewish people" to exist at the same time that their members or patrons participated in a continuing debate about the meaning of Jewishness. Lower East Side Jews could "be" Jewish by belonging to a *landsmanshaft*, for example, or just by virtue of living in the neighborhood. After all, independent *mohelim* (circumcisers) would usher their newborn sons into the covenant of Abraham; rabbis without congregations would marry them; *hevre kadisha* (burial societies) would bury their dead; and, if they felt the call to worship during the Days of Awe, Rosh Hashanah, and Yom Kippur, dozens of makeshift services sprung up in rented halls, theaters, and other ordinarily unsanctified spaces. Unlike the Jews of Johnstown, these Jews did not need synagogues to service their religious needs.

The complex mosaic of Jewish institutions on the Lower East Side fostered and sustained ideological competition between groups, struggling over the heart and soul of the rising generation of American Jews. Created by the residents of the neighborhood themselves, these institutions proliferated along ideological lines, which in turn sustained, and indeed created, Jewish identities.

This institutional diversity and intense contest over ideas existed on the level of rhetoric, producing words and texts: newspapers, magazines, pamphlets, books, and broadsides. A contingent of Jewish radicals, for example, created a Jewish vegetarian society, the Better Health and Correct Eating Institute, which published magazines, broadsides, and cookbooks. On the cover of one of these vegetarian publications, an Orthodox man, presumably a *shochet* (ritual slaughterer), stood with a knife in hand, while the caption read, "Lo Tirtzakh" (you shall not kill).[30] On the Lower East Side, a small but visible contingent of anarchists annually sponsored a Yom Kippur ball, an atheistic bacchanalia designed to irritate the majority. In 1890 the sponsors of the ball issued tickets reading: "Grand Yom Zom [presumably a play on *tzom*, or fast] Kippur Ball with theatre. Arranged with the consent of all new rabbis of Liberty. Kol Nidre Night and Day in the year 6851 (5651), after the invention of the Jewish idols, and 1890 after the birth of the false Messiah. . . . Music, dancing, buffet, Marseillaise and other hymns against Satan."[31] They splashed their posters all over the streets, making it impossible for anyone to ignore their behavior.

At the other end of the ideological spectrum, the trustees of the Henry Street Synagogue angrily disbanded a Sabbath afternoon young people's *minhah,* or afternoon, service organized by students of the Jewish Theological Seminary for the youth of the Lower East Side. "To speak *goyish* [non-Jewish] in a *Makom kadosh* [holy place]," they vehemently shouted, when the English-language sermon was announced, amounted to blasphemy.[32] No such breaches of sacred tradition would take place on their premises.

Zionism, a force in the neighborhood, also raised the hackles of some. As a teenager, Abba Hillel Silver and a group of his friends organized a Zionist group, the Dr. Herzl Zion Club, which met at the Educational Alliance. Julia Richman and Henry Fleishman, along with other directors of the Educational Alliance, expressed dismay that in their building local youngsters spoke Hebrew and named a club for as un-American a hero as the Zionist leader. When asked to cease such problematic behavior, Silver faced Richman and the others and responded that any language good enough for the Psalms of David or the prophecies of Isaiah should surely be good enough for the Educational Alliance of East Broadway.[33]

Massive labor strikes on the Lower East Side, in the garment industry, and in other Jewish trade groups like the bakers and the printers publicly pitted Jewish workers against Jewish employers.[34] Rallies, parades, and protest meetings were as common on the landscape of the Lower East Side as the more mundane activities of ordinary life.

Sheer numbers made possible this highly developed institutional network. The institutional richness of the Lower East Side drew Jews from other New York neighborhoods. Jews who had left the neighborhood and New York Jews who had never lived there used Lower East Side stores, restaurants, theaters, movie houses, and meeting halls. While they had created similar institutions, in Harlem, for example,[35] New York Jews continued to function within a wide Lower East Side net that defied place of residence. Lawrence Levine's parents were immigrants from Lithuania who had settled around 1910 in Harlem and had never lived on the Lower East Side. But they regularly "went to its Yiddish theaters, restaurants, vereine [societies] . . . to see a *real* Yiddish community." Bringing their children with them, they traveled from the upper to the lower reaches of Manhattan to consume Jewish culture in its authentic setting.[36]

Jewish institutions and amenities drew Jews from other "better" neighborhoods to New York's southern area. The *Jewish Daily Forward* reported in 1926 on the "downtown" restaurants that served as lodestones for both authentic food and social comfort:

> Within a radius of a few blocks are Moskowitz's and Lupowitz's Roumanian Rathskeller, Kumonin's, Pearlman's Oriental, Phillip's Russian Bavaria . . . of course, Schwartz's "Little Hungary" on Houston Street . . . the food most frequently, Roumanian cooking with steaks running high in favor. On Saturday nights the automobiles of uptown guests line the curbs and their owners . . . beam in the warmth of familiar speech and countenance and gorge themselves on the delicacies with which no night club lobster *a la Newburg* can compare. . . . One can get jazz in any cabaret—but not with such food. A platter of bread anticipates the appetite, and abundant pickles, sour tomatoes and kraut. The waiters are . . . disdainful of finicky appetites. Eat and drink, and be merry, for tomorrow you're uptown again. Here a man may talk in Yiddish . . . and draw neither stares nor sneers.[37]

Because of these kinds of nonresidential engagements with the Lower East Side, however fleeting, Harlemites or even Jews who in the mid-1920s already owned cars and lived well beyond the areas of urban concentration could be occasional Lower East Siders.

Sheer numbers also brought to the surface the tensions and debates that ripped through modern Jewish life. Different groups of Jews—Orthodox and anarchist, socialist and communist, Americanizers and resisters, Zionists and Yiddishists—each with a different vision of the meaning of Jewish life and its future in America, struggled with each other. In the process they constructed an image of a neighborhood, or better, *the* neighborhood. They vied with each other and in the process resorted to institutions to sustain their causes, and to the printed word as the vehicle for promulgating their beliefs.

The Lower East Side—the zone of first Jewish settlement in New York—was a zone of words, oral for sure, as attested to by the powerful culture of the theater and by descriptions of talk of all kinds. But the power of the Lower East Side memory took on its transcendent meaning from the realm of print. The Lower East Side emerged as the center of Yiddish journalism and literature in America. Through newspapers published there and through novels, poems, and plays created, printed, and sold there, the basic concerns of the Jewish immigrants emerged as subjects of literary and journalistic concern. These texts explored the crises of migration, the gulf between generations, the breakdown of families, the political strife between neighbors, the rootlessness of the children who belonged neither in the "world" of their "fathers" nor in the world of the Americans that they yearned to enter. These pieces of writing made several points, regardless of their tone, style, or ideology.

They emphasized the idea that the migration to America had heralded a new era in Jewish history for which the old texts, the canon of the past, no longer sufficed. Because the traditional sacred texts had lost their salience, or part of it, the new ones—the newspapers, books, and plays—would fill the void. In different ways immigrant eastern European Jews across America recognized this, too. But the texts that they read by and large emanated from New York, and from the Lower East Side.[38]

The *Forward* (*Forverts*), that powerful organ of public opinion and arbiter of politics, ideology, literature, and theater of the Lower East Side, was read all over the country. Founded in 1897 and with a daily circulation of over 198,000, in 1916, this newspaper functioned as one of the centripetal forces in Jewish immigrant life in America. It pushed the Lower East Side onto its pages, and into the consciousness of Jews everywhere in America. Published on the Lower East Side, with its office building on East Broadway dominating the neighborhood's skyline, the *Forward* (as well as its editor, Abraham Cahan) played a role in almost every aspect of eastern European Jewish life in America: its literature, theater, politics, and trade unionism.

The *Forward* (as well as the other Lower East Side Yiddish news-papers, *Der Tog*, the *Morgen Zhournal*, and the *Yiddishe Tageblatt*) owed its existence to the Lower East Side, but it helped shape a national Jewish culture. It resonated with Jews far beyond the Lower East Side, or Manhattan, or even New York. Its readers lived in Brooklyn, the Bronx, and Harlem. They also made their homes in Cleveland or Chicago or Tulsa or Milwaukee. The *Forward* actu-ally printed twelve separate daily out-of-town editions, for Chicago, Philadelphia, Boston, Baltimore, and so on.[39] Eastern European Jews went to these places, and there they also confronted the con-flicts between parents and children, between tradition and moder-nity, between wanting to be authentically Jewish at the same time they hoped to become thoroughly American.

In these other places they came to accept the idea that the news-papers and other products of American Jewish life came first from New York, and in particular from the Lower East Side. Ruth Sapin-sky grew up in a small town in southern Indiana at the end of the nineteenth and early twentieth century. She remembered her mother's New York–shaped reading habits: "Her favorite paper (and what a favorite!) was the *Yiddishe Gazetten*, a news and literary weekly from New York. It arrived, as a rule, on Friday morning, and I would stop any game to run indoors with the precious *Gazetten*, so eager, I knew, was Mom to see her paper, her link to the great outside world." Sapinsky's mother not only devoured the New York (Lower East Side) Yiddish paper in Indiana but also passed on her "saved-up copies of the *Yiddishe Gazetten*" to Auntie Dvorie, a poor relative.[40]

Living wherever east European immigrant Jews did, they came to believe that New York *was* the normative Jewish experience, with the Lower East side at its heart. Writing about Chicago in *The Ghetto*, his sociological work of 1928, Louis Wirth explored the development of Jewish journalism in "the second city": "In 1887 Leon Zolotkoff established the first Yiddish newspaper in Chicago. This organ, at first a weekly, but soon a daily, exercised a tremen-dous pressure in welding the orthodox, Yiddish-speaking group together. It gave local Yiddish writers an opportunity to exercise their talents and brought to the Yiddish group the movements *that were stirring the ghetto in New York.* [emphasis added]."[41]

So, too, in the realm of theater, Yiddish New York set the terms, and the rest of the Jews of America followed suit as best they could. New York Yiddish theatrical groups traveled around America, bringing bits and pieces of the "Jewish Rialto" to the hinterlands. "The Chicago Yiddish theater," Wirth noted, "like the Yiddish press, is for the most part but a sideshow of the New York ghetto. The Yiddish newspapers and the Yiddish theater draw their talent from New York. And if there happens to be discovered a literary genius or an *actorke* on the local scene, the wider and more appreciative audience of Second Avenue—the Yiddish Broadway of New York—soon snatches them off."[42]

Words on paper and words on the stage drew immigrant Jews into a New York and Lower East Side orbit regardless of where they made their American homes. So, too, pictures—moving ones— linked the immigrant Jews all over America and in eastern Europe through the neighborhood as a spatial icon. Yiddish films, which not only traveled across America, to play to immigrant audiences, but also actually went back to eastern Europe as part of the constantly recycling diaspora culture,[43] marked off the Lower East Side as the spot from which to tell the immigrants' American tale. The "typical" Yiddish film of the early decades of the century had to have a shot of the Lower East Side—identifiable to all by the swarming crowd of pushcarts, haggling housewives, running children, and Yiddish signs—in order to establish the authenticity of both its Jewishness and its Americanness. The films also added a cinematographic element to the inner Jewish debate, albeit in melodramatic form, about Jewishness, group loyalty, family, and success. In their sentimentality, they touched upon the deep complexities of immigrant adjustment to a country so different from the ones they had left.

Indeed, because Jews consumed these films (and the *Forverts* and much of American Jewish popular music) before migration, they may actually have come to America with a fixed "picture" in their minds about New York's Jewish quarter. In that imaginary world made by the movies and other cultural products, America emerged as a liberating land of opportunity yet one that shook the foundations of communal and familial coherence.

The political theorist Benedict Anderson wrote a book about the role of the press around the world in transforming people who did not necessarily see themselves as sharing a past or a present, let alone a future, into something that he termed an "imagined community." Although he focused in this much-cited book on the complicated process of creating nations out of the legacy of colonialism, his thinking may help in understanding the construction of the Lower East Side.[44]

The neighborhood came to be a singular entity, an icon, a locus of the sacred for American Jews, and a metaphor for their "imagined community" because of its very complexity. Competition and chaos, created by the migration and the breakdown of traditionally constituted and homogeneous Jewish communities, led to institutions, and institutions led to the explosion of words.[45] Those words, most skillfully manipulated in the press but developed as well in literature, theater, political rhetoric, religious discourse, and talk of all kind, became a powerful force binding the jumble of Jews, ordinarily divided among themselves, into a belief that despite all sorts of differences they *did* live in a single neighborhood.

What went on in these streets revealed a microcosm of the debate over the meaning of Jewish life in the modern world, the localized version of the inner Jewish debate over modernity and its consequences for the Jewish people. Jews removed physically from the neighborhood worried about it, joined in the disputational fray, and issued a torrent of commentary about the neighborhood and the conflicts it engendered. So much happened among the immigrant Jews in New York, and so much of it could be seen, that it drew the attention of outsiders. It attracted a wide array of observers, both economically better-off, culturally more Americanized Jews and non-Jews, concerned with what they perceived to be the deterioration of American life in the age of industrialization.

The Jews—settlement workers, charitable society donors, social workers, rabbis, publicists—who found elements of Lower East

Side life distasteful wrote voluminously about it in order to refashion it. They saw in the Lower East Side all that they feared about the future of American Jewry. Jews had achieved a level of Americanization and seeming acceptance as worthy members of society, at the same time that they built up an American Jewish life. The influx of the eastern Europeans, and as they saw it, the patterns of life developing on the Lower East Side, threatened to undo this slow but steady progress.

They focused on the labor agitation, the socialist politics, the anarchists, and the noisy street life throbbing with ideology, and found such ideas inappropriate to America. They saw the dirt, the crowding, the vocal and vociferous public behavior, and deemed them to be out of step with a middle-class American celebration of the neat division of the world into public and private behaviors. Here they saw Jews, their sisters and brothers, doing in public what ought to be done in private. Jews in the modern world had a responsibility to each other to stamp out uncivil behavior, and the Lower East Side embodied, boldly, that uncivility.[46]

As one of many possible examples, we might turn to one publication, the *American Hebrew,* an English-language weekly magazine, published in New York and edited by Philip Cowen.[47] Like almost all nationally circulating Jewish publications of the early twentieth century, it emanated from New York. Not only did it physically roll off of New York presses, but its staff lived there, it advertised New York goods and services, and it drew upon New York examples to fill its pages.[48]

Founded in 1879, the *American Hebrew* catered to, and was written by, well-off but traditionally oriented American Jews. This magazine, with its economically comfortable, culturally Americanized, and religiously traditional readers who lived all over America, paid close attention to the migration from eastern Europe and the doings of the immigrant Jews on the Lower East Side, "our brethren in the lower part of the city."[49]

The magazine depicted the neighborhood in exotic terms. Its reporters sent back dispatches from its depths of the unfamiliar. In 1886 "Rambler" jotted down some quite positive impressions of the neighborhood, beginning the piece, "A Walk in the Jewish

Quarter," with the admission, "I must confess that the late cry of danger impending from the 'Russianization of American Jews' was the principle stimulus towards this journey."[50] An 1895 article bore the title "Between Mincha and Ma'arib [afternoon and evening prayers]: A Peep at the East Side." Discussing a sermon by the Slutzker Rav, Zvi Hirsch Maslianski, the reporter commented, "It may be news to many readers that on the east-side, the sermons as a rule are not delivered during the forenoon service but between four and six in the afternoon."[51]

But the magazine also portrayed the neighborhood as connected to the fate of its readers. It sought at one and the same time to distance itself and its readers from the Lower East Side, to prove that the immigrants had positive characteristics,[52] and that its readers had an obligation to help the unfortunate residents of the city's lower regions to lead more wholesome lives, "lest they be the prey of spreadeagle Judaic-ministers," namely, Reformers.[53] The *American Hebrew* saw the numbers and recognized that the eastern Europeans represented the future majority of American Jewry, forecasting in 1886 that the incoming Russian and Polish Jews "will ere long be the preponderant element of our people in this country." The readers of the *American Hebrew*, the editorial continued, "owe" their coreligionists involvement and service. "But we owe it much more to ourselves," the writer commented. If the newcomers "speak their jargon, earn a pernicious livelihood by peddling and remain a class, their characteristics will . . . soon be regarded as peculiarly Jewish," and all Jews, including those who read this publication, would be stigmatized.[54]

In describing the immigrants' religious practices, educational choices, political behaviors, or lifestyles, the *American Hebrew* always located them on "the East Side" or "in the lower regions" of the city. It understood the physical concentration of the immigrants as noteworthy and assumed that their behavior in part grew out of their residential decisions. "Once an immigrant breathes the atmosphere of the East Side," it speculated in wonderment in 1903, "strange as it may seem, it is difficult to get him to change his place of residence, to where the air and surroundings are healthier and purer."[55]

148 CHAPTER THREE

The writer erred. Immigrants left the Lower East Side as soon as they could. But the magazine's staff could not see this. Worried about the impact of residential clustering on the immigrants, they instead created a stagnant ghetto, where its residents had segregated themselves behind its mythic walls. The commentators believed that the Lower East Side bred crime. They editorialized about the scourge of prostitution, something they believed stemmed from neighborhood conditions. They scorned the recreational life as made up of cheap "music halls and low theaters."[56] The editors covered with alarm the radical movements of the neighborhood and the threat of atheism, which they believed might engulf the Lower East Side's young people and give all Jews a bad name.

Most of all, the *American Hebrew* wrote about what it saw as the chaos of religious practice on the Lower East Side, where immigrant rabbis performed marriage ceremonies without ever checking to see if couples had obtained a marriage license and, with equal disdain for civil law, granted *gittin* (religious divorces), not knowing that a civil divorce also had to be obtained in America. "Twice or thrice," editorialized the magazine in 1894, "we told the Russian rabbis of the east side that the rites of divorce which some of them sell to unhappy husbands of the Jewish faith are not legal papers."[57]

Such Lower East Side behavior brought dishonor on the rest of American Jewry. These Jews' mode of worship met with objections as well. Lower East Side worshipers wept and wailed, swayed and spat. They squandered money on *hazzanim* (cantors), "while the average Jewish congregation in selecting its spiritual head seeks one who will attract by his eloquence and learning." Not so in the "downtown" congregations.[58] The residents of the Lower East Side, "the poorer among our coreligionists," it noted, "go to the *chevras* and other temporary places of worship." No mere neutral matter of preference, according to the *American Hebrew*, the "evil of these latter (minyanim) consist in that they keep so many Israelites from permanently connecting themselves with a *properly* [emphasis added] organized and conducted congregation."[59]

Readers of the magazine lived all over America, although New York ers predominated. The *American Hebrew* pointed out to all of them the need for religious order and organization. It told them of their collective responsibility to help Lower East Siders no matter where they—the potential ameliorators—lived. They all had a stake in, for example, the fledgling Jewish Theological Seminary, which the publication supported because the school would produce English-speaking American rabbis who could be a traditional bulwark against Reform and a rational, cultivated antidote to Lower East Side/eastern European–style fanaticism.

Readers of the *American Hebrew*, wherever they were, shared in this discourse about the Lower East Side as a problem. That sharing did not, however, go the other way. New York Jewish readers did not read the local Jewish press from Baltimore, Chicago, or Los Angeles, where similar articles focused on the problems of the immigrant Jews in their local ghettos. Articles about those places were put in the "Out of Town" columns. The Jewish journalistic reportage about the pathologies and promises of the Lower East Side became a national issue; the problems and achievements of Maxwell Street in Chicago or East Baltimore remained local.

So, too, Jews who had more ample resources and felt more integrated into American society than the new immigrants created institutions to reshape the problematic nature of the Lower East Side, as they saw it. The Educational Alliance, the Henry Street Settlement, the Hebrew Immigrant Aid Society (HIAS), the National Council of Jewish Women, the Hebrew Institute, the Baron de Hirsch Fund, and the Jewish Endeavor Society were just some of those philanthropic, service-oriented efforts to help the immigrants and their children on the Lower East Side.

The histories of every other Jewish community in America also include the details of these kinds of helping enterprises. The books and articles written about Buffalo, Detroit, or Atlanta Jewries include the names of helpers, generous with time and money, and the names of the helping institutions they built to assist the immigrants. Their names, however, have remained relegated to the rolls of local community events and notable people. They achieved no recognition beyond the boundaries of Atlanta, Milwaukee, or Buffalo.[60]

The Jewish community in Philadelphia, for example, produced a remarkable group of philanthropists with a broad vision of the cultural needs of American Jewry and a strong sense of the importance of building institutions to shape the religious lives of the new immigrants. This "Philadelphia group" has been the subject of some considerable scholarship, particularly *When Philadelphia Was the Capital of Jewish America* (1993). Yet of the notable accomplishments of the "group" highlighted in this book, the majority involved New York efforts. Many of the book's details focused on the efforts of these Philadelphians to build New York—that is, national—Jewish institutions.[61]

But the New York Jewish philanthropic experience as it focused on the exigencies of the Lower East Side took a different turn, and that helped make the neighborhood an icon of Jewish memory for all American Jews. Jewish philanthropists who wanted to help poor immigrant Jews saw the Lower East Side as the place where they could do the most good. Jewish publications, like the *American Hebrew*, appealed to these women and men regardless of residence to play a role in reshaping New York's immigrant Jews and their blighted neighborhood. As such, well-off Jews across America had a stake in the Lower East Side, or, better yet, they believed that they had a stake in it.

Second, local Jewish philanthropies and social service agencies in other cities did not define place as *the* problem. Chicago's middle-class Jews, in league with the immigrants, created an impressive array of institutions for exactly the same reasons that analogous institutions developed on the Lower East Side.[62] In smaller cities, with lesser populations, only a modest number of such institutions emerged, but they did develop and attempt to help the new immigrants.[63] But only in the case of New York, and its Lower East Side, did philanthropy and the provision of services go hand in hand with an intense discourse about the liabilities of geographic place.

Indeed, the author of a history of the Jewish community in Brownsville, himself a community leader in the neighborhood, noted that, "unlike the East Side—which became the concern of the social reformers—and the older settlers, the 'Uptown German' Jews, who sought to help the newcomers in their Americanization, Brownsville was left largely to itself." The book went on to describe the existence of crime, disease, overcrowding, poverty, and all sorts of other ills among the immigrant Jews of Brownsville. Brownsville could take care of itself; the Lower East Side needed to be helped from the outside.[64]

By the beginning of the twentieth century, Jews around America heard, and participated in, a discussion about why the immigrant Jews should leave New York for more wholesome and salubrious surroundings. Philadelphian Cyrus Sulzberger depicted the wretched conditions prevalent among the immigrants in New York at the meeting of the National Conference of Jewish Charities, in 1901. Representatives from the Jewish charitable establishment across America heard him cry out, "Go back to your communities and tell them . . . to take these thousands of newcomers off New York's hands." At that same meeting, another speaker chided the charity workers, "Are you going to let them rot there, or are you going to help us get them out?"[65] Leo N. Levi, B'nai B'rith official, asserted that New York's immigrant Jews lived in "a worse hell than was ever invented by the imagination of the most vindictive Jew-hater of Europe."[66]

As a result of this kind of rhetoric, and the substantial financial backing of the Baron de Hirsch Fund and that of Jacob Schiff, the Industrial Removal Office (IRO) was created in New York in 1901. Until its demise in 1922, it sent over seventy-five thousand Jewish newcomers out of New York and into fifteen hundred smaller communities.[67] The IRO, in its usual mode of operation, sent immigrants (usually men) to particular places where it knew reasonable employment prospects existed, and helped them to secure jobs. Initially the IRO funded them so that they could save money for the time when they would reunite with their families. Shortly thereafter the men would communicate with the IRO, letting officials know that they could now provide for wives and children.

What made New York and its Lower East Side sui generis in this context was that all of the other cities were designated by the IRO as places to receive New York's surplus. Not surprisingly the IRO sent Jewish immigrants to small communities—Champaign, Illinois; La Crosse, Wisconsin; Gary, Indiana; Galveston, Texas; Cedar Rapids, Iowa—all places quite unlike the Lower East Side in terms of Jewish numbers, density, and diversity. But the IRO also sent New York's Jewish newcomers to Cleveland, St. Louis, and Chicago, places that had attracted immigrant Jews directly from eastern Europe and that had neighborhoods that closely resembled the Lower East Side. It is not necessary to belabor what made New York different from, say, Ellwood, Indiana. Few Jews lived in the latter. By their very small number, they achieved a kind of integration through anonymity, and with so few Jews present, schisms, factions, and ideological strife could not break out. Elias Margolin, who served as an IRO agent there, favorably scoped out prospects for immigrants: "Living expenses in this town are low. . . . [It] seems a veritable paradise to an Eastside Jew of the tenements. Be careful not to send a very Orthodox Jew because kosher meats can be procured only by sending to Indianapolis for it."[68]

But what could have inspired the IRO to send immigrant Jews to Detroit, Cleveland, or Chicago? Each city housed large immigrant Jewish communities, replete with shabby housing, militant unions, lowbrow Yiddish popular entertainments, crime, and *landsmanshaft* minyanim, all the elements of Lower East Side life so problematic to American Jews. Chicago, in particular, had a huge Jewish community, about two hundred thousand in the years right after World War I. As in New York, most of these people were immigrants from eastern Europe who, in a typically bifurcated manner, fell into either the "orthodox" or the "socialist" camp. Large numbers worked in the garment trades, split up into hundreds of societies and congregations, lived in poor housing, relished the cultural life of the Yiddish theater, and even supported a lively outdoor market culture around Maxwell Street.[69] If the IRO wanted to send Jews to places where they could be weaned of eastern European–style Jewish practice, socialist politics, or Yiddish culture, it not only should have not sent them to Chicago, but should have sent them out of the Second City. But it only sent immigrant Jews out of New York.[70]

This fact again suggests that New York occupied a special place in the consciousness of American Jews of the early twentieth century. That should not be surprising, however, because New York occupied a special place in the consciousness of Americans at that very time. New York's role in American culture and culture production endowed it with power beyond what simple numbers warranted.

And, coincidence or not, the majority of the Jewish immigrants from eastern Europe chose to remain in New York, America's largest city and the second-largest city on the face of the earth. What happened in New York in the realm of politics, theater, art, letters, mass entertainment, fashion, and education rippled outward to the rest of America. That power of New York to define culture played a powerful role in the projection of the Lower East Side as a space that mattered.

In each of these realms the coincidence of New York's power as a culture producer and the Jewish immigrant presence had its own historical trajectory that influenced future developments, including the eventual projection of an iconic Lower East Side. The American world of fashion and clothing concentrated in New York, and immigrant Jews made up the single largest element of the labor force that sewed those clothes.[71] That confluence has created a situation in which historians have been drawn to the subject of these New York Jewish garment workers to a degree unmatched by their interest in, say, Jewish garment workers in Chicago, likewise eastern European immigrants.

New York produced America's popular entertainment. By the 1880s it captured the world of music production and marketing, creating much of it in midtown, in the area dubbed Tin Pan Alley. The tunes Americans all over the country sang, played, and listened to were New York's. Young Jews flocked to the New York world of popular music and entertainment, creating a cultural phenomenon that produced George and Ira Gershwin, Irving Berlin, and legions of others who, despite their newness to American culture, helped define the nation's musical vernacular.[72]

But in the context of explaining the emergence of Lower East Side memory as an icon of American Jewish culture, New York's

centrality in late-nineteenth- and early-twentieth-century American Progressive reform bears particular emphasis. Much of the
Progressive thrust that gave the era its name either developed in
New York or reached its most visible articulation there. Historian
Allen F. Davis, in his study of the social settlement movement,
noted that when cities around the country needed personnel or
ideas to implement the vision of Progressivism, they "looked to
New York."[73] Without diminishing the national breadth of the Progressive effort, the struggles of reformers to make an impression
on other places, particularly Chicago and Boston, or the tremen-
dous influence of non–New Yorkers like Jane Addams, Grace and
Edith Abbott, and Florence Kelly, New York served as America's
greatest laboratory for creating a more progressive society.

New York's influence as a center for reform might be demonstrated briefly in the realm of housing. Lawrence Veiller, who lived
at the Lower East Side's University Settlement, was appalled by the
physical conditions of the neighborhood's dwellers and organized
an exhibit to document the dirt, crowding, unsanitary conditions,
and lack of air and light in the tenements on and around Eldridge
Street, where the settlement stood. Governor Theodore Roosevelt
saw the exhibit and duly created a State Tenement House Commission, naming Veiller its secretary. The commission drafted a new
housing code, which the legislature in Albany quickly passed, man-
dating safety and sanitation standards and setting up a permanent
Tenement House Department to enforce the legislation. Veiller
then became a national expert on tenement reform and housing
codes. Reformers around the country consulted with him, and several states borrowed New York's legislation for the benefit of their
own poor. The Chicago City Homes Association, that city's progressive housing organization, "borrowed the idea of the New York
Tenement House Exhibit." Not surprisingly, when housing activists went national to create the National Housing Association in
1910, Veiller and his New York coworkers spearheaded the effort.[74]

In all the Progressive Era crusades in New York—better housing,
factory safety, labor organizing, antiprostitution, playgrounds, and
wholesome recreation—Jews emerged as prime subjects of discus-

sion and objects of reform. The immigrant Jews who arrived in massive numbers after the 1880s, the problems they endured, and their ways of life caught the attention of New York reformers to a degree unequaled by other Jews in other cities.

Non-Jews, caught up in the flurry of reform activism that characterized the late nineteenth and early twentieth century, operated in most large American cities: Chicago, Boston, Philadelphia, Baltimore, Cleveland, and so on. But to them Jews did not constitute *the* problem. To much of New York's powerful reform community, the problem of the Jews and the problems caused by industrialization, urbanization, and the legacy of laissez-faire constituted the essence of what needed fixing.

To further solidify New York's premier status in the Progressive moment, it housed America's publishing industry. Books and magazines of all kinds went forth from New York, and most publishing companies had their editorial and corporate offices there: D. Appleton, Harper and Brothers, John Wiley, G. P. Putnam's Sons, Charles Scribner's Sons, E. P. Dutton, Henry Holt and Company, Doubleday, McGraw-Hill, Horace Liveright and Company, Harcourt Brace, Delacorte Press, Simon and Schuster, W. W. Norton, and Grosset and Dunlap represent just some of the names of New York City publishing companies in the late nineteenth and early twentieth century.

Obviously, these companies brought out books of every imaginable kind. But in the Progressive Era a market developed for books exposing the evils of industrialization and the plight of the poor. Almost all the notable books of that genre came from New York publishing houses, linking that city to the culture of Progressivism. Almost all mentioned the Jews of New York as exemplars of the problems of the industrial age.[75]

Likewise, most of America's nationally circulating magazines, *Harper's Monthly* (1850), *Putnam's Monthly* (1853), *Leslie's Weekly* (1858), *Scribner's Monthly* (later the *Century*; 1870), *McClure's Magazine* (1893), and a host of others emanated from New York.[76] According to one source, by 1880, "publishers in the city produced a quarter of the country's magazines and two thirds of those with a circulation of more than 100,000."[77] Magazine publishers also jumped on the Progressive bandwagon, publishing reams of articles about the poor, the immigrants, and the slum dwellers who benefited little from the promise of American life.

In this journalistic outpouring from New York, the Jews, the new immigrants from the czarist lands, and their neighborhood received prominent attention. Nearly all articles published about immigrant Jews in the United States in the late nineteenth and early twentieth century appeared in magazines published in New York. From 1905 to 1910, of the 44 articles indexed in the *Reader's Guide to Periodical Literature* under the category "Jews in the United States," 6 appeared in magazines published outside of New York; from 1910 to 1914, 4 out of 23 rolled off the presses in other cities. For the entire period, from 1890, when the *Reader's Guide* began to index magazine articles, until 1918, 21 articles on Jews in the United States, mostly dealing with immigrant issues, came out in magazines published in other cities, compared with 108 in New York.

Magazines coming out of New York, like the prestigious nationally circulating *Outlook*, carried articles such as "Book Stores and Readers in East Side New York." *Current Literature*, in 1903, ran an article entitled "Queer East Side Vocations," and the *Literary Digest* offered, "How New York Corrupts the East Side Boy." The writers, editors, and publishers focused on a particular space within New York to examine the Jews. By the end of the 1930s, the phenomenon of reportage about the Lower East Side had become so familiar that *The WPA Guide to New York City* could write of it (and only it): "The dramatic, intensely human story of the Lower East Side is a familiar chapter in the epic of America; a host of writers—some seeking out the Lower East Side and others originating there—have described its people."[78] The fact of the Jewish visibility and representation in the magazines with national circulation spelled the nationalization of what would later be called the "Lower East Side."

In the hundreds of journalistic treatments of New York's immigrant Jews, in the voluminous book-length treatments of urban life, industrial society, and the consequences of immigration, and in the vast photographic record of that day and place,[79] New York's

Jews came to stand for much of what observers loved and hated about cities and modernity. In their engagement with the novelties of the new age, they found the immigrant Jews, and located them on the Lower East Side. William Dean Howells, one of America's preeminent novelists, predicted in *Harper's Monthly* in 1915 that soon "a Russian or Polish Jew, bred on our East Side . . . [shall] burst from his parental Yiddish, and from the local hydrants, as from wells of English undefiled, slake our drought of imaginative literature."[80] Journalistic observers shared with readers far beyond the banks of the Hudson River their impressions of the Jews and their neighborhood, and as such fixed in the popular consciousness the inextricable bond between New York, Jews, and a particular set of streets that later came to be called the Lower East Side.

Images of the Lower East Side circulated across New York and around America through words and pictures. Hutchins Hapgood's 1902 scketches of Lower East Side "types," bundled together in a single volume, *The Spirit of the Ghetto*, benefited visually from the illustrations of Jacob Epstein. Abraham Walkowitz painted scenes of Lower East Side life, and his role in the 1913 Armory Show brought the neighborhood and its artists into the mainstream of American avant-garde art. So, too, a whole range of artists, including Jo Davidson, William Gropper, Chaim Gross, Samuel Halpert, and William Meyerowitz, spent part of their childhood years in New York's ghetto, got their earliest training in its settlement houses, and went on to depict it in paint and pencil, in bronze and marble. They, like the photographers, emphasized street scenes with crowds of people, pushing and shoving each other, milling around pushcarts, with the looming, dark tenement buildings soaring above them. The products of their studios created a set of images of the Lower East Side that were widely exhibited and expansively reproduced. That viewers around the country saw them helped make the Lower East Side scenes emblematic of the eastern European Jewish immigrant experience in America.[81]

Artists from outside the neighborhood were also drawn to it. Painters like George Bellows, John Sloan, George Luks, Jerome Myers, and William Glackens found the Lower East Side a throbbing observatory of human beings using space in ways they perceived to be quite different and more intense than those employed by other Americans as they interacted with their physical environments. Indeed, the Ashcan school of American painters was launched on the sidewalks of New York's Lower East Side, and the reproductions of that group's work diffused the details of the neighborhood's people and places far beyond its borders. Glackens, for example, produced many Lower East Side streetscapes for *Collier's* magazine, a mass-market publication read by Americans all over the country. His commentary, "The crowded city street, with its dangers and temptations, is a pitiful makeshift playground for the children," brought the idea of the eastern European Jewish immigrant neighborhood as a crowded and perilous place to a broad audience. It also helped secure the association between the Lower East Side and that which was essential to Jewish life in the United States.[82]

The observers of New York's Jews, insiders and outsiders, left more words, pictures, and photographs about it than any observers provided about Chicago's Maxwell Street neighborhood, Baltimore's Lombard Street, or Boston's West End. More written and visual evidence about America's immigrant "Jewish problem" focused on the Lower East Side than did the texts and images depicting other neighborhoods where immigrant Jews lived at precisely that time. This distinction certainly explains why later architects of memory have turned to the Lower East Side for the source of ideas and images.

The words of Jacob Riis, Hutchins Hapgood, Julia Richman, Lillian Wald, Margaret Sanger, William Dean Howells, Hamlin Garland, Abraham Cahan, Henry James, and the many others who commented on the Lower East Side provided a powerful factor in explaining the area's salience for future generations of American Jews. Those in later generations who were in need of memory had fewer words and pictures to draw upon to describe the immigrant moment in Chicago, Boston, or Pittsburgh. New York and its immigrant enclave provided the texts from which they fashioned their texts of memory.

Figure 28. The Lower East Side has been the most photographed and documented Jewish neighborhood in the long history of the Jewish people. This is Lewis Hine's study of a market day, 1912. (New York Public Library)

Thus Jacob Riis's words and the products of his dry-plate camera and flash produced a torrent of images about New York's Jews unmatched by the words and pictures describing all other Jewish immigrant neighborhoods combined. The sheer aggregation of images of New York were consumed by more Americans than those depicting any other immigrant zone.[83] So, too, the vast photographic legacy of Lewis Hine, Jessie Tarbox Beals, and others made the visual images of the Lower East Side familiar, close to universal, and recognizable as synonymous with Jewish life in the immigrant generation. Hine, for example, armed with a 35-millimeter camera, left some of the most enduring photographs of New York's immigrant Jewish neighborhood. Since the 1960s these photographs have accompanied numerous historical studies

Figure 29. Lower East Side photographs emphasized the intensity with which the immigrants used the streets. That use, in turn, helped to make them so photogenic. (Photofest).

of the Lower East Side. They have graced museum exhibits dealing with the immigrant Jewish experience, have been put to use to sell Jewish themes on consumer products, and have come to be the most recognizable graphic representations of that pivotal era and place in modern Jewish history.

Hine came to New York from his country home in Hastings-on-Hudson, New York, in 1900 and initially taught nature to middle-class "German Jewish" children at the Ethical Culture School. Here he discovered photography. In the course of one of his first projects, photographing immigrants at Ellis Island, he discovered a swath of Jewish life, seemingly far different from that of his pupils uptown. Hine went on to have a long, distinguished career in social commentary photography. In 1907 he became the chief photographer for the landmark *Pittsburgh Survey*, offering a relatively callous public a stark depiction of wretched living conditions, overworked children, and unsafe workplaces in Steeltown.

But from the point of view of American Jewish history and memory, Hine's photographs of the Lower East Side—its crowded streets, its constricting tenement apartments crammed with people, its men, women, and children ground down by work but bustling in public spaces—emerged not just as one photographer's vision but as *the* fixed images of immigrant Jewish life.[84] He did not provide those kinds of shots for Maxwell Street, Pitkin Avenue, Half Street, or Boyle Heights, despite the similarities between these places and Rivington, Essex, Delancey, and Orchard Streets of the Lower East Side. American Jews whose families encountered America first in Chicago, Brownsville, Washington, D.C., or Los Angeles probably had the street scenes of the Lower East Side impressed on their consciousness more clearly and graphically than the street scenes of their own hometowns.

A Place in Memory

If in the late nineteenth and early twentieth century New York came to serve as a point of reference for Americans concerned with cities, industrialization, and immigrants, it did so even more for Jews. For them New York's Lower East Side functioned as the source of cultural production, the embodiment in one city of a national experience. The Lower East Side claimed its sacred and exemplary status because of being in New York, America's largest city, its greatest port, and the place where, indeed, most European immigrants landed. After 1870, the majority of Jews who immigrated to America came through New York, and most stayed there. As New York became America's premier Jewish city, *it* set the terms of Jewish accommodation, created institutions for all American Jews, produced the nationally (and internationally) circulating texts, and left its mark on a greater number of them than perhaps any other city in Jewish history— or Jewish memory—other than Jerusalem. When the children and grandchildren of the immigrant generation came to create a communal narrative for themselves as American Jews, they, regardless of where they lived or where their parents had first set up their American homes, turned to New York and, by extension, to the Lower East Side, as the place through which to remember.

A few examples indicate the breadth of the late-twentieth-century New York canvas upon which Jewish memory has been depicted. The writer Calvin Trillin grew up in Kansas City and remembered his Jewish childhood. "I think that I assumed that the real Jews were in New York. In fact, New York was a code word for Jewish in Kansas City. . . . We were farm-club Jews," he assessed, but New York Jews played in the major league. His parents, returning from a trip to New York, marveled "at encountering Jewish policemen and cabdrivers and waiters." In New York, he opined for them, "Jews do everything."[85]

Steven Spielberg, born in Cincinnati, took on the Jewish immigration narrative through his cartoon immigrant mouse Fievel in *An American Tail* (1986). Fleeing the land where cats attacked innocent mice, the Mouskewitz family chose to go to America, where "the streets are paved with cheese." Singing their theme song, "There Are No Cats in America," the family entered the immigrant ship, in the rodent section of steerage, awaiting their new opportunities in the good land. Onboard young Fievel announced that he was going to America. A wiser immigrant corrected him, in a voice notable for its distinctive New York accent. No, he told Fievel, he was actually going to New York, a place unlike any other in America.

Perhaps Boston-born journalist Theodore White stated it most clearly in his autobiography. He introduced himself as having been born "in the ghetto of Boston on May 6, 1915." Boston played a central part in his memoir as he traced his career from that ghetto to *The Making of the President—1960*, the work that catapulted him to national prominence. He played a bit of Jewish geography with his readers as he set the scene of his life. "Each of the Jewish communities," he claimed, "then a-borning in America was to be different," each taking on the color and flavor of the larger urban culture in which it found itself. But:

> Only New York had a community of Jews large enough to create a
> culture of its own, in which Yiddish newspapers could thrive, and
> Yiddish artists, poets, playwrights, actors could develop an audience
> of their own . . . . *Never, in all the history of the Jews since Titus plowed*
> *the Temple and sent them into exile, had so many Jews been gathered in one*
> *place and at one time. New York's Jewry, before it dissolved into the suburbs,*
> *and across the country, was unique in history* [emphasis added].[86]

White's comment provides a link between the two factors that created Lower East Side memory, the one growing out of the actual
details of Jewish life in New York and America at the time of the
great immigration, and the other a product of the decades after
World War II when the neighborhood reached iconic status.

In the years after World War II, American Jews needed a Lower
East Side, a place of origin through which they could represent
themselves, and a venue from which to describe the loss of Jewish
authenticity in the face of collective, and individual, achievement,
the underlying themes of Trillin's memoir, Spielberg's cartoon
and its sequel, *Fievel Goes West*, and White's autobiography. At the
heart of the sanctification of the Lower East Side lies the theme
of personal success, bought at the price of Jewish coherence, a
price the authors no doubt felt was worth what it got them, but
not without a degree of regret.

The theme of the loss of coherence in modern Jewish culture
had a transnational history, which began taking shape several decades before the sacralization of the Lower East Side. It was in ac-
tive formation precisely when the masses of eastern European Jews
settled below Houston Street. Indeed, their migration to America
might be seen as a social manifestation of a deeper cultural moment, when Jews began to feel the diminution of traditional culture, which they simultaneously welcomed and regretted.

This leitmotiv in modern Jewish expression gloomily focused on
the seemingly inevitable waning of "authentic" Jewish life. Poetry,
novels, and autobiography depicted the erosion of both piety and
intense communal cohesion.[87] Yet at the same time these precise
works embraced modernity, indeed, by their very form as well as
their content. Writers and intellectuals sought it out, describing

the changes as personally liberating yet communally destructive. Eastern European Jewish writers described the inexorable process of the fraying of the links between their own lives and those of their childhood years, when they had lived as part of an intensely Jewish organic whole.[88]

At the end of the nineteenth century, the Hebrew poet Chaim Nahman Bialik explored in minute but lyrical terms the anguish of loss of faith and loss of community. One critic has described Bialik as having written from a "sense of the lost unity, safety and joy of childhood," a common enough device in poetic expression, but in his works it was encoded into the Jewish encounter with modernity. His poem "L'vadi" (By myself) made very clear that he expressed not just personal angst but a Jewish generational metaphor:

> The wind has carried them all away, the light has drawn them all off.
> A new song has refreshed the morning of their lives.
> But I alone, a tender bird, have been forsaken,
> Under the wings of the Shechina [a female embodiment of the divine].
> Alone, alone I have remained, but with the Shechina.
> Her broken right wing trembled over my head.
> My heart knew hers: She trembled for me,
> Her son, her only one.[89]

The sober realization of the inevitable dissolution of traditional Jewish life dominated Yiddish and Hebrew novels produced in the years both before and after World War I. Popular images notwithstanding, the loss of coherence dominated the works of the Yiddish writer Sholem Aleichem (who, when he came to America in 1906, did not choose to live on the Lower East Side, making his home in Harlem instead).[90] This mournful theme of the evaporation of authenticity achieved a powerful voice in S. Y. Agnon's magisterial novel *A Guest for the Night* (1939), set in the aftermath of the devastation of World War I. A young man, long a rebel against the old way of life, had been away from Szibusz, a small town so obscure that "only one born there, one raised there, and lived there knows how to pronounce its name." He returned for just a night and was shocked to find that the town had decayed in his absence, Jewish life eroded, symbolized by the loss of the key to the study house. Now an outsider, he attempted in vain to find the key, so as to re-create the intense piety and retrieve the wholeness of the world that he himself had rejected.[91]

So, too, the wildly popular Yiddish song "Kinder Yorn," by Mordecai Gebertig, nostalgically mourned the passage of time and the loss of place. Gebertig, a carpenter and poet, along with his wife and children, was killed in the Kraków Ghetto in 1942. But in the 1930s his song, which could be heard in Jewish schools, community meetings, and family gatherings around the diaspora, became something of an anthem of the moment:

> Childhood years, sweet childhood years.
> You will always be in my memory.
> The small town still stands before my eyes,
> But like a dream it all has flown away.
> Childhood years, you will never come back to me.[92]

In America a series of popular songs written by immigrants for mass-market Yiddish audiences rhapsodized about towns like "Belz," which the immigrants had left and would never return to. Lower East Side memory culture owed some of its origins to this powerful theme of twentieth-century diaspora culture, a culture that stood poised between "tradition" and "modernity."

But the specific roots of the process by which the Lower East Side emerged as American Jewish sacred space took hold only after the immigrants and their children had become American and lived far beyond the neighborhood's borders. Two phenomena in particular shaped the American Jewish consciousness of the Lower East Side as Jewish sacred space.

First, the destruction of European Jewry during World World II and the literal disappearance of older Jewish communal sites not only made America the most populous Jewish community in the world but also robbed American Jews of a "back there," which they could use to measure the distance they had traveled as they enjoyed comfort and success in the expansive American climate of the late 1940s and 1950s. The Holocaust and the subsequent cold

war made Eastern Europe utterly inaccessible to those who might
have wanted to reengage with the spaces of childhood or with
their parents' birthplaces.

No more did letters arrive in the morning mail informing American Jews of the ordinary life-cycle events of friends and family
back home, of deaths, births, marriages, *bnei mitzvah*, which had
linked diaspora Jews to each other. Gone were the pleas from rela-
tives still in Poland or Lithuania asking for money in times of want.
No longer did American Jews, through their *landsmanshaftn*, the
community societies representing hundreds of towns in eastern
Europe, get reports of dire communal needs in those places, re-
quests for a new roof for the study house, a new wing for a hospital,
a communal soup kitchen, or the like.[93]

In the *yizkor bukh* (memorial book) written for the destroyed
town of Zabludow, in Poland, one Holocaust survivor remembered a notable character of the town, Esther-Khaye, the *zogerin*
(woman prayer leader). Before the war she had played a role in
maintaining the transoceanic chain of communication. Among
her many ritual functions in this Polish Jewish town in the years
before World War II, Esther-Khaye had the task of praying over
the graves of the mothers and fathers of the immigrants, who were
physically unable to do so. As the memorial book described:

> Either an American comes from across the sea to see his parents
> who are in the True World [dead], and comes to Esther-Khaye,
> or she receives orders from America. Esther-Khaye does her work
> thoroughly; when she beseeches on behalf of an American she
> speaks quite differently. She displays her true talent. Then the wide
> sea separating Zubudove from America doesn't exist for her, it be-
> comes all one city. And later in a letter, she sends her client greet-
> ings from his near and dear ones. She is faithfully paid for this.[94]

It seems safe to conjecture that Esther-Khaye perished, as did
nearly all those "near and dear" to American Jews. No old town
survived to call home, and no cemetery stood that housed the remains, both physical and metaphoric, of the memories of the past.

So, too, on a larger scale the American-European links were
severed. Jewish organizations in America—Zionist, socialist,

religious, and literary—could not exchange news any more with their European counterparts. They no longer had to defer to, or rebel against, the decisions of their colleagues in Europe, who mostly set the prewar worldwide Jewish agenda. The schools and institutes in Europe no longer produced the personnel who would come to America and bring with them "authentic" ideas about education, literature, or religion. American Jews no longer had to find out what went on at the symposiums on Jewish culture that once took place in Warsaw or Vilna. They could not read the journals, novels, manifestos, or poems, let alone see the plays and films produced by European Jewry. All had their doors closed on them and ground to a silent halt.

The end of World War II and the end of European Jewry coincided with the rise of both American Jewish history as a field of study and the veneration of the Lower East Side. Although other factors also shaped the first of these, namely, the earlier lowering of the bar against Jews in American academia and the maturation of the immigrants' children, the tragic events of the war hovered over the beginning of the historical enterprise.

Salo Baron, one of the earliest American-based scholars of Jewish history, issued the first call for the systematic study of the history of American Jews in 1942 at the 450th anniversary of the "discovery of America." The moment, he noted, hardly seemed right for American Jews to think about themselves and their past, let alone to celebrate it, because at that very moment, "the fate of the Jewish people is being decided now for generations to come." Yet Baron, in this talk, challenged American Jews to contemplate their own history.[95]

Between Baron's words in 1942 and Oscar Handlin's publication of *Adventure of Freedom* in 1954, the worst happened, and American Jewry emerged as the single largest Jewish community in the world. Handlin, in the introduction to his book, made the connection. "The year we celebrate," he remarked, "is 1654," the three hundredth anniversary of a Jewish presence in North America. "But," he went on, "we cannot forget that the year in which we celebrate is 1954. Nor can we, in the midst of our joy and well-being, blot out from memory the tragic decade that has just closed. Jews have not recovered from the shock of the six million victims of the European catastrophe." Thus began the first survey of the history of the Jews of the United States written by a professional American historian.[96]

In a similar vein the historian and journalist Abraham Menes, writing on the history of the Jewish labor movement in the United States for a special issue of *Judaism* to mark that same tercentenary, specifically embedded the significance of the "East Side" in the destruction of European Jewry. This article may have been the first postwar piece of Jewish letters that elided "American" Jewish and "East Side." It effortlessly concluded that "the foregoing [material in the article] traces the general contours of the Jewish labor movement in America," without ever looking beyond Delancey or Houston Street.

More to the point, the apocryphal nature of Menes's narrative about the Lower East Side manifested itself as he wrote about the neighborhood as a sacred place of miraculous rescue. After exploring some matters in Jewish demographic history, clouded by the shadow of the Holocaust, he postulated: "Tragic and painful beyond compare as the catastrophe in Europe has been for us, it would have been still more crushing to us as a people had it not been preceded by the miracle of mass immigration from Europe which commenced in the 1880's. The pioneers of the East Side, and of other Jewish sections in other large cities of America, played a leading role in bringing about this miracle."[97] Thus, in Menes's writing, the denizens of the Lower East Side had played a sacred role as a "saving remnant," those whose escape allowed for the survival of Jewish life. So, too, Emma Beckerman, a Lower East Side memoirist who came to New York from "a small Austrian town" in 1904, prefaced her autobiography with a clear linkage between that migration, her life in America, and the Holocaust. She noted that her parents in Galicia "struggled with . . . discrimination, and then decided to emigrate to America." Straightforward enough, she went on: "Could I have foreseen the future I would have blessed that cruel oppression; it saved our lives, for we were already in America when Hitler came to power some years later."[98]

Thus, on the level of lived life, American Jews after the war, had no place to turn to experience what they believed to be "traditional" Jewish culture. That culture which had once served as the yardstick of the authentic had literally gone up in smoke. American Jews in essence had nowhere to turn for the imprimatur of authenticity other than to look within their own borders, to their neighborhood of first settlement, the Lower East Side.

The tragic passing of the baton to American Jewry coincided with another set of linked developments, the Jewish rush to America's suburbs, the maturation of the immigrants' children, and their seizing control of the Jewish communities in America. This transformation had antecedents in the prewar decades. Jews had been leapfrogging out of areas of first settlement, such as the Lower East Side, from the beginning of their time in America. Until the 1920s, as long as immigration continued as a palpable force in American Jewish life, immigrant neighborhoods kept getting replenished with newer newcomers. With the passage of immigration restriction in 1924, green recruits ceased to take the place of those Jews engaged in the act of abandoning all areas of first settlement around America for newer sections of the cities, which boasted bigger apartments, even private houses, lawns, and middle-class privacy. By the close of World War II and the massive suburban building boom of the 1950s, the balance of Jewish life shifted from central cities to newer neighborhoods with few, or indeed no, Jewish historical memories connected to them from which Jews could draw.

Additionally, Jews had become American not just in ideology but also in nativity. A population that had once been notable for its foreign birth no longer stood out, at least in that way. By 1940 a majority of American Jews had been born in America. With each succeeding decade that percentage dropped further.[99] The immigrants themselves aged and died. So, too, the direct connections that linked American Jews to the immigration experience increasingly were unhinged. With the passage of time, then, personal recollections of eastern Europe faded. On a personal level, by and large, the European bond was fully severed.

Their very Americanness and their nearly universal middle-class status made it less problematic to identify with the immigrant milieu. The more comfortable and acculturated Jews became in America, the more at ease they were in discussing where they had come from, the "authentic" culture of the eastern European shtetl associated with their grandparents, and the early years of their families' experiences in America. They could look back to the place where those experiences had been played out—the Lower East Side—and talk about them lovingly from the ease of postwar acceptance.

In the decades after World War II, accelerating with particular vigor in the 1960s, Jews began to disperse across America. While New York City and its suburbs have remained the largest Jewish community during the half century since the 1950s, Jews from New York took advantage of professional opportunities all over America. They were a people on the move.[100]

Among the items in their cultural repertoire that these transplanted New Yorkers brought with them was a little bit of the Lower East Side. It was probably not the experience of having lived on the Lower East Side that they carried with them to California, Florida, or just about any metropolitan area in the United States. Rather, these ex–New Yorkers would have transported the idea of the Lower East Side, the site of Jewish shopping for goods of various kinds, food in particular. They took to other American cities the residual aura of having had some contact with this repository of an authentic Jewish cultural site.

For American-born Jews living on the suburban fringes of America's cities, the Lower East Side became their "old world," their *alte heym*. With no towns across the Atlantic whose names resonated to them, with no bonds drawing them to think about those ancestral places, the Lower East Side emerged as the place that all Jews could somehow share as their collective "shtetl," the emblem for them all of the places they had left.

The first scholarly history of the eastern European Jewish immigration to New York, Moses Rischin's *The Promised City*, made no prefatory remarks that linked the history of the Lower East Side to the American Jews' suburbanization. But in his preface to the 1977 reprint of the book, Rischin made that connection palpable.

He noted that when he wrote the book, based on his Harvard dissertation, "the embers of New York's classic Lower East Side still smouldered on East Broadway. . . . Newspaper offices, bookstores, theaters, synagogues, settlement houses, schools, storefronts, and tenements, however blighted and mouldy, sustained more than the illusion of direct continuity with a vital, earlier time." The Lower East Side that he wrote about had been "the densest and most pulsating concentration of humanity in history," and it lost all of that because of the "decentralization of population and economy . . . the seductive pull of the sun-warmed cheaper-energy regions, suburban, ex-urban, and minicity alternatives."[101]

Jews were heading to those kinds of places also, and when they consumed the texts of Lower East Side memory in their new homes, they could do so painlessly. They did not have to live there. After all, they had Scarsdale, Great Neck, Skokie, Silver Spring, Shaker Heights, Brookline, and the other Jewish suburbs around America that they could call home. But the Lower East Side was accessible to them as the new "old world." It had within it just enough residue of the past, just enough markers of times gone by, to seem authentic. It even still had some Jews, many of whom sold pickles, bread, kosher meat, and Jewish books.[102] The fact that Lower East Side Jews were generally older and poorer and seemingly more traditional than those who dwelled in the "gilded ghettos," as Jewish sociologists called the suburban communities, made the neighborhood's past more palpable, more authentically Jewish, and more special. Jews in the New York suburbs, or those visiting New York from other suburbs, could go to the Lower East Side, buy Jewish products, and literally consume authenticity.[103] In the immediate years after World War II, Jewish schoolchildren from affluent neighborhoods within New York were taken on field trips to the Lower East Side. Here they visited matzo factories, toured the press rooms of Yiddish newspapers, observed Jews at prayer at a *shtibel* (storefront synagogue), and then returned to the Upper West Side, thrilled by their trip to the "picturesque . . . intensive Jewishness" of the old neighborhood."[104]

Additionally, by the 1940s the key institutions in American Jewish life had definitely passed over to the control of the children and grandchildren of the eastern European immigrants. College educated, thoroughly American, economically secure, they no longer had to face the "German Jews" as their superiors who shaped Jewish communal life and cultural production. The descendants of the immigrants from the "shtetl" now sat in the boardrooms of the American Jewish Committee, the B'nai B'rith, and the Union of American Hebrew Congregations, as well as the local communal bodies. The vast majority of Reform rabbis, once the pillar of German Jewry, now came from eastern European Jewish families. They now edited the magazines for national distribution and wrote the novels, poems, plays, and songs that made up American Jewish culture. In their hands, their memories of America, told through the medium of the Lower East Side, became the singular Jewish story.

On some level, the sacralization of the Lower East Side might actually be seen as their revenge against the "yekkes," a term of derision directed at German Jews. A key element in the images of the Lower East Side involved the disdain of those "yekkes" toward the newcomers, their efforts to make the eastern Europeans into something more civil, refined, and bourgeois than they appeared. But, as the memory emerged and got told as the communal narrative, the immigrants resisted their social betters and refused to acknowledge the German Jews' power to make them over.

The memory culture of the Lower East Side, and of the Jewish past in America, posed the new immigrants, loud and assertive, and the German Jews who greeted them as utterly separate, different, and unequal in power. The "yekkes," sometimes called "uptown" Jews, tried to transform the newcomers, tone them down, clean them up, and wean them from their passions. In the stories told about the Lower East Side as American Jews' sacred space, their efforts were for nought. In their space the eastern European downtowners resisted and won.

In the decades to come, the architects of Lower East Side memory and history would use the images of that space to announce their collective triumph over the "Germans." Irving Howe and Kenneth Libo boldly stated that "the Eastern European Jews were different from all other ethnic groups—and indeed from the earlier Sephardic and German Jewish contingent." Unlike those others, particularly the German Jews, the Jews of eastern Europe came to America as part of a "collective utopian experiment," they wrote, and provided the "major source of Jewish energy" in America."[105]

The sacralization of the Lower East Side began slowly in the 1940s, particularly in the immediate aftermath of World War II. The neighborhood's emergence as an icon of American Jewish memory ought, indeed, to be thought of in generational terms. The earliest text that celebrated the neighborhood as the incarnation of Jewish authenticity was directed at children, Sydney Taylor's *All-of-a-Kind Family*. Those youngsters of the 1950s, the target audience for Taylor's books, grew up to be the Jewish young adults who in the 1960s in particular seized upon the romance of the Lower East Side. They wrote and bought *The Jewish Catalog*, which offered the chance to find a "do-it-yourself" Jewish life and depicted the Lower East Side as the closest approximation of Jerusalem in the diaspora.[106] These young Jews were the first generation to go to college and university and to find Henry Roth's *Call It Sleep* on the syllabi of literature classes, or to hear professors of American history refer to Abraham Cahan and *The Rise of David Levinsky*.[107] In their years of young adulthood, the women's movement discovered Anzia Yezierska's *Bread Givers*, hailing her and her novel as examples of an autonomous woman's voice rebelling against the limitations of patriarchy. Feminist bookstores stocked *Bread Givers* on their shelves, and young Jewish women, challenging still-present restrictions upon them in Jewish institutions, had a Lower East Side role model whose words they could consume.

These young Jews, perhaps embodied in someone such as Paul Cowan, participated in the countercultural criticism and political turmoil of the 1960s and saw in the memory of the Lower East Side a Jewish way of life that did not seek to make compromises with middle-class American culture, a culture against which they actively rebelled. They perceived the Lower East Side as a place where Jews had resisted the rule of bourgeois respectability, where they made their last stand for cultural authenticity. That is, they invented a Lower East Side that fit their own ideals of cultural integrity.

In a cultural era pulsating with social criticism and with a disdain for the blandness of suburban culture, the Lower East Side beckoned as an imagined alternative. Paul Berman, like Paul Cowan a writer for the *Village Voice*, discovered a meaningful Jewishness for himself sometime in the late 1960s in a confluence of the decade's turmoil with the literary remnants of the Lower East Side: "I read all sorts of novels, and I saw myself in the old Jewish world of the Lower East Side of fifty years before, where a characteristic personality—a least in the novels—was someone whose life revolved around a passion for ideas: Marxist ideas, or literature, or religion, or whatever. . . . I went on sort of a Jewish kick."[108] Berman's "whatever" was key. It did not matter what was the focus of the passion. It was the intensity that mattered.

This engagement with ideas, as it appeared in the imaginary Lower East Side of memory, emerged as the opposite of the world these particular Jews lived in—comfortable, respectable, and compromising. A filmmaker of this same generation described his reengagement with Judaism, also through the medium of the Lower East Side: "I am a romantic about it. . . . A high point of my life, and not just professionally, was our re-creation of the Lower East Side for a film I worked on. All the stills that you see about Jewish life on the Lower East Side, we made them move. . . . And I loved it. I yearned for it. . . . Not that I would exchange my life now for that. I know the problems were overwhelming—it was dirty, it was crowded, it was poor. . . . But it was perfect for me: like stepping into a still photograph."[109] That imagined passion moved many young Jews of that generation, or at least those who went on to create texts of American Jewish culture. Here they had examples of Jews who seemed to live life to its fullest, who valued ideas and eschewed conventional success.

Leslie Epstein, author of a powerful Holocaust novel, *King of the Jews*, experienced his epiphany as a young Jew when writing a story that took him eight years to compose, "about this little old man . . . on New York's Lower East Side," who had dedicated his life to proving that Mozart was Jewish. In the process of writing his Lower East Side story, Epstein, who then turned his literary lens on the ghetto of Lodz, exclaimed, "The dam broke, I became insufferable."[110] Here once again the Lower East Side as an imagined place of ideas, intensely felt, and the power of its imagery served as a springboard to the exploration of Jewish themes and a segue to the Holocaust.

On some level the Holocaust served the same purpose. These Jews who came of age in the 1960s and 1970s, and who had seized upon Lower East Side memory, had also been youngsters when another book, *The Diary of Anne Frank*, captured the world's attention. It told a very different kind of story of childhood than that of Mama's girls in *All-of-A-Kind Family*, published one year earlier. The publication of the *Diary* and the canonization of both the book and its author also made up part of the childhood legacy of the Jewish "baby boom."

This same generation called upon the images of the Holocaust in their own political struggles of the 1960s and played a key role in making the Holocaust a central tenet of American Jewish identity. When, as adults, they became teachers, leaders of communal institutions, or writers (the creators of texts) or even just members of congregations and organizations (consumers of texts), they moved the Holocaust from behind a kind of Jewish veil into public prominence. It, like the Lower East Side, offered a particularistic Jewish narrative that could also be understood in dramatically universalistic terms.

The linkages between Holocaust consciousness and Lower East Side memory shared a generational trajectory and a history of representation. Within a two-year period Irving Howe's *World of Our Fathers* and the television series *Holocaust* twinned these two icons of identity. Both came to be *the* primary ways in which American Jews represented their history to the larger world. They emerged as the most identifiably Jewish idioms by which American Jews explained themselves to their non-Jewish neighbors.[111]

Not coincidentally, the "discovery" of the Lower East Side as a powerful theme in American Jewish memory culture and the "discovery" of the Holocaust as a cornerstone of American Jewish identity happened together. Indeed, both received fixed names with capital letters in the 1960s. Until then, Jews referred to them in various ways—"ghetto," "East Side," "old East Side," "Delancey

Street," and "the catastrophe," "Hitler's times," "the Six Million"; the various terms were interchangeable. American Jews did not know exactly how to use them before that decade, nor had they become crystallized enough to be cornerstones of memory. In the period from the end of World War II until the 1960s, American Jews struggled with the terms' meaning in relatively nonpublic ways and had not fixed on a single proper noun to represent them.

In the 1960s the Lower East Side, as a shrine of memory, became universalized and firmly established. After that, *all* American Jews referred to it; *all* public presentations of Jewishness emanated from the image of the Lower East Side. As a brief point of contrast, in the 1950s the sociologist Nathan Glazer wrote a slim book, *American Judaism,* as part of the Chicago History of American Civilization Series. In that decade he could still note that New York City Jews lived in multiple "ghetto areas," and that in terms of eastern European immigrant Jewish culture, "It was not uncommon for a Jewish worker to read an antireligious Yiddish newspaper, vote Socialist, join a socialist union, and yet attend the synagogue weekly, or even daily, and observe most of the Jewish law."[112] That is, his New York Jewish immigrants could live in any number of places, and they found ways to soften their ideologies.

That Lower East Side memory culture has grown only stronger as the twentieth century draws to an end can be demonstrated in the tale of a book and its changing titles. In 1969 journalist Ronald Sanders published *The Downtown Jews: Portraits of an Immigrant Generation. The Downtown Jews* anticipated by a bit less than a decade the more commercially successful *World of Our Fathers* by Irving Howe, but it touched on many of the same themes and highlighted the same personalities. For a few years, *Downtown Jews* was the only popular-audience book on the subject, and Sanders enjoyed a kind of prominence on the Jewish lecture circuit. With the publication of Howe's magnum opus, the Sanders book was consigned to a decidedly lower status and obscured visibility. Yet in 1999 the *The Downtown Jews* was reissued. The publishing house took out a large, quarter-page advertisement in the *Forward,* a nationally circulating (now) English Jewish newspaper, trumpeting the forthcoming appearance of the book, the story of the "laborers, radicals, actors, poets, peddlers, journalists, intellectuals, and others, providing the area with one of the most vital and colorful subcultures in the city's history." But the title of the book changed. No longer did the phrase, "the Downtown Jews" suffice. The book had become now *The Lower East Side Jews.* Downtown lacked the power of memory which Lower East Side inspired.[113]

After the 1960s, scholars, in tandem with the vast multitude of American Jews, began telling the story of the single New York ghetto and the stark choices made between traditional religion and secular politics. In that watershed decade the Lower East Side achieved iconic status. In the years since, it has become even more firmly fixed as American Jews' special—that is, holy—space.

For American Jews, the 1960s saw the final triumph of the American Dream of acceptance and mobility. The final barriers in higher education, the professions, housing, and public accommodations crumbled. Anti-Semitism declined. Yet at the same time Jewish communal leaders and the committed grass roots of American Jewry recognized that victory rested upon the loss of a distinctive Jewish culture in America. Increased discussion of assimilation and intermarriage began to dominate communal concerns. In the rhetorical repertoire of American Jews, the Lower East Side stood as a symbol of Jewish life before the need to compromise, or the desire to fit in.

The story told of a remembered place where Jews could behave in public with loud, emotional intensity. They could grab at merchandise from pushcarts, argue with peddlers, and be "themselves," unconcerned with genteel standards of civil behavior. They clung to their narrow streets. They did not need the "goyish" world of compromise. They created a self-sufficient, self-sustaining Jewish—Yiddish—culture that existed in, but not of, Christian America. They could be Jews as they wanted.

In the midst of this conundrum—the sweet success of acceptance and the fear of "the vanishing American Jew," the title of a *Look* magazine article in the early 1960s[114]—a new element entered into American culture as a whole which facilitated the emergence of Lower East Side memory. Spurred on in part by the civil rights movement and the celebration of a distinctive African-American culture, many Americans began turning inward, exploring their own cultural repertoires. Dubbed the "ethnic revival," this development witnessed one community after another re-creating cultural forms from the past. What they actually did, rather than revive, was invent a series of communal rituals, institutions, and practices that allowed them to participate in this veneration of their particular pasts.

For Jews the return phenomenon of the 1960s had multiple roots, many of them independent of the general American mood, which saw the flowering of "Kiss Me I'm Irish" bumper stickers, Italian folk festivals, the revival of Polish dance traditions, and the like.[115] The explosive and televised trial of Adolph Eichmann in Jerusalem at the beginning of the decade and Israel's stunning victory in the Six-Day War of 1967 did not play just incidental parts in the shifting of American Jewish culture. These two events so thoroughly informed American Jewish consciousness of the late twentieth century that no event after them, including the sacralization of the Lower East Side, was untouched by their power.

The Eichmann trial, broadcast into American homes night after night, "was the first time that what we now call the Holocaust was presented to the American public as an entity in its own right."[116] From then on, accelerating with time, the catastrophic events of Europe of the 1930s and 1940s emerged from the hushed privacy of inner Jewish discourse into the open, public world of American culture.[117] Likewise, the Six-Day War changed Israel from being a source of affection for American Jews into a focal point of loyalty and identity.

American Jews did participate in the ethnic revival of these years along with the grandchildren of their fellow immigrants in steerage. They, too, began, both literally and figuratively, to search for "roots" and to talk about those idiosyncratically Jewish experiences to a mixed and broad audience. This was, after all, the decade in which the Broadway musical *Fiddler on the Roof* catapulted the shtetl into common American parlance. Jewish-owned businesses began pitching their products to mass markets, capitalizing on themes and terms of Jewish life. In these years Americans, regardless of who they were or where they lived, saw newspaper and billboard advertisements featuring an Indian man and a young black child munching on a piece of rye bread, graced with the words "You Don't Have to Be Jewish to Eat Levy's Rye." On television Uncle Sam, in Hebrew National commercials, bit into his ordinary non-kosher hot dog—that most iconic of American foods—as a voice thundered from above, advising him not to eat it. Instead, the voice of God shouted down, America should choose Hebrew National, because kosher products ensured a higher quality. They answered to an authority greater than the United States Department of Agriculture.[118]

Late 1960s public culture created an atmosphere that allowed for discussions of the particular and celebrations of the distinctive. American Jews had no past homeland that they had ever lived in which could provide the starting point for their late-twentieth-century American narratives, from which they could talk about their roots. Thus the Jews' search for communal origins and the public discussions of what they found in America inevitably brought them to that singular place, the Lower East Side, that place whose residents and observers had left a vast compendium of words and images which these later generations could draw upon. In May 1966 New York's Jewish radio station, WEVD, aired a program entitled "Shtetl on the Hudson," which described the Lower East Side as "twenty blocks, bounded on the east by a river and on the west, north and south by nostalgia. . . . It was poverty and squalor, but side by side walked ambition and the hope for a better life. In today's language, the Lower East Side of 1910 was a real swinging place."[119]

The Jewish migration out of the Lower East Side left behind a skeletal community, the one that indeed had drawn Paul Cowan back to his Judaism. Many of these merchants sold the remainders, and reminders, of an earlier time. Hi Kleinstein was still operating a brass shop in 1994, a store that at that point had been in existence for 121 years. He described himself and the other remaining vendors of the immigration era as "the last of the Mohicans." From the vantage point of his shop, he understood the trajectory of Lower East Side memory and its uses for American Jewish culture at the end of the twentieth century:

I'll tell you something funny. . . . From 1880, here's what happened: the Jews came over from Europe, *schlepping* their samovars, copper pots and *Shabbes* candlesticks on their backs. Their children became assimilated, they threw out their observance and they had no use for these old pieces. So they sold them to the brass dealers. And now I've lived long enough to see the grandchildren of the immigrants buy back all those things that the children threw out! Amazing.[120]

As American Jews drew upon the idea of the Lower East Side, the producers of American Jewish culture ensured its sanctity. In 1987 literary critic Morris Dickstein shared with readers of *Dissent* his journey out of the Lower East Side as a "real" place, and back to it as a magnet for the creation of memory. When he was a young boy, he and his family lived on the "crowded streets of the Lower East Side, with their grimy tenements and narrow sidewalks, their tiny candy stores, pushcart peddlers." In 1949, when he was nine, the family moved to Queens, but they "kept up the umbilical tie to the old neighborhood, which had the only good bakeries and delicatessens, the only real synagogues and yeshivas, the best bargains, and so on." But with time even that linkage became attenuated, "buried beneath an Ivy League demeanor and a not wholly convincing new personality as an intellectual and a citizen of the world. I belonged to the culture of the West, not the parochialism of the ghetto." Yet coincident with Dickstein's acquiring a pedigree education, a niche in the world of the American professions, and moving to the sophistication of New York's Upper West Side and its culture of cosmopolitanism, the 1960s complicated his easy journey outward. He recalled how "the protest movements of the 1960s . . . encouraged people to 'do their own thing,' and this lent impetus to a growing pluralism. After a long period of amnesia, I somehow remembered where I came from."[121] Dickstein's piece linked the retrieval of a past with its sacralization within two great events of the last half of the twentieth century: the suburban exodus immediately after World War II and the cultural upheavals of the 1960s. Together they allowed him to tell his American Jewish story.

That specialness, that mythic collective memory which resided in, and on, the Lower East Side catapulted it from being just a particular neighborhood where many Jews had once lived to its mythic status. Its sanctity grew out of the power, however invented, of its memory. Historians themselves endowed it with sanctity, and this only confirmed the truth of its singularity.[122] And because of the sanctity once received, it became repeatedly resacralized, enshrined in an ever-growing series of texts, artifacts, and performances, all of which constituted the culture of the veneration of the Lower East Side.

The memory and the simultaneous history of the Lower East Side of New York City, the central sacred space in American Jewish life, not only encapsulates the confluence between these two different ways of understanding the past but also offers a mirror in which to see Jewish self-understanding and Jewish presentation of self to the American, non-Jewish, public at large. Their seemingly paradoxical senses of pride and shame, achievement and loss, success and failure, as Americans and as Jews, all can be viewed in this Lower East Side tale.

The fact that the history of the Lower East Side actually deviated quite substantially from its memory does not diminish that memory, nor has it inhibited the production of historical scholarship, which has examined multiple aspects of its past. Americans Jews, including many historians, may remember it quite differently than it "really was," however, because the elements of the memory fulfill a range of contemporary needs that the data of the "real" history do not. By the multiple acts of remembering, American Jews have involved themselves in the process of creating a repertoire of palpable symbols of belonging to a people, with whom they identify and about whose fate they fret.

Each point in the sacred narrative—the Lower East Side as an all-Jewish neighborhood, a wholly eastern European one, as a poor and isolated neighborhood where the senses operated at a sharper level than elsewhere where other Jews lived and where the Lower East Side's residents later moved to—has played a role in shaping American Jewish identity in the recent past. American Jews have invoked the Lower East Side as a way to reconnect to an imagined past to which they could and would never return.

As they scour the neighborhood for the relics of the past, as they invoke its tastes, sights, sounds, and smells, however romanticized, they are searching for a way to be Jewish. At a time when rabbis and Jewish newspapers, organizations, and schools express openly their fears of a looming break in the continuity of the Jewish people, they and the masses of American Jews have sought out the Lower East Side, a place where they can stake a claim to their peoplehood in America. In their pilgrimages to the Lower East Side and in their many acts of claiming it as their sacred space, they have demonstrated a continuing search for meaning in their Jewish lives, a quest for a marker of the authentic which they can, when they wish, use to assess the quality of their own lives.

Where that quest may lead no historian can possibly predict. Criticizing such uses of the past as nostalgia tells us nothing. Nostalgia, indeed, assumes meaning, implying that something once mattered a great deal. That American Jews at the beginning of the twenty-first century continue to comb the Lower East Side for hints of who they were, and for hopes that the neighborhood as a sacred space will help them chart their future, bears witness to the power of memory in shaping identity.

NOTES

INTRODUCTION
The Stirrings of Memory

1. Sidney Taylor, *All-of-a-Kind Family* (New York: Follett, 1954); Bobbie Malone to author, personal correspondence, May 9, 1999.

CHAPTER ONE
The Lower East Side and American Jewish Memory

1. See, for example, Jeffrey S. Gurock, "From *Publication* to *American Jewish History*: The Journal of the American Jewish Historical Society and the Writing of American Jewish History," *American Jewish History* 81 (winter 1993–94): 155–270.

2. Quoted in Geoffrey Hartman, *Holocaust Remembrance: The Shapes of Memory* (Cambridge: Blackwell, 1994), 18.

3. The most authoritative statement about the Jewish engagement with memory and the distance between those memories and the field of history is Yosef Hayim Yerushalmi, *Zakhor: Jewish History and Jewish Memory* (Seattle: University of Washington Press, 1982). A scholar of Jewish history of the late Middle Ages and the early modern period, Yerushalmi has almost nothing to offer about American Jews and their construction of memory. See, for example, 99.

4. "We Mourn the Loss of Our Temple," in *Grandma Never Lived in America: The New Journalism of Abraham Cahan*, ed. Moses Rischin (Bloomington: Indiana University Press, 1985), 90–91.

5. Mark Wischnitzer, *To Dwell in Safety: The Story of Jewish Migration since 1800* (Philadelphia: Jewish Publication Society of America, 1948).

6. There is some confusion regarding the exact name of Yezierska's birthplace. She gave it variously as Plotsk, Plinsk, Ploch, or Plock. See "Introduction," by Blanche H. Gelfant, to Anzia Yezierska, *Hungry Hearts* (New York: Penguin Books, 1997), xi.

7. Anzia Yezierska, "America and I," in *America and I: Short Stories by American Jewish Women Writers*, ed. Joyce Antler (Boston: Beacon Press, 1990), 72.

8. One history of American Jews took its title directly from the Bible (Gen. 12:1). See Stanley Feldstein, *The Land That I Show You: Three Centuries of Jewish Life in America* (Garden City, N.Y.: Anchor Press, 1978).

9. Oscar Handlin, *The Uprooted* (New York: Grossett and Dunlap, 1951); Handlin, *Adventure in Freedom* (New York: McGraw-Hill, 1954).

10. Lee M. Friedman, *Pilgrims in a New Land* (Philadelphia: Jewish Publication Society, 1948).

11. Yezierska, "America and I," 82.

12. Calvin Goldscheider and Alan S. Zuckerman, *The Transformation of the Jews* (Chicago: University of Chicago Press, 1984), 163.

13. See Simon Kuznets, "Immigration of Russian Jews to the United States: Background and Structure," *Perspectives in American History* 9 (1975): 35–124.

14. Irving Howe and Kenneth Libo, *We Lived There, Too: In Their Own Words and Pictures—Pioneer Jews and the Westward Movement of America, 1630–1930* (New York: St. Martin's, 1984), 29.

15. Central Conference of American Rabbis, *Union Haggadah: Home Service for Passover* (n.p.: CCAR, 1923), 120–21; Mordecai Kaplan, Judith Kaplan Eisenstein, and Ira Eisenstein, *The New Haggadah for the Passover Seder* (New York: Behrman House, 1942).

16. Milton Hindus, ed., *The Old East Side: An Anthology* (Philadelphia: Jewish Publication Society of America, 1969), xxv–xxvi.

17. Morris Raphael Cohen, *A Dreamer's Journey* (Glencoe, Ill.: Free Press, 1949), 106.

18. Abraham Cahan, *The Rise of David Levinsky* (New York: Harper and Brothers, 1917), 156.

19. Hutchins Hapgood, *The Spirit of the Ghetto: Studies of the Jewish Quarter of New York* (New York: Schocken Books, 1966), vi.

20. Emma Beckerman, *Not So Long Ago: A Recollection* (New York: Bloch Publishers, 1980), 45, 63.

21. Irving G. Wyllie, *The Self-Made Man in America* (New York: Free Press, 1954).

22. Henry Steele Commanger, ed., *The Autobiography of Benjamin Franklin and Selections from His Other Writings* (New York: Modern Library, 1944), 6.

23. Anzia Yezierska, *The Bread Givers: A Struggle between a Father of the Old World and a Daughter of the New* (1925; New York: Persea Press, 1975).

24. Cahan, *The Rise of David Levinsky*, 3.

25. Quoted in Norma Feingold, *Water Street: World within a World* (Worcester, Mass.: Worcester Historical Museum, 1983), 18.

26. Cohen, *A Dreamer's Journey*, 16.

27. Delmore Schwartz, "The Ballad of the Children of the Czar," *Partisan Review* 4, no. 2 (January 1938): 29.

28. Mary Antin, *The Promised Land* (1912; New York: Penguin Books, 1997); Sophie Turpin, *Dakota Diaspora: Memoirs of a Jewish Homesteader* (Lincoln: University of Nebraska Press, 1984).

29. *A Voice of Conscience: The Prints of Jack Levine*, Brooklyn Museum of Art, April 23–June 20, 1999.

30. For the concept of an American Jewish "homeland" in New York, see Ira M. Sheskin, "Jewish Metropolitan Homelands," *Journal of Cultural Geography* 13 (fall, 1993): 119–32.

31. *The Compact Edition of the Oxford English Dictionary*, s.v. "sacred."

32. Quoted in Philip E. Hammond, *The Sacred in the Secular Age: Toward Revision in the Scientific Study of Religion* (Berkeley: University of California Press, 1985), 3.

33. Mircea Eliade, *Myths, Dreams and Mysteries*, trans. Philip Mairet (New York: Harper Colophon, 1975), 34–35; see also Peter Berger, *The Sacred Canopy: Elements of a Sociological Theory of Religion* (Garden City, N.Y.: Doubleday, 1967).

34. For one analysis of the process of sacralization, see Johannis J. Mol, *Identity and the Sacred: A Sketch for a New Social-Scientific Theory of Religion* (New York: Free Press, 1976).

35. Quoted in Jack Santino, *All around the Year: Holidays and Celebration in American Life* (Urbana: University of Illinois Press, 1994), 171–73.

36. The imagined centrality of the Lower East Side to Jewish culture in America has gone beyond the boundaries of the Jewish world. General publications, for example, also assume an organic connection between the idea of the Lower East Side and Jewish culture, particularly that transplanted from eastern Europe, in America. Thus the following item appeared in, the *Chronicle of Higher Education* on June 11, 1999: "In the world of Yiddish studies, ZACHARY M. BAKER, is the answer man, a resource for information about Eastern European Jewry perfectly placed as the head librarian at the YIVO Institute for Jewish Research. Now Mr. Baker is taking his smarts far from the Lower East Side and Ellis Island, to a part of the world not especially known for *Yiddishkeit*. This fall he becomes the curator of the Judaica and Hebraica collections at the Stanford University Libraries" (A46). YIVO, where Baker worked, and where the vast

library for the study of Yiddish culture was housed, was far removed from the Lower East Side. It made its home on West Fifty-fifth Street, not even close by a stretch.

37. Pamphlet, "Media Projects, Inc.," Dallas, Texas.

38. Irving Howe and Kenneth Libo, *How We Lived: A Documentary History of Immigrant Jews in America, 1880–1930* (New York: St. Martin's, 1979); Howe and Libo, *We Lived There, Too: In Their Own Words and Pictures—Pioneer Jews and the Westward Movement of America, 1630–1930* (New York: St. Martin's, 1984).

39. Tom Tugend, "Jolson *Shul* Saved in L.A.," *Washington Jewish Week,* July 16, 1998, 21; also *Forward,* July 17, 1998, 12.

40. Quoted in Max Vorspan and Lloyd P. Gartner, *History of the Jews of Los Angeles* (San Marino, Calif.: Huntington Library, 1970), 117.

41. U.S. Census Office, *Vital Statistics of New York City and Brooklyn, Eleventh Census, 1890* (Washington, D.C.: U.S. Census Office, 1894), 234.

42. Selig Adler and Thomas E. Connolly, *From Ararat to Suburbia: The History of the Jewish Community of Buffalo* (Philadelphia: Jewish Publication Society of America, 1960), 256.

43. Gerald Sorin, *The Nurturing Neighborhood: The Brownsville Boys Club and Jewish Community in Urban America, 1940–1990* (New York: New York University Press, 1990), 9–28.

44. *A Colorado Jewish Family Album: 1859–1992* (Denver: Rocky Mountain Jewish Historical Society, 1992), 14.

45. Steven Lowenstein, *The Jews of Oregon: 1850–1950* (Portland, Ore.: Jewish Historical Society of Portland, 1987), xii, 75–76.

46. David G. Dalin and Jonathan Rosenbaum, *Making a Life, Building a Community: A History of the Jews of Hartford* (New York: Holmes and Meier, 1997), 51, 52.

47. No scholar has yet written a history of the Lower East Side. Moses Rischin's pioneering work, *The Promised City: New York's Jews, 1870–1914* (Cambridge, Mass.: Harvard University Press, 1962), came closest and certainly set the stage for all subsequent histories. But he used the Lower East Side as a backdrop for his larger interest, the eastern European Jewish transformation in America. Neither did Irving Howe, in *World of Our Fathers: Journey of the East European Jews to America and the Life They Found and Made* (New York: Harcourt Brace Jovanovich, 1976), despite his constant use of and references to the Lower East Side as the place where the journey ended and the new life began. Likewise, such important books as Andrew Heinze, *Adapting to Abundance: Jewish Immigrants, Mass Consumption, and the Search for American Identity* (New York:

Columbia University Press, 1990); and Elizabeth Ewen, *Immigrant Women in the Land of Dollars: Life and Culture on the Lower East Side, 1890–1925* (New York: Monthly Review Press, 1985), take the Lower East Side as their setting but do not historicize the demographic, residential, and economic transformations of the neighborhood.

48. See, for example, Hutchins Hapgood, *Spirit of the Ghetto* (New York: Funk and Wagnalls, 1902); Jacob Riis, *How the Other Half Lives: Studies among the Tenements of New York* (New York: Charles Scribner, 1890); Robert Hunter, *Poverty* (New York: Macmillan, 1904), for just a few examples.

49. For a compendium of Abraham Cahan's English writings on the "east side," see Moses Rischin, ed., *Grandma Never Lived in America: The New Journalism of Abraham Cahan* (Bloomington: Indiana University Press, 1985).

50. Quoted in Alon Schoener, *Portal to America: The Lower East Side, 1870–1925* (New York: Holt, Rinehart and Winston, 1967), 105.

51. Milton Reizenstein, "General Aspects of the New York Ghetto," in *The Russian Jew in the United States,* ed. Charles Bernheimer (Philadelphia: Winston, 1905), 44.

52. *Encyclopaedia Britannica,* 11th ed., s.v. "New York."

53. A systematic history of the Lower East Side would ask if the inner divisions within the "Lower East Side" had a class basis as well, and it would explore how often Jews moved. New Yorkers generally had a tradition in the nineteenth century and early twentieth of moving a great deal, with May 1 being "Moving Day." This almost ritualistic phenomenon has been explored for the earlier part of the nineteenth century by Kenneth Scherzer in *The Unbounded Community: Neighborhood Life and Social Structure in New York City, 1830–1875* (Durham, N.C: Duke University Press, 1992). If Lower East Side Jews changed residences as frequently as other New Yorkers, how much did they stay within their subethnic zone, and how much did they stay in the larger neighborhood?

54. Rischin, *Promised City,* 77–78.

55. Konrad Bercovici, *Around the World in New York* (New York: Appleton-Century, 1938), 88–95.

56. Federal Writers Project, *The WPA Guide to New York City* (New York: Random House, 1939), 108.

57. Ibid.

58. Ibid., 113–24.

59. Quoted William H. A. Williams, *'Twas Only an Irishman's Dream: The Image of Ireland and the Irish in American Popular Song Lyrics, 1800–1920* (Urbana: University of Illinois Press, 1996), 168–69.

60. Samuel Orntiz, *Haunch, Paunch and Jowl* (New York: Boni and Liveright, 1923), 49.

61. Henry Roth, *Call It Sleep* (New York: Cooper Square Publishers, 1934).

62. Quoted in Mario Maffi, *Gateway to the Promised City: Ethnic Cultures in New York's Lower East Side* (New York: New York University Press, 1995), 133.

63. Roy B. Helfgott, "Women's and Children's Apparel," in *Made in New York: Case Studies in Metropolitan Manufacturing*, ed. Max Hall (Cambridge, Mass.: Harvard University Press, 1959), 19–134, 329–39.

64. Irving Howe, in *World of Our Fathers*, transformed the Triangle Shirtwaist fire into a Lower East Side event. He wrote, "In the spring of 1911, the nerves of the East Side broke," and "investigations, recriminations, exonerations: none could quench the grief of the East Side" (304, 305).

65. David Lifson, *The Yiddish Theater in America* (New York: Thomas Yoseloff, 1965); Nahma Sandrow, *Vagabond Stars: The World History of Yiddish Theater* (New York: Harper and Row, 1977); Federal Writers Project, *WPA Guide to New York City*, 123–24.

66. Federal Writers Project, *WPA Guide to New York City*, 124.

67. Roy Rozenzweig and Elizabeth Blackmar, *The Park and the People: A History of Central Park* (Ithaca, N.Y.: Cornell University Press, 1992), 361, 388.

68. A history of the neighborhood would in fact analyze the movement of Jews outward to other neighborhoods, Brownsville and Williamsburg, as well as Harlem and the Bronx. Thomas Kessner, in his important book *The Golden Door: Italian and Jewish Mobility in New York City, 1880–1915* (New York: Columbia University Press, 1977), found that Jews left the neighborhood earlier and more thoroughly than did their Italian coresidents. What we do not learn from Kessner, since it was not his interest, were the differentials associated with Jewish longevity in the neighborhood. Did shopkeepers stay longer, for example, than garment workers? Likewise Deborah Dash Moore, in *At Home in America: Second Generation New York Jews* (New York: Columbia University Press, 1981), studied the emergence of Jewish neighborhoods in the Bronx and Brooklyn. As such, the Lower East Side functioned as the place that many left, rather than as that where some stayed. Who were those in the years 1910–29, when her narrative began, who remained?

69. Jeffrey Gurock and Jacob J. Schacter, *A Modern Heretic and a Traditional Community: Mordecai M. Kaplan, Orthodoxy, and American Judaism* (New York: Columbia University Press, 1997), 23.

70. Heinze, *Adapting to Abundance.*

71. Letter from Stephen Long, director, Resource and Study Center, Lower East Side Tenement Museum, to author, July 21, 1998.

72. Quoted in Hasia Diner, *A Time for Gathering: The Second Migration, 1820–1880* (Baltimore: Johns Hopkins University Press, 1992), 80.

73. The geographic concentration of Jews in these Lower East Side streets of the 1840s has been well documented in an early comprehensive history of immigration to New York City: Robert Ernst, *Immigrant Life in New York City, 1825–1863* (New York: King's Crown Press, 1949), 46.

74. The only book to study this neighborhood is Stanley Nadel's very impressive *Ethnicity, Religion, and Class in New York City, 1845–1860* (Urbana: University of Illinois Press, 1990). Nadel proves the density of the Jewish presence in this area and the overlapping space of *Kleindeutschland* and the Lower East Side.

75. Diner, *Time for Gathering,* 78.

76. Lorna Sass, "The Great Nosh: Some Landmark New York Delis," *Journal of Gastronomy* 4 (1988): 38; see my forthcoming *Memories of Hunger: Immigrant Foodways and Ethnic Identities* (Cambridge, Mass.: Harvard University Press).

77. Eddie Cantor, *My Life Is in Your Hands* (New York: Harper and Brothers, 1928), 20–21, 288.

78. See Kerry M. Olitzky, *The American Synagogue: A Historical Dictionary and Sourcebook* (Westport, Conn.: Greenwood Press, 1996), for the various addresses of these and other "Lower East Side" synagogues.

79. Deborah Dash Moore, *B'nai B'rith and the Challenge of Ethnic Leadership* (Albany: State University of New York Press, 1981).

80. Nathan M. Kaganoff, "Organized Jewish Welfare Activity in New York City (1848–1860)," *American Jewish Historical Quarterly* 56 (September–June 1966): 27–49.

81. See Diner, *A Time for Gathering,* for a fuller discussion of this phenomenon.

82. Judah David Eisenstein, "The History of the First Russian-American Jewish Congregation," *Publications of the American Jewish Historical Society* 9 (1901): 64–65.

83. Judah David Eisenstein, *Ozar Zichronotai* (Treasure of my memories) (New York: Privately published, 1929), 11.

84. Jeremiah J. Berman, "Jewish Education in New York City, 1860–1900," *YIVO Annual of Jewish Social Science* 9 (1954): 247–75.

85. Kessner, *Golden Door,* 154.

86. Sorin, *Nurturing Neighborhood,* 14.

87. Alfred Kazin's memoir, *A Walker in the City* (New York: Harcourt Brace, 1951), of growing up in Brownsville may be the most gripping and eloquent American Jewish autobiography. It certainly has been hailed, and deservedly so, as the most evocative memoir of a child of eastern European Jewish immigrants.

88. Hapgood, *Spirit of the Ghetto.*

89. Notably, the names "Lower East Side" and "Harlem," unlike "Little Italy" or "Chinatown," do not refer to a particular ethnic group. That Americans by and large understand the former to imply a Jewish experience and the latter, African-American, demonstrates the intensity of the association. Neither neighborhood needs, in contemporary parlance, the ethnic labels to convey its group specificity.

90. Arcadius Kahan, "Vilna: The Sociocultural Anatomy of a Jewish Community in Interwar Poland," in *Essays in Jewish Social and Economic History*, ed. Roger Weiss (Chicago: University of Chicago Press, 1986), 149–60.

CHAPTER TWO
The Texts of Memory

1. Daryl Lyman, *The Jewish Comedy Catalog* (Middle Village, N.Y.: Jonathan David, 1989), 128–30.

2. On Mickey Katz, see Herbert J. Gans, "The 'Yinglish' Music of Mickey Katz," *American Quarterly* 5 (fall 1953): 213–18; Donald Weber, "Taking Jewish American Popular Culture Seriously: The Yinglish Worlds of Gertrude Berg, Milton Berle, and Mickey Katz," *Jewish Social Studies* 5 (fall 1998-winter 1999): 124–53.

3. According to Lloyd Gartner, in *A History of the Jews of Cleveland* (Cleveland: Western Reserve Historical Society, 1978), by 1920 about seventy-five thousand eastern European Jews had arrived in Cleveland. They made their homes heavily in that city's Woodland Avenue district, and indeed there were many butchers, *shochtim* (slaughterers), and other provisioners of kosher food. In 1906, Jewish women in Cleveland, like their Lower East Side counterparts, joined with Jewish trade unionists on strike to protest the high cost of kosher meat; see 101, 11, 162, 176–77.

4. For a synopsis of "Like Father, Like Clown," see Ray Richmond and Antonia Coffman, *The Simpsons: A Complete Guide to Our Favorite Family* (New York: Harper Collins, 1997), 67.

5. The Source for Everything Jewish; for online: http://jewishsource.com.

6. An interpretive essay such as this can hardly catalog the entire range of texts of Lower East Side memory. It can suggest a way of looking at a few obvious, almost iconic, ones, and several more obscure ones culled from local rather than national sources. I make no claim here, then, to providing an exhaustive survey of these texts. The ones presented here are intended as representative of certain categories of Lower East Side artifacts.

7. According to Althea K. Helbig and Agnes R. Perkins's *Dictionary of American Children's Fiction, 1859–1959: Books of Recognized Merit* (Westport, Conn.: Greenwood Press, 1985), only one children's book on an American Jewish topic predated *All-of-a-Kind Family*. That book, John R. Tunis', *Keystone Kids* (New York: Harcourt Brace, 1943), has not had the same longevity as *All-of-a-Kind Family*.

8. Mary Arbuthnot, review of *All-of-a-Kind Family*, *Publishers Weekly*, October 13, 1951, 1577.

9. *Library Journal*, October 15, 1951, 172.

10. Other 1950s titles include Nora Benjamin Kubie, *Joel*; Mina Lewitin, *Rachel and Herman*; Leota Harris, *Freckle Face Frankel*; Arbuthnot, review of *All of a Kind Family*.

11. The same year Gladys Malvern published, *"Behold Your Queen!"* (New York: Longmans, 1951) a juvenile fictional rendition of the story of Queen Esther.

12. *Library Journal*, October 15, 1951, 78.

13. Laura Ingalls Wilder, *Little House on the Prairie* (New York: Harper, 1935).

14. Esther Forbes, *Johnny Tremaine: A Novel for Old and Young* (Boston: Houghton Mifflin, 1943).

15. For the wide appeal of *All-of-a-Kind Family*, see Mary Hill Arbuthnot, *Children and Books* (Chicago: Scott, Foresman, 1957), 420–21. Arbuthnot, a specialist in children's literature, recommended it for use at Sunday school and summer camps, as well as home reading.

16. See the entry "Children's Literature," in *Jewish Women in America: An Historical Encyclopedia*, ed. Paula E. Hyman and Deborah Dash Moore (New York: Routledge, 1997), vol. 1, 220.

17. See "Taylor, Sydney (1904–1978)" in *Jewish Women in America: An Historical Encyclopedia*, vol. 2, 138–39.

18. "TAYLOR, Sydney (Brenner)" in *Something about the Author: Facts and Pictures about Authors and Illustrators of Books for Young People*, ed. Anne Commire (Detroit: Gale Research Company, 1971), vol. 28, 203.

19. Sydney Taylor, *All-of-a-Kind Family* (New York: Follett, 1951), 34.

20. Ibid., 67–68.

21. Ibid., 73–74.

22. Sydney Taylor, *More All-of-a-Kind Family* (New York: Follett, 1954), 158.

23. Ibid., 144–45.

24. Ibid., 1.

25. Ibid., 77–78.

26. Ibid., 80–81.

27. Ibid., 135–38.

28. See, for example, Jianhua Yu, "Immigrant Life and Its Cultural Implications in the Fiction of Jewish Immigrant Writers of New York's Lower East Side, 1890–1930" (Ph.D. diss., University of East Anglia, 1991); K. Dittmar, "Jewish Ghetto-Literature: The Lower East Side, 1890–1924," *Amerikastudien* 26 (1981): 170–292.

29. A fourth novel of the historic Lower East Side had a somewhat different history. Mike Gold's *Jews without Money* (New York: Horace Liveright, 1930) had actually never gotten lost. It became a popular book among left-wing readers from the time of its initial publication, and although it changed publishers a number of times, it never went out of print. It is the case, however, that it was reissued in 1965 by a mainstream publishing company, Avon, and as such became available, or at least acceptable, to a wider audience. See also Eric Homberger, "Michael Gold, Ethnicity, and the Left in the 1930's," *Revue Française d'Etudes Americaines* 16 (1993): 31–41.

30. Leslie A. Fiedler, *Love and Death in the American Novel* (New York: Criterion, 1960), 463.

31. Henry Roth, *Call It Sleep* (New York: R. O. Ballou, 1934).

32. The *New York Herald Tribune* focused on its "crude bitterness," which "makes Erskine Caldwell's work monotonous" by comparison. See *New York Herald Tribune*, February 16, 1935, 9.

33. Bonnie Lyons, *Henry Roth: The Man and His Work* (New York: Cooper Square, 1977).

34. Walter Rideout, *The Radical Novel in the United States, 1900–1954: Some Interrelations of Literature and Society* (Cambridge, Mass.: Harvard University Press, 1956), 186–90.

35. Alfred Kazin, "Neglected Books," *American Scholar* 25 (autumn 1956): 478, 486; Leslie Fiedler, "Henry Roth's Neglected Masterpiece" (1960), in *The Collected Essays of Leslie Fiedler* (New York: Stein and Day, 1971), vol. 2, 271–79.

36. Walter Allen, "Afterword" to Henry Roth, *Call It Sleep*, 442.

37. Since the initial reissue, editions of *Call It Sleep* have been published in 1963 (in England), 1966 (in Spanish, published in Barcelona), 1991, 1995, and 1996. See *New Essays on* Call It Sleep (New York: Cambridge University Press, 1996); Horst Immel, *Literarische Gestaltungsvarianten des Einwanderromans* (Frankfurt am Main: Peter Lang, 1987); and Mario Materassi, *Rothiana: Henry Roth nella critic italiana* (Florence: Giutina, 1985).

38. *New Republic*, February 2, 1918, 31.

39. "Introduction," by John Higham, to Abraham Cahan *The Rise of David Levinsky* (New York: Harper and Brothers, 1960), xi.

40. Likewise, Cahan's short stories saw life, died, and then were revived in the late 1960s. Thus, *The Imported Bridegroom and Other Stories* was first published in 1898 by Houghton, Mifflin; *Yekl* had been published in 1896 by Appleton. In 1968 a small press, Garrett, released *The Imported Bridegroom*, and in 1970 Dover published a volume of Cahan stories as *Yekl and The Imported Bridegroom*.

41. Isaac Rosenfeld, "The Fall of David Levinsky," in *Preserving the Hunger: An Isaac Rosenfeld Reader*, ed. Mark Schechner (Detroit: Wayne State University Press, 1988), 152.

42. It is virtually impossible to cite the number of places where Cahan is quoted and the number of scholarly articles that have referenced *The Rise of David Levinsky*. Ronald Sanders, *The Downtown Jews* (New York: Harper and Row, 1969), is subtitled *Portraits of an Immigrant Generation*. It is, however, a loosely constructed biography of Cahan. In the index to Irving Howe, *World of Our Fathers: The Journey of the East European Jews to America and the Life They Found and Made* (New York: Harcourt Brace Jovanovich, 1976), no name appears more often that Abraham Cahan, no newspaper more frequently than the *Jewish Daily Forward*, nor any novel more than *The Rise of David Levinsky*. Moses Rischin, *Grandma Never Lived in America: The New Journalism of Abraham Cahan* (Bloomington: Indiana University Press, 1985), has brought together Cahan's English newspaper writings, while Isaac Metzker's *A Bintel Brief: Sixty Years of Letters from the Lower East Side to the Jewish Daily Forward* (Garden City, N.Y.: Doubleday, 1971) transformed Cahan's advice column in the *Forward* to canonical status. See also Sanford E. Marovitz, "The Lonely New Americans of Abraham Cahan," *American Quarterly* 20, no. 2, pt. 1 (1968): 196–210.

43. A similar story might be told of Hutchins Hapgood's journalistic treatment of the neighborhood, *The Spirit of the Ghetto: Studies of the Jewish*

Quarter. Published in part in a number of magazines (*Atlantic Monthly, The Critic, The Bookman,* and others) and then brought out in book form in 1902 by Funk and Wagnalls, *Spirit of the Ghetto* was intended to offer a fresh look at the immigrant Jews of New York's East Side. Rather than presenting any single Jew as typical of the immigrants, Hapgood sought to show that many Jews lived there, expressing diverse views about Jewishness and America. He offered portraits of "the old and new woman," rabbis, poets, radicals, "submerged scholars," and many others. After its 1902 publication, *The Spirit of the Ghetto* lay on library shelves. In 1965 Funk and Wagnalls reissued it, with Schocken paperback editions coming out in 1966 and 1967.

44. *International Book Reviews,* October 1925, 719; *New York Tribune,* October 25, 1925, 20.

45. *New York Times,* September 13, 1925, 8.

46. "Introduction," by Blanche H. Gelfant, to Anzia Yezierska, *Hungry Hearts* (New York: Penguin Press, 1997), xvii.

47. Joyce Antler, *The Journey Home: Jewish Women and the American Century* (New York: Free Press, 1997), 27.

48. Yezierska, *Hungry Hearts,* xix.

49. Alice Kessler Harris, "Organizing the Unorganizable: Three Jewish Women and Their Union," *Labor History* 17 (winter 1976): 14–28; Harris "Where Are the Organized Women Workers?" *Feminist Studies* 3 (fall 1975): 92–110.

50. Yezierska, *Bread Givers,* 297.

51. Cahan, *Rise of David Levinsky,* 525–26.

52. Henry Roth, *Call It Sleep* (New York: Avon, 1962), 138.

53. Ibid., 147.

54. Just as the retrieval of these novels represented a new and different interest in America in the Lower East Side so, too, some memoir literature. Rose Cohen's, *Out of the Shadow* was first published in 1918 by G. H. Doran. This autobiography of a young woman growing up on the Lower East Side was reissued in 1971, and then again in 1995 by Cornell University Press with an introduction by the labor historian Thomas Dublin.

55. Belva Plain, *Evergreen* (New York: Delacorte, 1978).

56. Gloria Goldreich, *Leah's Journey* (New York: Harcourt Brace, 1978).

57. Meredith Tax, *Rivington Street* (New York: William Morrow, 1982); *Tax Union Square* (New York: William Morrow, 1988).

58. Janet Robertson, *Journey Home* (New York: Simon and Schuster, 1990).

59. On the romance genre and its formulaic nature, see Janice Radway, *Reading the Romance: Women, Patriarchy, and Popular Literature* (Chapel Hill: University of North Carolina Press, 1991).

60. Emily Maxwell, *An Easter Disguise* (New York: Zebra Books, 1994).

61. Plain, *Evergreen*, 29; Goldreich, *Leah's Journey*, 27; Tax, *Rivington Street*, 80.

62. Goldreich, *Leah's Journey*, 103; Robertson, *Journey Home*, 62.

63. Goldreich, *Leah's Journey*, 102.

64. For this see my forthcoming book *Memories of Hunger: Immigrant Foodways and Ethnic Identities* (Cambridge, Mass.: Harvard University Press).

65. Tax, *Rivington Street*, 9.

66. Plain, *Evergreen*, 587.

67. On Rose Pastor Stokes, see Herbert Shapiro and David L. Sterling, eds., *"I Belong to the Working Class": The Unfinished Autobiography of Rose Pastor Stokes* (Athens: University of Georgia Press, 1992).

68. Plain, *Evergreen*, 18–19.

69. Goldreich, *Leah's Journey*, 449.

70. Plain, *Evergreen*, 30.

71. Ibid., 587.

72. Radway, *Reading the Romance*, 74.

73. Allon Schoener, "Reflections on the Lower East Side: Portal to America" (talk presented at conference, May 10, 1998, New York University).

74. Allon Schoener, ed., *Portal to America: The Lower East Side, 1870–1925* (New York: Holt, Rinehart and Winston, 1967), n.p.

75. Milton Hindus, ed., *The Jewish East Side, 1881–1924* (Philadelphia: Jewish Publication Society, 1969), xxiii.

76. One description of the exhibit is provided in Jenna Weissman Joselit, "Telling Tales: Or, How a Slum Became a Shrine," *Jewish Social Studies* 2, no. 2 (n.s.) (winter 1996): 59–61.

77. Allon Schoener, lecture, New York University, May 10, 1998.

78. *Washington Post*, November 27, 1980.

79. Jacob A. Riis, *How the Other Half Lives: Studies among the Tenements of New York* (New York: Charles Scribner's, 1890), 128.

80. *Washington Post*, November 27, 1980.

81. Friedman, *The Jewish Image in American Film*, 28; Thomas Cripps, "The Movie Jew as an Image of Assimilation," *Journal of Popular Film* 4 (spring 1975): 190–207.

82. See J. Hoberman, *Bridge of Light: Yiddish Film between Two Worlds* (Philadelphia: Temple University Press, 1995).

83. *The Naked City* (1947) took place in part in the Lower East Side. A few characters with distinctive New York Jewish accents and a streetscape with the words "Bosser Kosher" (kosher meat) constituted the Jewish content to the film.

84. See Joyce Antler, "Hester Street," in *Past Imperfect: History According to the Movies*, ed. Mark C. Carnes (New York: Henry Holt, 1995), 178–81.

85. Rabbi Roseman credited the idea of writing a "choose-your-own-adventure" book to his wife, a reading specialist who used these kinds of books to help youngsters with reading problems learn to enjoy reading. Telephone interview with Rabbi Kenneth Roseman, Temple Shalom, Dallas, Texas, July 16, 1998.

86. Kenneth Roseman, *The Melting Pot: An Adventure in New York* (New York: Union of American Hebrew Congregations, 1984), 1.

87. Telephone interview, Philip Warmflash, August 4, 1998.

88. Telephone interview, Wendy Rosenthal, Camp Ramah, Ojai, California, July 10, 1998. Camp Ramah, in Eagle River, Wisconsin, also had a Lower East Side Day program in the 1980s. According to Jeffery Rubenstein, a former counselor, in a personal communication with the author, "they did a whole program on the Lower East Side, which involved the kids going through immigration processing as if they just arrived off the boat and then they went to the Lower East Side."

89. Howe, *World of Our Fathers*.

90. The phrase is Howe's, from *Margin of Hope: An Intellectual Autobiography* (New York: Harcourt, Brace, 1982).

91. Edward Alexander, *Irving Howe: Socialist, Critic, Jew* (Bloomington: Indiana University Press, 1998); see his autobiographical piece in Bernard Rosenberg and Ernest Goldstein, *Creators and Disturbers: Reminiscences of Jewish Intellectuals of New York* (New York: Columbia University Press, 1982), 264–87.

92. Irving Howe and Eliezer Greenberg, eds., *A Treasury of Yiddish Stories* (New York: Viking, 1954); Howe and Greenberg, *A Treasury of Yiddish Poetry* (New York: Holt, Rinehart and Winston, 1969); Howe and Greenberg, *Voices from the Yiddish: Essays, Memoirs, Diaries* (Ann Arbor: University of Michigan Press, 1972).

93. Alexander, *Irving Howe*, 79.

94. Nathan Glazer, "At the Trotsky Table," *CommonQuest* 3, nos. 3/4 (1999): 27.

95. Alexander, *Irving Howe*, 187.

96. *Congress Monthly,* March 1976, 17–18.

97. *Hadassah Monthly,* March 1976, 26–27.

98. Howe, *Margin of Hope,* 339–41.

99. Miriam Sagan, *Tracing Our Jewish Roots* (Santa Fe, N.M.: John Muir Publications, 1993), 22. Indeed, a scan of the index of this work of juvenile nonfiction reveals more references to the Lower East Side than to any other place in America, Europe, or elsewhere.

100. Elsa Okon Rael, *What Zeesie Saw on Delancey Street* (New York: Simon and Schuster, 1996); Rael, *When Zaydeh Danced on Eldridge Street* (New York: Simon and Schuster, 1997).

101. "Vaudeville with Vigor," *New York Times,* April 2, 1999; interview, Dale Davidson, May 6, 1999.

102. Richard Siegel, Michael Strassfeld, and Sharon Strassfeld, eds., *The Jewish Catalog: A Do-It-Yourself Kit* (Philadelphia: Jewish Publication Society, 1973). On the *havurah* movement, see Riv-Ellen Prell, *Prayer and Community: The Havurah in American Judaism* (Detroit: Wayne State University Press, 1989).

103. Siegel, Strassfeld, and Strassfeld, *The Jewish Catalog,* 76.

104. Sharon Strassfeld and Michael Strassfeld, eds., *The Third Jewish Catalog: Creating Community* (Philadelphia: Jewish Publication Society of America, 1980), 205–6.

105. Siegel, Strassfeld, and Strassfeld, *The Jewish Catalog,* 64–65, 76–77.

106. Paul Cowan, *An Orphan in History: Retrieving a Jewish Legacy* (Garden City, N.Y.: Doubleday, 1982).

107. Ibid., 176.

108. Ibid., 8–9.

109. Ibid., 17.

110. Ibid., 157.

111. Ibid., 197.

112. See, for example, Jacob Katz, *Out of the Ghetto: The Social Background of Jewish Emancipation, 1770–1870* (Cambridge, Mass.: Harvard University Press, 1972); John Murray Cuddihy, *The Ordeal of Civility: Freud, Marx, Levi-Strauss, and the Jewish Struggle with Modernity* (Boston: Beacon Press, 1974).

113. Translation in Paul Mendes-Flohr and Jehuda Reinharz, eds., *The Jew in the Modern World* (Oxford: Oxford University Press, 1980), 312–13.

114. Cowan, *An Orphan in History,* 212.

115. Robert L. Carringer, *The Jazz Singer* (Madison: University of Wisconsin Press, 1979).

116. The Samson Raphaelson story is reprinted in ibid., 147–67.

117. Most of the scholarly discourse about *The Jazz Singer* focuses—mistakenly, I believe—on the racial element. Jolson in the 1927 version and Diamond in the 1980 one, in different ways, "blacken up" in order to appear on stage. See Michael P. Rogin, *Blackface, White Noise: Jewish Immigrants in the Hollywood Melting Pot* (Berkeley: University of California Press, 1996); see my review, "Trading Faces," in *CommonQuest* 2, no. 1 (summer 1997): 40–44.

118. The screenplay is also reproduced in Carringer, *The Jazz Singer*; see 49.

119. Steve Whitfield, "Jazz Singers: A Hollywood Bomb—But Inadvertently, an Accurate Portrayal of the American Jewish Condition," *Moment* 6, nos. 3–4 (March–April 1981): 19–25.

120. Ronald Sanders, *The Lower East Side: A Guide to Its Jewish Past in 99 New Photographs* (New York: Dover, 1979), 72.

121. Ibid.

122. Gerald R. Wolfe, *The Synagogues of New York's Lower East Side* (New York: New York University, 1978), 3.

123. Telephone interview, Amy Waterman, July 21, 1998.

124. Ibid.

125. According to the Eldridge Street Synagogue staff, "We could have them every week," but because of limitations of space and staff they can accommodate the teenagers in special "Clean and Shine Day" efforts only twice a year. Ibid.

126. Promotional material from the Eldridge Street Synagogue courtesy of Allison Gottsengen, District of Columbia Jewish Community Center. The Eldridge Street Synagogue was highlighted in a DCJCC exhibit on American Jewish sacred spaces, January–July 1997.

127. On an even more recent manifestation of this phenomenon, see Yigal Schleifer, "Recrossing Delancey," *Jerusalem Report*, July 6, 1998, 32–34 (Subtitled, "The trendy bars and clubs of today's Lower East Side are part of what is drawing grandchildren of the immigrants who once filled the neighborhood").

128. Kenneth T. Jackson, ed., *The Encyclopedia of New York City* (New Haven, Conn.: Yale University Press, 1995), 697.

129. Quoted in Sanders, *The Lower East Side: A Guide to Its Jewish Past*, n.p.

130. Telephone interview, Ruth Abram, July 21, 1988.

131. Quoted in Jane Brown Gillette, "Urban Log Cabin: America's Immigrant Past Resurfaces at 97 Orchard Street," *Historic Preservation* 46 (January/February 1994): 24–25.

132. Telephone interview, Ruth Abram, July 21, 1997.

133. Menu, Sammy's Roumanian Steak House; Jack Kugelmass, "Green Bagels: An Essay on Food, Nostalgia, and the Carnivalesque," *YIVO Annual* 19 (1990): 57–80.

134. *AJHS Recorder* 2, no. 4 (December 1961): 3.

135. Strassfeld and Strassfeld, *Third Jewish Catalog*, 89–90.

136. Oscar Israelowitz, *The Lower East Side Guide* (New York: Israelowitz, 1988); Ruth Limmer, *Six Heritage Tours of the Lower East Side: A Walking Guide* (New York: New York University Press, 1997); Strassfeld and Strassfeld, *The Third Jewish Catalog*, 213–22.

137. Strassfeld and Strassfeld, *The Third Jewish Catalog*, 213–22. The only other tour of the sort in the book is of Jewish Los Angeles, and that section, appropriately, is broken up into "Fairfax Avenue," "Pico-Robertson," "West Side," "Beverly Hills," "Westwood," "Venice," and "Jewish Valley." To do the L.A. Jewish tour requires a car; the Lower East Side is a singular whole, to be done on foot.

138. Advertisement, *Forward*, May 21, 1999, 3.

139. Telephone interview with Seth Kamil, July 7, 1998; Gabe Levenson, "A Lower East Side Sukkot," *Jewish Week*, October 9–15, 1992.

140. Many of the tour guides for Big Onion tours are history graduate students. They walk an interpretive line between narrating the history of the neighborhood as it conforms to the data of historical scholarship and as it reflects what the visitors want to hear. Annie Polland, a Big Onion tour guide and history student at Columbia University in 1999, confirmed that visitors to the Lower East Side tours want to be told that the neighborhood was an all-Jewish enclave. Telephone interview, April 30, 1999.

141. Telephone interview, July 7, 1998.

142. Brochure, "Big Onion Walking Tours: N.Y.C.: Walking Tour of Jewish New York for Student and Adult Groups," n.d.; in possession of author.

143. I want to thank Beryl Benderly of Kehila Chadashah for giving me the *havurah*'s newsletter (February 1999), which contains a description of the annual trip to New York for the children in their school. The children and their chaperons went to the Museum of the Jewish Heritage, saw a

Broadway play, and then met their Big Onion tour guide at Ratner's, a Delancey Street restaurant. One of the boys in the group "discovered a hidden hundred-year-old Siddur [prayer book] hidden in an area of broken wall at the synagogue." The boy was so taken with his discovery, as were the staff members of the synagogue, that he developed a keen interest in its history and was invited to come back and help work on the restoration.

144. Sarah Schulman, "When We Were Very Young: A Walking Tour through Radical Jewish Women's History on the Lower East Side, 1879–1919," in, Melanie Kaye/Kantrowitz and Irena Klepfisz, *The Tribes of Dina: A Jewish Women's Anthology* (Montpelier, Vt.: Sinister Wisdom, 1976, 232–53).

145. Handbill, Radical Walking Tours by Bruce Kayton, summer/fall 1999 schedule; in author's possession.

CHAPTER THREE
The Wellsprings of Memory

1. Barbara Blumberg, *Celebrating the Immigrant: An Administrative History of the Statue of Liberty National Monument* (Boston: U.S. Department of the Interior, National Park Service, 1985).

2. Jacques Le Goff, *History and Memory,* translated by Steven Rendall and Elizabeth Claman (New York: Columbia University Press, 1992), 51.

3. Quoted in ibid., 95.

4. Places become redefined because the process of redefinition serves deeper cultural needs. I was influenced in this kind of cultural history of space by Henry D. Shapiro, *Appalachia on Our Mind: The Southern Mountains and Mountaineers in the American Consciousness, 1870–1920* (Chapel Hill: University of North Carolina Press, 1978). Shapiro's provocative book, he declared, "is not a history of Appalachia. It is a history of the idea of Appalachia; and hence the invention of Appalachia. It attempts to examine the origins and consequences of the idea that the mountainous portions of eight or nine southern states form a coherent region inhabited by a homogeneous population possessing a uniform culture" (ix).

5. Yael Zerubavel, *Recovered Roots: Collective Memory and the Making of Israeli National Tradition* (Chicago: University of Chicago Press, 1995);

Mark A. Raider, *The Emergence of American Zionism* (New York: New York University Press, 1998), 69–124.

6. *American Jewish Yearbook: 5660/1899–1900* (Philadelphia: Jewish Publication Society of America, 1900); *American Jewish Yearbook: 5674/ 1913–1914* (Philadelphia: Jewish Publication Society, 1914), 427.

7. *American Jewish Yearbook: 5661/1900–1901.*

8. Figures from Gerald Sorin, *A Time for Building: The Third Migration, 1880–1920* (Baltimore: Johns Hopkins University Press, 1992), 70; Ira Rosenwaike, *Population History of New York City* (Syracuse, N.Y.: Syracuse University Press, 1972), 84.

9. *Encyclopaedia Britannica*, 11th ed., s.v. New York (City).

10. Lee Shai Weisbach, "The Jewish Communities of the United States of the Eve of Mass Migration," *American Jewish History* 78 (September 1988): 79–108.

11. Evelyn Levow Greenberg, "Life in the Old Southwest," *The Record* 3, no. 2 (November 1968): 3–10; Robert Shosteck, "An Economic Study of the Southwest Jewish Community, 1855–1955," *The Record* 3, no. 2 (November 1968): 21–35.

12. Ewa Morawska, *Insecure Prosperity: Small-Town Jews in Industrial America, 1890–1940* (Princeton, N.J.: Princeton University Press, 1996).

13. Richard Plunz, *A History of Housing in New York City: Dwelling Types and Social Change in the American Metropolis* (New York: Columbia University Press, 1990).

14. Robert G. Barrows, "Beyond the Tenement: Patterns of American Urban Housing, 1870–1930," *Journal of Urban History* 9 (August 1983): 395–420.

15. Quoted in Irving Cutler, *The Jews of Chicago: From Shtetl to Suburb* (Urbana: University of Illinois Press, 1996), 51.

16. Residents of Hull House, *Hull House Maps and Papers* (New York: Thomas Crowell, 1895), 94–95.

17. David G. Dalin and Jonathan Rosenbaum, *Making a Life, Building a Community: A History of the Jews of Hartford* (New York: Holmes and Meier, 1997), 51.

18. Alter F. Landesman, *Brownsville: The Birth, Development and Passing of a Jewish Community in New York* (New York: Bloch Publishing, 1971), 83.

19. Riis, *How the Other Half Lives*, 65.

20. Richard Sennett, *The Uses of Disorder: Personal Identity and City Life* (New York: Knopf, 1970), 47–48, 196–98.

21. Henry Roth, *Call It Sleep* (New York: R. O. Ballon, 1934), 143.

22. Anzia Yezierska, *Red Ribbons on a White Horse* (New York: Charles Scribner, 1950), 25–26, 149.

23. Quoted in Nahma Sandrow, *Vagabond Stars: A World History of Yiddish Theater* (Syracuse, N.Y.: Syracuse University Press, 1977), 102.

24. For one discussion of this phenomenon, see Kenneth T. Jackson, *Crabgrass Frontier: The Suburbanization of the United States* (New York: Oxford University Press, 1985), esp. 45–72.

25. Hasia R. Diner, *A Time for Gathering: The Second Migration, 1820–1880* (Baltimore: Johns Hopkins University Press, 1992), 129–30, 222–24.

26. Morawska, *Insecure Prosperity*, 140.

27. Moses Rischin, *The Promised City: New York's Jews, 1870–1914* (Cambridge, Mass.: Harvard University Press, 1962), 105–7.

28. Daniel Soyer, "Traditions of Grass-Roots Organization and Leadership: The Continuity of *Landsmanshaftn* in New York," *American Jewish History* 76 (September 1986): 25–39.

29. Daniel Soyer, *Jewish Immigrant Associations and American Identity in New York, 1880–1939* (Cambridge, Mass.: Harvard University Press, 1997), 88.

30. Aaron H. Frankel, *Lo Tirtzakh: Ein Ubhandlung Iber "Vegetarianism"* (New York: B. Rabinowitz, 1899).

31. Quoted in Rischin, *The Promised City*, 155.

32. Elias Solomon, *"This Was My Portion": A Message to My People* (privately published, 1951), RG 15A, Rabbinical School Alumni File, 27, Jewish Theological Seminary Archives.

33. Marc Lee Raphael, *Abba Hillel Silver: A Profile in American Judaism* (New York: Holmes and Meier, 1989), 6.

34. Elias Tcherikower, *The Early Jewish Labor Movement in the United States* (New York: YIVO, 1961); Herberg Will, "The American Jewish Labor Movement," in *American Jewish Yearbook* (Philadelphia: Jewish Publication Society, 1952), 3–74.

35. Jeffrey Gurock, *When Harlem Was Jewish: 1870–1930* (New York: Columbia University Press, 1979), 60, 65.

36. Communication from Lawrence Levine to the author, February 16, 1999.

37. Zelda F. Popkin, "Jewish Cabarets on the East Side," *Jewish Daily Forward*, May 9, 1926. Thanks to Riv-Ellen Prell for this article.

38. Ruth Wisse, in her study of the culture of Yiddish poetry in immigrant New York, described the café culture of the Lower East Side: "In

small cafeterias clustered around Rutgers Square, writers, editors, and educated readers gathered after a day's work to argue. . . . The cafeteria debates had the flavor of the yeshivas and houses of study where some of the participants had spent their youth. . . . The competitive male camaraderie of traditional Jewish society stimulated a new kind of culture, at once freed of religious restraints yet reminiscent of them." Ruth Wisse, *A Little Love in Big Manhattan* (Cambridge, Mass.: Harvard University Press, 1988), 4.

39. Mordecai Soltes, *The Yiddish Press: An Americanizing Agency* (New York: Teachers College, Columbia University, 1925), 24.

40. "Memories of a Hoosier Girl, 1893–1906," in *The American Jewish Woman: A Documentary History*, ed. Jacob Rader Marcus (New York: KTAV, 1981), 443–44.

41. Louis Wirth, *The Ghetto* (Chicago: University of Chicago Press, 1928), 185.

42. Ibid., 225.

43. J. Hoberman, in *Bridge of Light: Yiddish Film between Two Worlds* (Philadelphia: Temple University Press, 1995), has offered an important challenge to historians who separate American and modern eastern European Jewish history. Although they are almost always analyzed separately, Hoberman has indicated a reason to think of them as part of a transnational cultural milieu. The films he studied, as well as the actors, directors, and film crews, went back and forth until World War II brought this to a halt.

44. Benedict Anderson, *Imagined Communities* (London: Verso, 1981).

45. Certainly European Jews were undergoing this same internal differentiation, and communities that *may* have once been highly structured and undifferentiated were also enduring internal restructuring. The American variant on this process was, however, much more extreme and telescoped through a shorter prism of time. See Ezra Mendelsohn, *On Modern Jewish Politics* (New York: Oxford University Press, 1993).

46. John Murray Cuddihy, *The Ordeal of Civility: Freud, Marx, Levi-Strauss, and the Jewish Struggle with Modernity* (Boston: Beacon Press, 1974).

47. Philip Cowen, *Memories of an American Jew* (New York: International Press, 1932).

48. For the places of publication of American Jewish periodicals in the early twentieth century, see the various issues of the *American Jewish Yearbook*.

49. *American Hebrew,* July 3, 1890, 162.

50. *American Hebrew,* December 13, 1886, 115.

51. *American Hebrew,* September 6, 1895, 433.

52. For example, "Our up-town readers would be surprised to learn that on the East side—say up to 8th street—there are over one hundred and twenty-five congregations in a healthy flourishing condition. . . . In the members of the Beth Hamedrash [Beth Hamedrash Hagadol, a Lower East Side synagogue] can be counted several bankers, lawyers, importers and wholesale merchants, besides a fair sprinkling of the American element." *American Hebrew,* January 24, 1888, 41.

53. *American Hebrew,* October 8, 1886, 128.

54. *American Hebrew,* August 13, 1886, 2.

55. Quoted in Robert Rockaway, *Words of the Uprooted: Jewish Immigrants in Early Twentieth-Century America* (Ithaca, N.Y.: Cornell University Press, 1998), 18.

56. *American Hebrew,* November 9, 1888, 1.

57. *American Hebrew,* September 7, 1894, 556.

58. *American Hebrew,* August 13, 1886, 9.

59. *American Hebrew,* September 3, 1886, 49.

60. Milwaukee provides one notable exception. Lizzie Kander Black, a local leader of the National Council of Jewish Women, established a settlement house for the Jewish immigrant women of the neighborhood, and, to raise funds, she decided to issue a cookbook. That book, *The Settlement Cookbook*, ranks among America's most popular and enduring ones, although its association with Jewish immigration and philanthropy is not well known. See Louis J. Swichkow and Lloyd P. Gartmen, *A History of the Jews in Milwaukee* (Philadelphia: Jewish Publication Society, 1963), 227; Selig Adler and Thomas E. Connolly, *From Ararat to Suburbia: The History of the Jewish Community of Buffalo* (Philadelphia: Jewish Publication Society of America, 1960); Robert A. Rockaway, *The Jews of Detroit: From the Beginning, 1762–1914* (Detroit: Wayne State University Press, 1986); Steven Hertzberg, *Strangers within the Gate City: The Jews of Atlanta, 1845–1916* (Philadelphia: Jewish Publication Society, 1978).

61. Murray Friedman, ed., *When Philadelphia Was the Capital of Jewish America* (Philadelphia: Balch Institute Press, 1993). In the index, the local institutions Gratz College and Dropsie College warrant six and seven citations, respectively; the Jewish Theological Seminary in New York appears thirteen times, and such individuals as Cyrus Adler, Alexander Kohut, Sabato Morais, Solomon Solis-Cohen, and Mayer Sulzberger, Philadelphians with many entries in the index, played key roles in the seminary's founding and early history, making this as much a New York

NOTES TO CHAPTER THREE

book as it was intended as an antidote to the New York focus of American Jewish history and an effort to restore Philadelphia to its place of honor in that history.

62. Cutler, *The Jews of Chicago.*

63. Albert Gordon, *Jews in Transition* (Minneapolis: University of Minnesota Press, 1949), 12–42; W. Gunther Plaut, *Jews of Minnesota: The First Seventy-Five Years* (New York: American Jewish Historical Society, 1959), 140–55; Max Vorspan and Lloyd P. Gartner, *History of the Jews of Los Angeles* (San Marino, Calif.: Huntington Library, 1970), 171–83; Selig Adler, *From Ararat to Suburbia: The History of the Jewish Community of Buffalo* (Philadelphia: Jewish Publication Society, 1960), 214–77.

64. Landesman, *Brownsville,* 5.

65. Quoted in Rockaway, *Words of the Uprooted,* 13.

66. Ibid., 11.

67. Ibid., 1.

68. Ibid., 50.

69. See Wirth, *The Ghetto.*

70. On the IRO's activities sending immigrants to Chicago, see Rockaway, *Words of the Uprooted,* 139–41; see also references to Detroit, 122–24 and to Cleveland, 34.

71. Nancy L. Green, *Ready-to-Wear and Ready-to-Work: A Century of Industry and Immigrants in Paris and New York* (Durham, N.C.: Duke University Press, 1997).

72. David A. Jasen, *Tin Pan Alley: The Composers, the Songs, the Performers, and Their Times* (New York: Donald I. Fine, 1988).

73. Allen F. Davis, *Spearheads for Reform: The Social Settlements and the Progressive Movement, 1890–1914* (New York: Oxford University Press, 1967), 69.

74. Steven J. Diner, *A Very Different Age: Americans of the Progressive Era* (New York: Hill and Wang, 1998), 220; Davis, *Spearheads for Reform,* 69.

75. Jacob Riis, *How the Other Half Lives: Studies among the Tenements of New York* (New York: Scribner's, 1890); Robert Hunter, *Poverty* (New York: Macmillan, 1904); Charles B. Spahr, *America's Working People* (New York: Longmans, Green, 1900); Peter Roberts, *Anthracite Coal Communities* (New York: Macmillan, 1904); Walter A. Wyckoff, *The Workers* (New York: Charles Scribner, 1897); John Spargo, *Bitter Cry of the Children* (New York: Macmillan, 1907); Lawrence Veiller and R. W. de Forest, eds., *The Tenement House Problem* (New York: Macmillan, 1903); and Arthur C. Holden, *The Settlement Idea: A Vision of Social Justice* (New York: Macmillan, 1922)

are just a few of the reform-minded, problem-oriented books of the Progressive Era published in New York City. See also Jane Addams, *Twenty Years at Hull House* (New York: Macmillan, 1910); Residents of Hull House, *Hull House Maps and Papers* (New York: Thomas Crowell, 1895); and Robert A. Woods and Albert J. Kennedy, *The Settlement Horizon: A National Estimate* (New York: Russell Sage, 1922).

76. Frank Luther Mott, *A History of American Magazines* (Cambridge, Mass.: Harvard University Press, 1957), vol. 4, 1885–1905; John William Tebbel and Mary Ellen Zuckerman, *The Magazine in America* (New York: Oxford University Press, 1991).

77. Mary Ellen Zuckerman, "Magazines," in *Encyclopedia of New York City*, ed. Kenneth T. Jackson (New Haven, Conn.: Yale University Press, 1995), 713–74.

78. Federal Writers Project, *The WPA Guide to New York City* (New York: Random House, 1939), 108.

79. See Peter B. Hales, *Silver Cities: The Photography of American Urbanization, 1839–1915* (Philadelphia: Temple University Press, 1984); Alan Trachtenberg, *Reading American Photographs: Images as History, Mathew Brady to Walker Evans* (New York: Hill and Wang, 1989).

80. William Dean Howells, "Editor's Easy Chair," *Harper's Monthly* magazine, May 1915, 958.

81. Norman Kleeblatt and Susan Chevlowe, eds., *Painting a Place in America: Jewish Artists in New York 1900–1945: A Tribute to the Educational Alliance Art School* (Bloomington: Indiana University Press, 1991).

82. Rebecca Zurier, Robert W. Snyder, and Virginia M. Mecklenburg, *Metropolitan Lives: The Ashcan Artists and Their New York* (New York: Norton, 1996), 22.

83. See Keith Gandal, *The Virtues of the Vicious: Jacob Riis, Stephen Crane, and the Spectacle of the Slum* (New York: Oxford University Press, 1997).

84. Naomi Rosenblum, Walter Rosenblum, and Alan Trachtenberg, *America and Lewis Hine* (New York: Aperture, 1977).

85. Calvin Trillin, *Messages from My Father* (New York: Farrar, Straus and Giroux, 1996), 101–2.

86. Theodore H. White, *In Search of History: A Personal Adventure* (New York: Warner Books, 1978).

87. Simon Rawidowicz delivered a lecture in 1948, "Israel the Ever-Dying People," asserting that this theme of impending loss has been a powerful leitmotif throughout Jewish history. "The world," wrote Rawidowicz, "makes many images of Israel, but Israel makes only one image of itself: that of a being constantly on the verge of ceasing to be, of disap-

pearing. The threat of doom, of an end that forecloses any new beginning, hung over the people Israel even before it gained its peoplehood." See this essay in Simon Rawidowicz, *Israel, The Ever-Dying People and Other Essays* (Rutherford, N.J.: Fairleigh Dickinson University Press, 1986), 53–63.

88. See, for example, Alan Mintz, *"Banished from Their Father's Table": Loss of Faith in Hebrew Autobiography* (Bloomington: Indiana University Press, 1989).

89. Ruth Nevo, ed., *Shirim Nevharim: Hayim Nahman Bialik* (Jerusalem: Dvir, 1981), xi, 32.

90. Dan Miron, *Der Imazh Fun Shtetl: Dray Literarishe Shtudies* (Tel Aviv: Peretz Farlag, 1981).

91. S. Y. Agnon, *Oreach Natan Laloon* (A guest for the night) (Tel Aviv: Shocken Press, 1939), 9.

92. Mordecai Amitai, ed., *Ha-Ayara Boyeret* (The town is burning) (Israel: Sifrut Poalim, 1967), 17.

93. Soyer, *Jewish Immigrant Associations.*

94. In Jack Kugelmass and Jonathan Boyarin, *From a Ruined Garden: The Memorial Books of Polish Jewry,* 2nd expanded edition (Bloomington: Indiana University Press, 1998), 105–6.

95. Salo W. Baron, *Steeled by Adversity: Essays and Addresses on American Jewish Life* (Philadelphia: Jewish Publication Society, 1971), 15.

96. Oscar Handlin, *Adventure in Freedom* (New York: McGraw-Hill, 1954), vii–viii.

97. Abraham Menes, "The East Side Matrix of the Jewish Labor Movement," *Judaism* 3 (fall 1954): 366–80.

98. Emma Beckerman, *Not So Long Ago: A Recollection* (New York: Bloch, 1980), n.p.

99. Edward Shapiro, *A Time for Healing: American Jewry since World War II* (Baltimore: Johns Hopkins University Press, 1992), 130–34.

100. Sidney Goldstein and Alice Goldstein, *Jews on the Move: Implications for Jewish Identity* (Albany: State University of New York Press, 1996).

101. Moses Rischin, *The Promised City: New York's Jews, 1870–1914* (Cambridge, Mass.: Harvard University Press, 1977), viii–ix.

102. Elaine Segal, "I Want to Stay in Business . . . I Like to Be in Business," *Smithsonian* 25, no. 1 (1994), 80–91.

103. See, for example, Albert I. Gordon, *Jews in Suburbia* (Boston: Beacon Press, 1959).

104. Quoted in Jenna Weissman Joselit, *New York's Jewish Jews: The Orthodox Community in the Interwar Years* (Bloomington: Indiana University Press, 1990) 9–10.

105. Irving Howe and Kenneth Libo, *We Lived There, Too: In Their Own Words and Pictures—Pioneer Jews and the Westward Movement of America, 1630–1930* (New York: St. Martin's Press, 1984), 27–28, 30.

106. On the *Jewish Catalog* as a text of the Jewish counterculture, see the critique of it by Marshall Sklare, "The Greening of Judaism," *Commentary* 58, 6 (December 1974), 70–77.

107. I first read *The Rise of David Levinsky* as a sophomore at the University of Wisconsin in Madison in a survey course in American history taught by Professor Stanley Kutler. Given the nature of the curriculum at the time and its single-minded emphasis on works of Anglo, Christian origins, I was shocked, but pleasantly, to read this book in a course taught by a college professor who I recognized to be a fellow Jew.

108. Quoted in Sara Bershtel and Allen Graubard, *Saving Remnants: Feeling Jewish in America* (Berkeley: University of California Press, 1992), 27–28.

109. Ibid., 21.

110. Ibid., 24.

111. On the process by which American Jews seized upon the Holocaust as an icon of memory and as a fixture of identity, see Peter Novick, *The Holocaust in American Life* (Boston: Houghton Mifflin, 1999).

112. Nathan Glazer, *American Judaism* (Chicago: University of Chicago Press, 1957), 67, 83.

113. Ronald Sanders, *The Downtown Jews: Portraits of an Immigrant Generation* (New York: Harper and Row, 1969); *Forward*, October 29, 1999, 15; Ronald Sanders, *The Lower East Side Jews: An Immigrant Generation* (Mineola, N.Y.: Dover, 1999).

114. Thomas B. Morgan, "The Vanishing American Jew," *Look* (May 1964), 42–46.

115. The "ethnic revival" needs to be understood both as a general phenomenon and in terms of the specific histories of individual ethnic group experiences, each of which had its own trajectory. Irish Americans, for example, were inspired and energized by the brewing "Troubles" in Northern Ireland, which revived a deep political and religious issue that had been dormant for decades. Italian and Greek Americans found their numbers in America replenished by an upsurge in immigration from their homelands after the passage of legislation in 1965, making a new influx possible. Polish, Czech, Slovakian, and other ethnic Americans from countries under Soviet domination also were influenced by political developments in their homelands.

116. Peter Novick, *The Holocaust in American Life* (Boston: Houghton Mifflin, 1999), 133.

117. Here I disagree with Novick. There was much talk of "Hitler's times" before the late-1960s. It took place, however, behind the Jewish veil.

118. See Gabaccia, *We Are What We Eat.*

119. This reference came from the National Jewish Archives of Broadcasting at the Jewish Museum. I want to thank Ari Kelman for bringing "Shtetl on the Hudson" to my attention.

120. Segal, "I Want to Stay in Business," 82.

121. Morris Dickstein, "Neighborhoods," *Dissent* 34 (fall 1987): 602–7.

122. A study of the historiography of the Lower East Side would need to consider the emergence in the 1960s of the historical paradigm of the "ghetto," that is, the urban Black neighborhoods that had become the focus of public policy debates as well as historical research. Historians, among others, analogized directly or indirectly from that far-ranging public discussion about the contemporary urban crisis to the historical experiences of immigrants, Jews, and others, who had clustered together in their areas of first settlement.

On the surface it seemed as though the 1960s ghetto model fit the classic immigrant neighborhoods of earlier in the century, the Lower East Side in particular. Poor people, marginal to the mainstream, lived together in dense settlement. But the ghetto model did not work. Neither the Lower East Side nor any of the other European immigrant neighborhoods ever matched the density and compulsory nature of African-American residential segregation. The immigrant "ghettos" had too many other groups living within these fluid borders, and those residents of the neighborhoods who sought to leave and live elsewhere could by and large do so undisturbed. See Sam Bass Warner and Colin B. Burke, "Cultural Change and the Ghetto," in *The Enduring Ghetto: Sources and Readings*, ed. David R. Goldfield and James B. Lane (Philadelphia: Lippincott, 1973), 49–62, for one article on why the 1960s paradigm of the ghetto did not hold for immigrant neigborhood patterns.

INDEX

sacred, concept of, 32
Sagan, Miriam, 94, 197
Sammy's Roumanian Steak House, 119–120
Sanders, Ronald, 176–177
Sanger, Margaret, 158
Sapinsky, Ruth, 143
Satz, Ludwig, 44
Schiff, Jacob, 151
Schoener, Allon, 80, 96
Schulman, Sara, 124
Schwartz, Delmore, 30
Schwartz, Maurice, 44
Scribner's Monthly, 155
Sennett, Richard, 134–135
settlement houses, 25, 124, 157; Henry Street Settlement,149; University Settlement, 154
Shapiro, Henry D., 200
Sharlack (Malone), Bobbie, 12
Shaw, George Bernard, 70
"*shtetl,*" idea of, 18
Shtetl on the Hudson, 179
Silver, Abba Hillel, 140
Silver, Joan Micklin, 86, 88, 101–104, 125
Simmel, Georg, 32
The Simpsons, 53–55, 104, 125
slavery, 21, 24
Sloan, John, 81, 157
Soyer, Daniel, 138
Spielberg, Steven, 86, 162–163
Stein, Gertrude, 70
strikes, 140
Sulzberger, Cyrus, 151
summer camps, 25, 90–92, 96, 109, 196
sweatshops, 24, 31, 45, 46, 69, 81, 90
synagogues/prayer quorums, 12, 34, 36, 121, 123–124, 138–140, 148, 171; Anshe Chesed, 47; Beth Hamedrash Hagadol, 48; Bialystoker Shul, 124; Eldridge Street Synagogue, 45, 106–114, 124, 198, 200; First Romanian Synagogue, 123; Kehal Adath Yeshrun Anshe Lubtz, 110; Norfolk Street Shul, 124; Rodeph Shalom, 47; Sharey Shamayim, 47
Synge, John, 69

Tax, Meredith, 73–74, 77–78
Taylor, Sidney, 10, 12, 13, 59, 60–65, 95, 173
Tenement Museum, 114–118
tenements, 3, 24, 31, 55, 65, 71, 74–75, 80–82, 94, 107, 133–134, 154, 157, 161
tercentenary of Jewish Settlement in America, 35, 167, 168
Thanksgiving, 32–33, 130
Thomas, Danny, 105
Thomashefsky, Boris, 44
Tolstoy, Ivan, 69
Triangle Shirtwaist Company, 44, 124
Trillin, Calvin, 162–163
Tsvey Shvester, 84
Turpin, Sophie, 30

Uncle Moses, 84
Union of American Hebrew Congregations, 23, 172
United Jewish Appeal (Federations), 35, 122

Veiller, Lawrence, 154
Village Voice, 98, 100, 174
"A Voice of Conscience: The Prints of Jack Levine," 31

Walkowitz, Abraham, 157
Warmflash, Philip, 90–91
Washington Post, 83
Waterman, Amy, 112
Weber, Max, 81
Weisser, Maude, 55–56, 125
West of Hester Street, 33
White, Theodore, 162–163
Wilder, Laura Ingalls, 60
Wirth, Louis, 143–144
Wisse, Ruth, 202–203
Wolfe, Gerald, 111